9/07 card ~~$4.95~~ B 4.50 29541

Cambridge Studies in Social Anthropology

GENERAL EDITOR: JACK GOODY

18

PERSPECTIVES IN MARXIST ANTHROPOLOGY

OTHER TITLES IN THE SERIES

1 *The Political Organization of Unyamwezi*
R. G. ABRAHAMS

2 *Buddhism and the Spirit Cults in North-East Thailand*
S. J. TAMBIAH

3 *Kalahari Village Politics: An African Democracy*
ADAM KUPER

4 *The Rope of Moka: Big-men and Ceremonial Exchange in Mount Hagen, New Guinea*
ANDREW STRATHERN

5 *The Majangir: Ecology and Society of a Southwest Ethiopian People*
JACK STAUDER

6 *Buddhist Monk, Buddhist Layman: A Study of Urban Monastic Organization in Central Thailand*
JANE BUNNAG

7 *Contexts of Kinship: An Essay in the Family Sociology of the Gonja of Northern Ghana*
ESTHER N. GOODY

8 *Marriage among a Matrilineal Elite: A Family Study of Ghanaian Senior Civil Servants*
CHRISTINE OPPONG

9 *Elite Politics in Rural India: Political Stratification and Political Alliances in Western Maharashtra*
ANTHONY T. CARTER

10 *Women and Property in Morocco: Their changing relation to the process of social stratification in the Middle Atlas*
VANESSA MAHER

11 *Rethinking Symbolism*
DAN SPERBER (translated by Alice L. Morton)

12 *Resources and Population: A study of the Gurungs of Nepal*
ALAN MACFARLANE

13 *Mediterranean Family Structures*
J. G. PERISTIANY (ed.)

14 *Spirits of Protest. Spirit mediums and the articulation of consensus amongst the Zezuru of Zimbabwe*
PETER FRY

15 *World Conqueror and World Renouncer. A study of Buddhism and Polity in Thailand against a historical background*
S. J. TAMBIAH

16 *Outline of a Theory of Practice*
PIERRE BOURDIEU (translated by Richard Nice)

17 *Production and Reproduction: A Comparative Study of the Domestic Domain*
JACK GOODY

PERSPECTIVES IN MARXIST ANTHROPOLOGY

MAURICE GODELIER

translated by
ROBERT BRAIN

CAMBRIDGE UNIVERSITY PRESS
CAMBRIDGE
LONDON NEW YORK NEW ROCHELLE
MELBOURNE SYDNEY

Published by the Press Syndicate of the University of Cambridge
The Pitt Building, Trumpington Street, Cambridge CB2 1RP
32 East 57th Street, New York, NY 10022, USA
296 Beaconsfield Parade, Middle Park, Melbourne 3206, Australia

Note: This English edition includes Part I, chapters 1, 2 and 3; Part II, chapter 1; Part IV, chapters 1 and 2; and Part V, chpaters 1, 2, 3 and 4 of the French edition, *Horizon, trajets marxistes en anthropologie,* which have here been renumbered consecutively.

First published in France 1973
Published in Great Britain 1977
Reprinted 1978 (twice), 1981

First printed in Great Britain
Reprinted in the United States of America

Library of Congress Cataloguing in Publication Data
Godelier, Maurice.
Perspectives in Marxist anthropology.
(Cambridge studies in social anthropology; 18)
Translation of some of the essays from the author's
Horizon, trajets marxists en anthropologie.
Includes bibliographical references.
CONTENTS: Structural causality in economics and some
ideas concerning Marxism and anthropology: Anthropology
and economics. The concept of social and economic formation.
The concept of the tribe. – Dead sections and living
ideas in Marx's thinking on primitive society: An
attempt at a critical evaluation. [etc.]
1. Economics, Primitive. 2. Dialectical materialism.
3. Ethnology. I. Title.
GN448.2.G63213 1977 335.43'8'3012 76-11081
ISBN 0 521 21311 8 hard covers
ISBN 0 521 29098 8 paperback

Contents

Introduction

> Il n'existe plus de point fixe d'où l'un d'entre nous pourrait espérer ressaisir, fût-ce en sa simple forme, la configuration du savoir et, par là en proposer la fermeture. Ce n'est pas la tentation qui manque, mais l'instrument qui permettrait d'y céder d'une manière convaincante. Ni du côté du Sujet, ni du côté du Concept, ni du côté de la Nature nous ne trouvons aujourd'hui de quoi nourrir et achever un discours totalisant. Mieux vaut en prendre acte et renoncer à livrer sur ce point un anachronique combat d'arrière-garde.
>
> Jean T. Desanti, *Matérialisme et Epistémologie*[1]

In 1958, we set ourselves two questions and in order to answer them we were obliged to pursue a strange itinerary – from philosophy to economics and then on to anthropology.[2] The two questions were: 'Is there a *hidden* logic in economic systems and what constitutes the *necessity* for their appearance, their reproduction or disappearance during the course of history?' and 'What are the epistemological conditions for a theoretical knowledge of these logical and necessary steps?' The two questions are really one; we are recognising two aspects of the problem of economic rationality. A vast question, the reply to which we did not seek in the philosophy of economics or history, but in all the diverse fields of knowledge which deal with economics. In 1965 we concluded from the route we had taken that 'no true economic rationality exists'[3] and that the problem was to work out the structural analysis of social relations in such a way that we could analyse 'the causality of structures', each in turn and, in particular, the causality of modes of production on different social structures, thereby bringing about an understanding of the mechanisms of their reproduction and change. Some of the texts which follow discuss this problem, but in this introduction we should like to present a kind of practical outline of the operative steps, which to us now, seem necessary if further progress is to be made.

The task of discovering and reconstructing by thought the modes of production which have developed or are still developing in history, is something *more than* and *different from* setting up an economic anthropology, or any other discipline with a similar baptismal name. The task implies the investigation of several theoretical problems – one by one – all of which are implicit in a knowledge of societies and their history, that is to say the problems inherent in the discovery of laws, not of 'History' in general (which is a related concept without an object), but laws pertaining to the different economic and social formations which are analysed by historians, anthropologists, sociologists and economists alike. These laws exist and express the unintentional structural properties of social relations, their hierarchy and articulation on the basis of determined modes of production.

Unlike the Marxism which is usually practised, a Marxism which soon turns to vulgar materialism, we maintain that Marx – in characterising infrastructure and superstructure and stating that the profound logic of societies and their history depended in the last analysis on changes in their infrastructure – did nothing less than bring to light for the first time a hierarchy of functional distinctions and structural causalities, without in any way prejudicing the *nature* of structures, which in every case perform these functions (kinship, politics, religion...), nor the *number of functions* which a structure may support. In order to arrive at this profound logic we must go further than a structural analysis of forms of social relations and modes of thought and try to decipher the 'effects' of structures on each other through the various processes of social practice and place them in the hierarchy of causes determining the functioning and reproduction of economic and social formations.

In adopting Marx's materialism as the epistemological horizon of critical work in the social sciences, we must discover and examine, by ways yet to be found, the invisible network of causes linking together forms, functions, modes of articulation and the hierarchy, appearance and disappearance of particular social structures.

If we follow such routes we shall arrive at a position where the distinction and differences between anthropology and history disappear and where it will no longer be possible to construct a single autonomous, fetishised domain where economic relations and systems are analysed. We shall arrive at a position beyond impotent functionalist empiricism and the limitations of structuralism.

In following these routes there is no question of 'returning to Marx', nor, for the anthropologist, of a resumption and a defence of Marx's ideas about primitive society and the beginnings of class society, although, as we have shown in our critical assessment of his ideas, his live ideas still outweigh the dead. Marx's contribution has been to provide an ensemble of hypotheses and methods which are devised for the analysis of the structures and conditions behind the appearance and evolution of one mode of production only – the capitalist mode of production – and related bourgeois society; this ensemble, however, has a general exemplary value. We shall show how this 'open' ensemble of hypotheses and methodological procedures not only belongs to the epistemological horizon of our own times, but actually provides the main guideline.

For Marx, the starting point in science is not to be found in appearances – the visible and spontaneous representation which members of a society devise from the nature of things, from their own activities or from the universe. For him – and this sets him apart from empiricists and functionalists – scientific thought cannot hope to discover any real links or inner relationships between things, if they start from their apparent links or superficial relationships. Scientific thought must ignore them; not in order to leave them unexplained as if beyond any rational knowledge, but in order to come back to them later and, having discovered the inner relationships and sequences of things, explain them with this new knowledge. In taking such a backward step, all illusions of a spontaneous awareness of the world dissolve one by one.

However, in this progression from the visible to the invisible, scientific thought finds out that all relationships between things, material goods, precious objects and values, are in fact relationships between men, relationships which men express and dissemble at the same time. The discovery that relationships between things involve the presence and determination of relationships between men is one which all anthropologists must understand and recognise as the aim of all their theoretical labours. In analysing commodities, money, capital, etc., Marx revealed his greatness by grasping the reverse order of those facts which, in the daily life and representations of people living and acting within a capitalist mode of production, are presented the other way round. He also revealed the phantasmic nature of social relations.

A theory of modes of production has yet to be constructed; it is impossible to read directly into the visible thread of social relations the exact nature of relations of production. Now – and we feel obliged to stress this point once again – Marx did not establish a doctrine which was meant to cover all infrastructures and superstructures once and for all. He did not propose an invariable form, content or place where relations of production might function. What he did establish was a differentiation in the functions and hierarchy within the causality of structures concerning the function and evolution of societies. There is no reason for denying, in Marx's name, as some Marxists do, that kinship relations sometimes involve relations of production, nor, on the other hand, to use this fact in order to find objections and make a refutation of Marx, as some functionalists and structuralists are wont to do. We must go beyond the morphological analysis of social structures in order to analyse functions and the changes in these functions and structures.

Accepting the fact that a structure may act as a support for several functions does not justify our confusing the different structural levels, nor neglecting the relative autonomy of these structures, which result from the autonomy of their inner properties. Marx's line of thought is not that of reductionist materialism, forcing all reality back onto economics, nor is it simplistic functionalism which hangs all society's structures onto the one which appears to predominate – whether it be kinship, politics or religion. Only by starting with this differentiation of functions and the relative autonomy of separate structures can we approach the problem of the causality between structures at different levels. In so far as a structure has *simultaneous* effects on all the structures which together make up a unique society, capable of reproducing itself, we try and discover in different *places* and at different *levels* – hence, a different *content* and a different *form* – the presence of the *same* cause, that is to say the requisite and simultaneous effects of a specific totality of unintentional characteristics in any given social relations. This does not mean 'reducing' one structure to another, but revealing the different forms of the active presence of a single structure in the very functioning of others. No container–contents or internal–external metaphor seems able to express correctly the mechanisms of intimate articulation or the reciprocal action of structures.[4]

A materialistic approach which takes Marx as its point of departure, cannot consist merely of a lengthy enquiry into the networks of structural causality without eventually seeking to evaluate the particular and unequal effect which these different structures may have on the functioning – i.e., particularly the conditions of *reproduction* – of an economic and social formation. In analysing the hierarchy of causes which determine the reproduction of an economic and social formation, materialism takes seriously Marx's fundamental hypothesis on the determining causality 'in the final analysis' for the reproduction of this formation, of the mode or modes of production which comprise the material and social infrastructure of this formation. Naturally, if we take this hypothesis seriously, it does not mean we convert it into some kind of dogma or facile prescription, blended with some magical and frankly frightening discourse, which barely masks the ignorance of its authors as they so unsubtly proclaim the failure of 'bourgeois' sciences. We need only list the number and complexity of problems which arise in trying to compare societies whose subsistence depends on hunting and gathering, such as the Bushmen, the Shoshones, the Australian Aborigines, in order to reveal the utter futility of such theoretical attitudes.[5]

A particularly notable example of the determining effect of modes of production on the organisation and reproduction of society is that of an original type of economy and society which appeared at the beginning of the seventeenth century among the Plains Indians of North America. As Symmes

C. Oliver has pointed out this type of society developed from the constraints of a hunting economy which came to rely on the use of the horse, and later guns, and was adapted to a specifically bison ecology; this implied the dispersal and independence of winter bands and their concentration and reciprocal dependence in summer.[6] What is specially remarkable in this case is the *convergence* and *standardisation* of the forms of social organisation which appeared in all the Plains tribes, in response to identical constraints. Yet these tribes differed profoundly in the beginning. Those of the north and west, the Cree, the Assiniboin and the Comanche, came from groups which till then were hunters and gatherers, living in bands of fluctuating composition. Those of the east and south-east were originally farming peoples who, particularly those of the south, lived in sedentary villages, under the centralised authority of hereditary chiefs and priests.[7] Very soon, less than a hundred years, a new mode of production involving a nomadic way of life became the norm for these tribes, without the original social relations undergoing total collapse or a radical disappearance, though there were changes in these relations caused by the addition of new functions or the suppression of old ones. These additions and suppressions corresponded to the constraints which arose as a result of the new conditions of production and social life. Those groups which were originally sedentary farmers organised in chiefdoms, were obliged to adopt a much more fluid and egalitarian form of social organisation, imposed by the need to split up regularly into nomadic bands where individual initiative played a large role. On the other hand, those groups which were originally nomadic bands of foot hunter–gatherers were obliged to adopt a more hierarchical form of organisation in order to impose the communal discipline necessary for the success of their great collective summer hunts. As Marx and Engels continually repeated, we cannot understand or analyse the forms and direction taken in changing from one mode of production and social life to another without fully accounting for the 'premises' which caused such changes to develop. Former relations of production and other social relations do not disappear suddenly from history, but they are changed; they influence the *forms* and *places* which will assume and manifest the effects of the new conditions in material life, within the former social structure.[8]

Thus, in continuities and ruptures such as these, the unintentional inner properties of social structures are always manifest, and the very contradictions which arise in these structures have their basis in these properties. Now, again on this point, the analysis of contradictions characterising the functioning and evolution of social relations, Marx has provided us with valuable analyses and, in particular, the distinction between internal contradictions within a structure as it relates to its functioning (like the worker–capitalist or peasant–lord relations constituting capitalist and feudal relations of production) and contradictions in structures which are interstructural. It is the combined play of these two kinds of contradiction which determine the specific conditions of reproduction in a particular economic and social formation.[9]

In short, whatever the internal or external causes or circumstances (the introduction of the horse in North America by Europeans) which bring about contradictions and structural changes within a determined mode of production and society, these contradictions and changes always have their basis in internal properties, *immanent* in social structures, and they express unintentional requirements, the reasons and laws for which remain to be discovered. It is in such properties and unintentional requirements that human intention and action take root and develop into the fullness of their social effects. If there are laws behind these structural transformations, then they are not 'historical' ones. In themselves, these laws do not change, they have no history; laws of change refer to constants because they reflect the structural properties of social relations.

History, therefore, does not explain: it has to be explained. Marx's general hypothesis concerning the existence of a relation of order between infrastructure and superstructure which, in the final analysis, determines the functioning and evolution of societies, does not mean that we may determine in advance the specific laws of functioning and evolution in the different economic and social formations which have appeared or will appear in history. This is because no general history exists and because we can never predict what structures will function as infrastructure or superstructure within these different economic and social formations. The epistemological horizon we have just outlined – with help from Marx and post-Marxist theoretical discoveries in the fields of mathematics, linguistics, information theory, structural analysis of kinship relations and myths – presents an open network of methodological principles, the practical applications of which, however, remain extremely complex. The 'open' nature of this horizon prevents from the start any theoretical course which would lead to a factitious, totalising synthesis. On the contrary, it permits us to observe all the cracks which could appear in the theoretical application of these social sciences and to sift and eject statements aimed at concealing these cracks by means of ideology or illusions.

To talk of Anthropology or History would be merely an abuse of language when referring to theoretical applications which could renounce an illusory totalisation, rather than rigorously implementing, for more modest objectives, an extremely complex methodology. Over and above the 'fetishist partitioning' and arbitrary divisions of human sciences, the question here is of a science of man which would truly aim at explaining its history, repaving the way, putting the past back in the future, that is to say, placing history once more within the possible. 'Possibility', said Kierkegaard, 'is the heaviest of all categories'[10] and we well know that the most difficult task in theoretical reasoning, as in practical actions, is to make an inventory and analysis of the 'possibilities' which coexist at a given moment in time.

So long as we do not know how to reconstruct, through scientific thought, the *limited* number of possible changes which any particular structure or particular combination of structures may carry out, history, as of yesterday and tomorrow, will stand over us like an immense mass of facts pressing with all the weight of its enigmas and consequences. To give an example of these enigmas: certain Mbuti bands hunt with the net in groups of seven to ten men; others hunt with the bow in groups of two or three scorning the use of the net, which they nevertheless know how to handle; others again prefer to hunt with the javelin. Along with levels of production techniques go alternatives and choice. One may digress from the norm only within certain limits. However, in all Mbuti bands, the social relations and ideology are the same. We must therefore go further with our analysis in order to explain the possibilities which depart from the norm, their occurrence or lack of occurrence in other aspects of social life. We ourselves have not been able to go so far, but we have at least recognised the problem.

In conclusion, we should like to return to one of those gaps, those empty, unthoughtout spaces we find unexplained in Marxist thought and the social sciences. This concerns the phantasmic nature of social relations, the question of religion, and from here to symbolic practice and ideology in general. This is a fundamental question since on it depends the possibility of understanding the various *forms* which are assumed by relations of domination and the exploitation of man by man, equally, therefore the possibility of reconstituting the various *processes* for the appearance of rank societies, caste and class societies which have gradually replaced former primitive societies.

In order to tackle this problem we turned initially to a paper by Marx which remained unpublished for some time, called 'Forms which precede capitalist production', and which formed part of the 1857 *Grundrisse.*[11] To separate the living ideas from the dead,[12] we made a critical assessment of this work. By 'critical', we mean the understanding of a text in the series of its contexts, contemporary to the time it was written and to our own times.[13] Now, among the live ideas there – thrown in as if by chance – there is one which, for our purposes, is vastly significant, though the theoretical consequences have as yet barely been noticed. It is the idea that in those ancient societies characterised by the Asiatic mode of production and by the exploitation of village communities and local tribes dominated by a State personified in the person of a 'despot', 'ultimately [this higher community exists and] appears as a person...This surplus labour is rendered both as tribute and as common labour for the glory of the unity, in part that of the despot, in part that of the imagined tribal entity of the god.'[14] The main thing which Marx is pointing out here is the fact that everything occurs 'as if' the conditions of reproduction in the mode of production and in society – the thing which assures the *unity* and *survival* of the community as a whole, its groups and members – really depended on the existence and actions of an imaginary tribal Being, a God, or on the person of an absolute despot, placed above the common run of mortals, sacrosanct. Here, therefore we find that man's relationship with his natural and social conditions of existence is both a real and a phantasmic one. Now, what Marx went on to say was that, to date, the mechanisms whereby 'the real conditions of life gradually assume an ethereal form', have never been thought out.

We can now see how vastly important was a paper Marx wrote, some years later in *Capital*, devoted to explaining the origin and content of the phantasmic nature of men's spontaneous representations concerning the essentials of commodities, money, capital, wages, etc.[15] In these representations everything is *presented inside-out*, relations between people appear to be relations between things and vice versa; what is cause appears to be effect.

What is immediately interesting is the analogy which exists between these mechanisms in the personification of things, the inversion of cause and effect which constitutes the phantasmic nature of market relations and the fetishised forms of social relations which produce an imaginary being, a god, as the living unity of a community, the source and condition for its Reproduction and its Well-Being. But since developed market relations, still less capitalist ones, do not exist in these primitive societies, what possibly could be the mechanism whereby the objective conditions of social life take on a mythical, phantasmic nature? With this end in view we examined Lévi-Strauss's *La Pensée sauvage* and *Mythologiques* and also made a lengthy analysis of the content and form of Mbuti religion.[16]

We soon noticed that religious observance among the Mbuti had a material basis, since the cult primarily consists in a great cycle of hunts of a more intense nature than is usual. This hunt, which results in a greater abundance of game to divide, involves cooperation and reciprocity between members of the band, irrespective of sex or age; a cooperation and reciprocity which are intensified and magnified for the period with the result that tensions within the group diminish, differences are temporarily softened and reduced, though not, of course, totally dismissed. Religious observance, therefore, actually constitutes a form of action, a political experience over specific social oppositions permanently generated by their mode of production and social being and which are constantly threatened by the break-up and fission of the bands.

At the same time, however, these observances – material, political, symbolic and aesthetic, along with the songs and dances which necessarily accompany them – revolve around a real and imaginary being, the Forest; they call upon the Forest and celebrate his watchful presence which brings good health and game in plenty, social harmony, life and it is the Forest which wards off epidemics, famine, discord and death. Religious observance is therefore primarily and totally orientated toward the conditions of reproduction of the Mbuti mode of production and way of life; it constitutes a veritable symbolic act, an imaginary action influencing these conditions.

Mbuti religion is therefore the place where, by imaginative means, an invisible join is located – a join which fuses their different social relations into a whole capable of reproducing itself, into a society living in a particular milieu. What is both revealed and concealed in this mode of representation, what is presented to their positive and illusory actions, is nothing other than the articulation, the invisible suture of their social relations, their inner foundation and form, in the guise and attributes of an omnipresent Subject, omnipotent and benevolent, the Forest. One can see the dangers of perceiving a simple, direct relationship – reflection-reflecting to reality-reflected – in analysing the content and function of Mbuti religion. The phantasmic nature of their social relations is not merely born from the fact that they represent to themselves, inside-out, the observance and conditions for reproducing their way of life, since, in fact, everything occurs as if it were not the hunters who catch game by their own skill and technique, but as if it were the gift of an omnipresent and benevolent Person. But the phantasm is itself *part of the content* of these social relations and not just the derisory and aberrant reflection of a reality which might have an existence apart.

This brief résumé will be sufficient to show how, starting with these analyses and their initial discoveries, we might tackle the problem of the various forms which relations of domination and the exploitation of man by man have taken in the course of different formational processes in rank, caste and class societies. For it should be noted that the Mbuti, who have a strongly egalitarian society, see themselves as being all equally dependent on the continual and benevolent intervention of the Forest (which, from an objective point of view is real since, never changing Nature themselves, they depend on it completely to reproduce themselves). Every one of them is a loyal minister of his faith and there are no shamans. They take it upon themselves to honour the Forest with supplementary labour, when they intensify their hunting forays and consume its produce at feasts which magnify the exceptional character of ritual life.

We can therefore understand why, when circumstances permitted, certain men, certain groups came to personify the common good themselves or to gain exclusive access to supernatural powers which were supposed to control the conditions for the reproduction of the universe and society. Such men or groups have appeared to be above the common run of mortals, near to gods; they have narrowed the distance, which from the beginning of time, has separated man from the gods. Taken from this point of view, it becomes clear how, in many societies where there are hereditary chiefs who use no physical violence over their dependants – such as the Trobriand Islanders, studied by Malinowski – the form which the chief's power takes and the ideological justification for such power comes from the fact that they control first and foremost the great fertility rites of the Land and Sea and that they appear to be the necessary intermediaries between clans, ancestors and gods. To stand apart from men and dominate them, to approach the gods and command obedience, are perhaps only two *simultaneous* aspects of the same process – a road and direction leading to class societies and the state. On this road stand the great figures of Assur, god-king of his city, and the Inca Shinti, son of the Sun, who ruled over Tahuantinsuyu, 'the empire of the four quarters'.[17]

But here what began as domination without violence became ideological oppression and economic exploitation, prolonged and sustained by armed violence. We need not, therefore, consider whether this is politics assuming a religious form or vice versa, since there are here two forms of the same process, two elements of the same content existing simultaneously on several levels. In the development of caste and/or class relations, however, it is of some importance whether the religious element dominates politics or the reverse. By working along these lines Marxism will produce an answer to those who object to the hypothesis that the mode of production, in the final analysis, is the determining causality; it might provide an answer to such authorities as Louis Dumont, who rightly points out that in India, for example, it is religion which has dominated the social organisation for thousands of years.

We now come to the end of this introduction with its incomplete analyses, orientated around shadowy areas, empty spaces, illusory flashes of illumination. We hope that, in the future, the reader will find the theoretical approaches which revolve continuously round Anthropology and History – from Lévi-Strauss, or Firth, to Marx and vice versa – less incomprehensible and exasperating and that he will never accept anything as truth which has not first been questioned and proved to be correct.

The reader will easily perceive that all the theoretical routes and detours we have taken, closely relate to a challengeable notion of economic rationality. In addition, he will find another mode of enquiry in the two papers dealing with the Baruya – a society living in the interior of New Guinea – where we carried out field work from 1967 to 1969, living and working in a society which saw its first white man in 1951 and which came under the control of the

Australian Government only in 1960. In 1967, when we arrived, colonial relations – nascent, we might add – had just abolished the distance separating, in time and space, two extreme forms in the protean development of history. Here was a classless society which had but recently closed the neolithic door behind it because of being able to exchange steel implements with distant tribes who had been in contact with Whites and which now found itself face to face with strangers who declared and imposed their 'right' (in the name of the 'superiority' of their own economic and social system), to 'pacify' them militarily, to 'civilise' them and then leave them to the care of anthropologists and other 'men of science'; in brief, they imposed the 'right' to subject them to the orders and for the benefit of a class society, no longer like the 'right' of Herodotus confronting the Scythians or Cortès before Montezuma, but the 'right' of capitalism and 'peace' imposed on colonised peoples.

Once again the question cropped up, right at the vibrant and painful juncture where two modes of production and two distinct and opposite social systems meet: the question concerning societies and their history, the reasons for their being what they are and doing what they do. Such a question, formed in such a way, obviously does not mean merely doing more scientific analysis regarding contradictions and reasons. What must always be added is action – action based on practical reasoning which fights against history for history's sake, and refuses to let it become Fate.

PART I

Structural causality in economics and some ideas concerning Marxism and Anthropology

The only safe inference is that social phenomena pursue no fixed sequences, or at least that their sequences are so intricate as to elude perception.

Robert Lowie,
'Social Organization',
Encyclopaedia of Social Sciences

In all earlier periods the investigation of these driving causes of history was almost impossible – on account of the complicated and concealed interconnections between them and their effects.

Friedrich Engels,
Four Theses on Feuerbach, *On Religion*, p. 255,
Lawrence and Wishart, 1957

I
Anthropology and economics†

Political Economy, however, as the science of the conditions and forms under which the various human societies have produced and exchanged and on this basis have distributed their products – political economy in this wider sense has still to be brought into being.
Friedrich Engels, *Anti-Dühring*, Lawrence and Wishart, 1953, p. 168

Is economic anthropology possible? At first sight this question is a meaningless one, since economic anthropology belongs to the domain of actual fact, of reality and not possibility. It is enough to recall one work which, at the beginning of this century, was to reorientate and put its mark on all modern anthropology, *The Argonauts of the Western Pacific*,[1] Malinowski's first great book, a work totally devoted to the analysis of economic relations and forms of competition and exchange among the peoples of the Trobriand Islands. And if we go back further still, to the founders of anthropological science, we immediately find a vast amount of work done by historians in comparative law, from Maurer[2] to Maine[3] and Kovalevski,[4] to mention only the greatest of them, who amassed a great variety of information on the various forms of property and labour available from the knowledge of ancient and medieval societies in East and West, information which they then compared with facts about the many living societies in Asia, America, Africa and Oceania which Europe had discovered one after the other in the course of colonial and imperialist expansion. To their mind, these facts were to have provided material for a theory of the evolution of mankind and, if one is obliged to criticise the narrowness and errors of the theory, it is an undeniable fact that the theory of a multilinear evolution of mankind is again a force in anthropology.

In order to be entirely convinced of the *reality* and theoretical importance of economic anthropology in the development of modern social anthropology, we need only note that Malinowski's *Argonauts* was followed by such celebrated works as *Primitive Polynesian Economy* (1939) by Raymond Firth, *The Nuer* (1940) by Evans-Pritchard and other significant, but less renowned works, such as *The Economics of the Central Chin Tribes* (1943) by Stevenson and *The Economic Organization of the Inca State* (1957) by John Murra or *Kapauku Papuan Economy* (1963) by Léopold Pospisil, etc.

Economic anthropology therefore exists not only as a fact but also as a right. And this question of right concerns its *real role, the relative significance of economic exchanges in the deeper logic of the functioning and evolution of human societies*, that is, the question of the relationship between economics, society and history. This theoretical question implies another, an epistemological one this time, concerning the conditions and modalities of theoretical practice which permit a scientific understanding of the economic structure of societies as studied by anthropologists.

However, we should stress at once, that while this second question more particularly concerns anthropologists and the practice of their profession, the first question, the fundamental one, *is in no way peculiar to anthropology and has not even begun to be asked in the present century*. No human science, whether it be archaeology, history, anthropology or sociology, demography or social psychology, can avoid confronting the problem of the relationship between economics, society and history, suggesting answers germane to each discipline. How many historians, as diverse as Fernand Braudel, Ernest Labrousse, Eric Will or Cyril Postan, would not subscribe to the following declaration of R. Firth – a type of theoretical summing up by a scientist who has observed and analysed the functioning and evolution of a Polynesian community on the island of Tikopia for thirty years:

> After publishing an account of the social structure, in particular, the kinship structure (*We, the Tikopia*, London, 1936), I analysed the economic structure of the society because so many social relationships were made most manifest in their economic content. Indeed the social structure, in particular the political structure, was clearly dependent on specific economic relationships arising out of the system of control of resources. With these relationships in turn were linked the religious activities and institutions of the society.[5]

Such a theoretical stand closely parallels that of André Leroi-Gourhan, who has deplored the fact that, in the works of archaeologists and sociologists, 'the techno-economic infrastructure is brought in, on the whole, only in so far as it affects the superstructure of matrimonial practices and rites. Continuity between the two aspects of the existence of groups has been expressed penetratingly by the best sociologists, more as an overflow of the social into the material than a two-way current *where the main impulse comes from material goods*. Accordingly one learns more about prestige exchange than day-to-day exchange, ritual prestations than commonplace services, the circulation of bridewealth than that of vegetables, much more about a society's mind than its body'.[6]

Reading such comments one might imagine that the question of the relationship between economics and history was already established in the minds of the greatest thinkers and in a way which strongly resembles Marx's celebrated thesis in his preface to *A Contribution to a criticism of Political Economy* (1859): 'The mode of production of material life conditions the general process of social, political and intellectual life. It is not the consciousness of men that determines their existence, but their social existence that determines their consciousness'.[7]

In fact, this is not so and among Marxists themselves there are several ways of understanding what is meant by economic *conditions* in the process of social life, the determining of social factors by economic ones. In order to show as briefly as possible – if not faithfully – the theoretical approaches used by anthropologists, reflecting their distinct and somewhat contradictory lines of thought about the relationship between economics, society and history, I shall limit myself to the major differences between functionalists, structuralists and Marxists. We should remember that these lines of thought exist not only in anthropology but in all the social sciences.

There are, in fact, three points central to the debates concerning economic anthropology:

– What is understood by economic reality, what are we aiming at in trying to analyse the economic system of a society?

– What are the boundaries of anthropology? What kind of societies are studied by anthropologists and is there a theoretical reason to justify these boundaries and subject matter?

– What is the causality of economic structures, their effect on the organisation and development of societies studied by anthropologists?

These three points are interconnected, but we shall tackle them separately for the convenience of presentation. We think that a critical synthesis of the main points arrived at should suggest a basic change in the theoretical analysis of these questions and for anthropology in general.

A DEFINITION OF ECONOMICS

Anthropologists deal with three opposing theses concerning a definition of economics, a situation which has existed among economists for over a century.[8] For Herskovits, Leclair, Burling, Salisbury, Schneider and all those who call themselves 'formalists', the aim of economic science is to study 'human behaviour as a relationship between ends and scarce means which have alternate uses'.[9]

This definition proceeds from a marginalist point of view, as professed by the majority of non-Marxist, western economists.[10] Karl Polanyi, George Dalton[11] and other adherents to a 'substantive' definition rather than a formal definition of economics, understand by 'the economy of a society', the social forms and structures of production, distribution and circulation of material goods which characterise a certain society at a particular moment in its existence. One recognises here the 'classical' definition of economics, that of Adam Smith and Ricardo, which dissenting economists of marginalist theory, like Piero Sraffa[12] are taking up again today.

Other anthropologists, like Marshall Sahlins, Jonathan Friedman, Maurice Godelier, Emmanuel Terray,[13] etc., reject any formal definition of economics, along with the substantivists, but consider the 'substantive' definition not exactly false but basically inadequate. They suggest analysing and explaining forms and structures of the process of material life in society with the aid of concepts elaborated by Marx – concepts which have not been perfected – on the 'mode of production' and on 'economic and social formation'.[14]

By 'mode of production' (in its restricted sense), they mean a combination – which is capable of reproducing itself – of productive forces and specific social relations of production which determine the structure and form of the process of production and the circulation of material goods within a historically determined society. They assume that to the mode of production (defined in a limited sense), there correspond, in a relationship of structural compatibility and causality, various determined forms of political, ideological etc., relations, and designate the totality of these economic and social relations analysed in their specific articulation under the same name of 'mode of production' (this time in the larger sense). For example, we speak of the 'slave' mode of production in Greek cities or ancient Rome, or the 'feudal' mode of production in France and medieval England. Moreover, it is often the case that a certain society is organised on the basis of several modes of production all interconnected in a specific way and dominated by one; therefore, in order to describe these connected wholes and modes of production, we have the notion of 'economic and social formation'. Thus in 19th-century France, there was a capitalist mode of production which gradually took over all industrial production and part of agricultural production and dominated the national economy; and in spite of the profound upheavals resulting from the 1789 revolution, continued to exist in agriculture, in crafts and small businesses, alongside precapitalist relations of production, based on the private ownership of small holdings or even on relations of production of a feudal or community type.

These are the three current themes we have to deal with. Let us look at their contradictions. Formalist theory – and this is its main weakness – assigns to economic anthropology the study of the variety in human behaviour involved in working out, in the best possible way, the determined and scarce means for achieving specific ends. In this way economic science loses its purpose, since all achieved human actions must be regarded as the accumulation of material wealth, political power or supernatural salvation. And economic science will dissolve and converge with praxeology – a new discipline, which to date has merely produced trivial observations on man's intentional behaviour.[15] Morever a scientific analysis starts off with aims and value systems which cannot be explained as far as their origins or bases are concerned and which appear to be contingent facts in a more or less haphazard individual or social history. The analysis of intentional economic behaviour among individuals and social groups – the analysis of their decisions and forms of actions, for example – provides a real basis for economic science; however the formalist definition of economics, in reducing the field of economic science to a single aim, prevents the final analysis of the situation by excluding those characteristics of social and economic systems which are neither desired nor often even known by those individuals or groups who are their agents, that is, the objective, but unintentional, characteristics which determine, in the last analysis, a deeper logic and development. Isolated from social relations, incapable of using and taking stock of history, a 'formal' definition of economics becomes at once inflated with all the old mythology of *homo oeconomicus*, which expresses and *legitimises* a 'bourgeois' view of society and economic 'rationality', understood as the maximisation of individual or group profit in competition in a society reduced to a mere market (of goods, power, values, etc.). It is this implicit or explicit 'mercantile' ideology of the formalist definition of economics, which Karl Polanyi, leader of the substantivists, harshly denounced, thereby aligning himself to a constant theme in the early and later writings of Marx.

In fact, it is not at all difficult to show that *in practice* the formalists have abandoned their own definition and are indeed studying the very objectives of economic science followed by economists of the classical and substantivist schools. In Samuelson's well-known treatise, the first few pages bring out the fact that economic science is the study of the ways of best 'economising' scarce resources; he then passes immediately from a general and formalist proposition to the analysis of the functioning of capitalist businesses and capitalist national economy, in fact to the determined social relations of production. We have the example of a recent work on the economics of pastoral society in Tanzania, written by the 'formalist' anthropologist, Harold Schneider, *The Wahi-Wanyaturu*; *Economics in an African Society* (1970).[16] In his introduction the author declares himself a firm partisan of the formal definition of economic science, understood as the study of the distribution of scarce resources between alternative ends, and he gives his reasons in the form of a syllogism. A study like this is always the study of a process in social competition. Among the Wahi, this rivalry centres around the control of herds of cattle and men; the formal definition of economics is thus validated by the facts and imposed by them. He takes up arms against those anthropologists who have overestimated the value of communal traditions within traditional African economic systems, thus hiding the fact that individuals may accumulate private wealth for themselves to a degree one has not dared to admit. It would be well worth showing up some of the naïvetés and pseudo-discoveries which such theoretical statements and counterstatements mask.

It is common knowledge – at least since the beginning of the 19th century – that cooperation in production among pastoral peoples is not so necessary as it is among agriculturalists; that livestock, the main source of production, is an immediate, or almost immediate, mobile source of wealth, which circulates in marketable or non-marketable forms and increases at great speed, in comparison with land in agricultural societies; that the adoption of marketable forms of exchange is made particularly easy among cattleherders and that these conditions also permit the phenomena of a rapid and vast accumulation of wealth in the hands of individuals or family groups, permitting a degree of social inequality also found among agriculturists, once the idea of private, feudal or state ownership of land gains ground. In this situation, it would be naïve and absurd, scientifically, to want to hide the facts of competition and market-exchange in a society of cattleherders in order to maintain at all cost the idea that social relations are egalitarian and communal. This kind of ideology transforms a sometimes valid hypothesis into a dogmatic statement. Schneider's great 'victory' over his absurd adversaries, his discovery that if there is competition there must exist something scarce (be it women, grazing-land, power, etc.) and his other discovery that if there is market exchange there is also a play between supply and demand – all which, in brief, seems to justify a whole-hearted adhesion to a traditional and formalist economic approach – this, in fact leads to a theoretical application and conclusion profoundly changed in character:

To employ the traditional, formal economic approach one must also augment it. Traditional economics is *insensitive to the constraints normative, cultural and ecological, that condition the play of the market.* Anthropologists, like myself are particularly aware of the existence of these constraints, so that I have had to *modify* formal approach to introduce them and thereby to make *more understandable* the way Turu make decisions in the market.[17]

This fundamental theoretical 'change' corresponds to the conclusions reached by Schneider, once having analysed (extremely well and in detail) Wahi ecological and technological constraints and their kinship and political relations. This analysis permits him to tackle, from a truer perspective, a study of their trading relations, thus realising *in practice* the substantivists' claims. It is indeed naïve to assume that social inequality and rivalry do not exist, or hardly so, in most non-western, precapitalist societies; but it is also absurd to maintain that in order to study rivalry and inequality, it is necessary to use a formal theory of economics, which does not, in fact, define economics but the form of any finalised behaviour; however, it is reassuring to note that in practice these differing premises or theoretical 'conclusions' have not been developed and cannot be confirmed.

This coming together of substantivists and formalists, caused by the modification, the flexibility, even the surrender, of formalist theses by their own defenders, provide us with an inkling that the quarrel over a definition of economies which has raged for twenty years in the *American Anthropologist*, *Current Anthropology*, etc., has less meaning or weight than its protagonists have claimed. That is because the two themes are merely two varieties of functionalist empiricism which have been common features in Anglo-Saxon economics and anthropology. Once one begins to study precapitalist and capitalist forms of trading relations, the proof of this merging becomes clear, since R. Firth, Salisbury, Schneider and the formalists on the one hand, Dalton, Polanyi and the substantivists on the other, agree – as all empiricists – that things are just as they appear, that wages are the price of labour, that labour is one factor of production among others, and therefore the source of the value of goods not only derives from the cost of social work, etc. Two theoretical currents therefore agree on the basic essentials of non-Marxist political economy and on the 'empirical' definitions of categories of value, price, wages, profit, income, interest, accumulation, etc. The difference, however, is that the substantivists refuse to apply these theoretical empirical categories to their analysis of *all* economic systems, confining them solely to an analysis of market economies. For these reasons Karl Polanyi quotes the young Marx and criticises economists who project onto all societies a 'mercantile' view of economics and social relations. And it is for the purpose of accounting for the diversity of precapitalist economic systems that Polanyi has proposed a general typology of economic systems.

He classifies these in three types, emphasising that within a given society the three types may coexist in differing proportions and that this typology does not exactly correspond to the three stages of a linear scheme of evolution. He distinguishes first, economies regulated by mechanisms of 'reciprocity', which express dependence on kinship relations or other institutions characteristic of primarily classless societies; secondly, economies regulated by mechanisms of 'redistribution', by means of a central authority, goods being received from the units of local production in the form of tribute or other prestations, economies which can be found in many societies characterised by rank, caste, or class, subject to some sort of chiefship or State; finally, economies 'integrated' by the functioning of an institution, 'disembedded' from social, political, religious or kinship relations – 'the market'.[18]

This typology limits itself to recording and classifying visible aspects of the functioning of different economic and social systems by means of superficial and mixed categories. Practices and ideas of reciprocity are not the same among the Congo Pygmies who hunt collectively with nets and live in bands of fluid composition without any lineage, organisation or chief, or among Andean farmers of precolonial, or even pre-Incan period, who lived in village communities, organised on a lineage basis, practising periodic redistribution of cultivated plots between domestic units. These farmers shared the cultivation of land by helping each other in various ways, usually under the authority of a chief, who more often than not never cultivated those lands which the community allotted to his use. In the same way it is true that trading mechanisms existed in Graeco-Latin times, the Middle Ages, in modern capitalism; however, in order to understand the functioning and form of these market relations, it is vital to look beyond them and discover their specific links with the modes of production in slave, feudal or capitalist systems. In each case, despite an apparent similarity between forms of marketing and circulating goods, the very mechanisms of this circulation, the settling of prices, the effecting of market profits are different, and this difference is based on the necessity for the various forms, both market and non-market, of the circulation of goods being *compatible*, functionally and structurally, with the dominant conditions of production and with the reproductive conditions of reproducing these modes of production. A methodological principle is possible by which one analyses the production and not the circulation of goods, if we wish to understand the real logic of an economic system. A second principle – on which all criticism of the empiricist approach in the social sciences is based – is that the analysis of an economic system is not to be confused with the observation of its visible aspects nor with the interpretation of spontaneous representations peculiar to the economic agents of this system and which, by their activity, reproduce it. It is a commonplace that capitalists appropriate to themselves the use of workers' labour against the payment of wages and that they also spend money in order to appropriate the other means of production – machines, raw materials, etc. Everything happens *as if* the wages paid for the work and *as if*, in the value of the goods produced at the end of the process of production, many other elements apart from human labour are involved. On the surface, therefore, capitalist profit has nothing to do with a mechanism exploiting the workers' manpower, since they receive a wage which seems equivalent to the cost consideration represented by the work.

One can easily see therefore how an anthropologist or an empirical economist, working from 'facts' and spontaneous representations of social relations in the minds of agents who intervene in production – whether capitalist or worker – cannot analyse the deep, invisible logic of capitalist modes of production and can merely 'reproduce' (in a manner more or less abstract, more or less complex) the obvious aspects of these relations, and – if one admits that the surplus-value is a fraction of the value of the goods which is *not* paid to those who produce – can only play a mystifying ideological role which reproduces, theoretically speaking, the spontaneous mystification engendered by the appearance of a capitalist mode of production. That is why Marx emphasised the gigantic effort of those 'classical' economists who were the first to break away from the purely apparent aspects of economic relations and who ceased to contrast (like the physiocrats) agricultural and industrial labour forces – one specific type of production with another – in order to discover manifestations of the same reality: the expenditure of a manpower which at any given moment a society has at its disposal. Unlike Aristotle who saw no means of explaining the commensurability of the worth of quite different goods, Adam Smith and Ricardo had begun to see in labour the common substance of the exchange value of goods which a society produces, in so far as those goods produced take the form of commodities.

Going further than the classic philosophers, Marx was to show that labour in itself has no price; manpower *alone* has a price, equivalent to the cost of all that is socially necessary for its reproduction. From this he could criticise the empirical categories of political economy and show that if wages are not equivalent to the value created by the use of manpower, but equivalent to the cost of reproducing this manpower, then the surplus-value is nothing more mysterious than the difference between the total value created by the use of manpower and the fraction of this value which is handed to the producer in the form of wages. Far from corresponding to reality, the 'facts', or at least their appearance and representation, the ideas corresponding to these 'facts', *conceal* this deep, invisible reality, thereby revealing precisely the *contrary*. One sees why the quarrel between formalists and substantivists, and the criticisms (up to a point, valid) directed by the substantivists against formalist theses in neo-marginalist political economics do not create conditions for true progress in our scientific knowledge of those economies as studied by anthropologists, or for true epistemological criticism in economic anthropology.

From this critical analysis of the problem of defining economics and the approaches adopted by formalist and substantivist trends, which, in spite of their opposition and real differences in meaning, can be found in the last analysis embedded in the very heart of empiricist epistemology, we may now establish two conditions of scientific knowledge of economic systems as studied by anthropologists. The analysis of the different modes of production and the circulation of goods must be conducted in such a way that:

(1) we shall look for – beyond the apparent, visible logic – an invisible underlying logic;

(2) we shall look for and find the structural and historical circumstances of their appearance, their reproduction and disappearance in history.

This is a problem found in modern scientific thought as well as in Marx's *Capital.* A mode of production is a reality which 'does not reveal itself' directly in any spontaneous and intimate experience of those agents who reproduce it by their activity ('indigenous' practices and representations), nor in any enquiries in the field or the knowledgeable external observations of professional anthropologists. A mode of production is a reality which requires to be reconstructed, to be reproduced in thought, in the very process of scientific knowledge. A reality exists as 'scientific fact' only when it is reconstructed within the field of scientific theory and its corresponding application. This conclusion follows modern practice in the natural sciences and Gaston Bachelard made it the essence of his 'rational materialism'. It is also the approach, or at least the theoretical aim, of those anthropologists who claim kinship with Marxism in anthropology. But in practice their approach proves most difficult, by the very extent of the constraints which they accept for establishing the epistemological rigours of their practice. In fact, it is not enough merely to compile, or reel off, a precise list of Marxist concepts on productive forces, relations of production, modes of production, etc., to *produce* scientific knowledge of any process of production. Moreover, a production process cannot be defined in advance with the aid of a few outlines, in general drawn from the configuration of concrete elements in the labour process, and a Marxist must prejudge neither the *nature* nor the *number* of the different modes of production which have been developed in history and which may be found, solely or combined, within any specific society.

The most common error, among Marxists, is to confuse the study of the production process in a society with that of the labour process, and to invent as many modes of production as there are labour processes.[19] For this reason one cannot speak of agricultural, pastoral, cynegetic or other 'modes of production'. The analysis then hardly differs from British functionalists, like R. Firth, Evans-Pritchard, who have certainly applied it without referring to Marxism at all, and even actually opposing it. The difference, however, is that Marxist categories have been plastered over the 'facts' which are then found to be translated and classified into a new theoretical vocabulary. A production process, in fact, consists not only of one or more labour processes (man's relationship to man on the material level in a determined environment on the basis of a determined technology) but man's relationship to man, producers and non-producers, in the appropriation and control of the means of production (land, tools, raw materials, manpower) and the products of labour (hunting, gathering, fishing, agriculture, breeding, grazing, planting, handicrafts, etc). These relations of production may be presented in the shape of kinship relations or relations of political or religious subordination, and the reproduction of the relations of production will then proceed through the reproduction of these kinship relations, of political or ideological subordination.

We shall return to this point at greater length, but let us now state, that anthropologists find it difficult to consider economic relations as a separate field, independent of social organisation, other social relations becoming, as a result, 'exogenous variables' in economic relations, an 'institutional framework', as non-Marxist economists phrase it, when analysing capitalist economies or the economics of 'under-developed' countries, etc. In fact, a scientific theory of society and history must endeavour to discover the corresponding structural relations and the causality existing between the levels and instances, which go to make a determined society, without denying the *relative autonomy* or *irreducibility* of these instances. If not, political economy becomes a fetishised theoretical domain, in the sense that one sees the analysis of economic relations to be confined to the analysis of what are or appear to be economic relations. Now, what is important is the analysis of the functions and the corresponding social relations, and not the objects; one should be capable of finding out, in a determined society, what it is that *functions as* relations of production and why this should be so. Otherwise we make a fetish of other societies projecting onto them everything which appears to be economics, kinship or religion in ours. Marx (as well as Evans-Pritchard and Karl Polanyi) periodically denounced such ethnocentrism. Now the problem becomes one of knowing whether objective criteria exist which would allow one to say that the study of a particular society belongs to anthropology or to another discipline. It is the problem of the content and boundaries of anthropology, and on this point too, anthropologists are in profound disagreement.

THE SCOPE AND BOUNDARIES OF ANTHROPOLOGY

Quite bluntly, there exists no principle or theoretical axiom which would give to anthropology an exclusive content, which would provide it with a restricted sphere of research devoted solely to the analysis of specific and exclusive realities.[20] Or rather, there does exist a principle as to the scope of anthropology, but it is primarily negative, based on practical grounds and not on any theoretical necessity. In practice, anthropology was founded when Europe discovered the non-Western world, along with the development of the different forms of Western colonial domination throughout the world, from the first forms of capitalist genesis to twentieth century world imperialism.[21] Little by little, a field of studies was evolved, peopled by all those non-Western societies which the West discovered during its period of world expansion and which historians abandoned to anthropologists when they found they could not substantiate their studies with written sources – which could also have dated buildings and material elements of a historic past – and when these historians saw it was necessary to use direct observation and verbal enquiries.

At the same time, and for the same reasons, entire sections of Western history, ancient and modern, were abandoned to ethnology or rural sociology – fields often confused with each other. Anthropology was handed the study of all aspects of regional or rural life which appeared to be survivals of precapitalist and preindustrialist modes of production and social organisation or which had very old ethnic and cultural characteristics – the Serbian zadruga, the family organisation of the Southern Slavs, Basque and Albanian customs, etc.; realities and facts which appeared rarely in written documents and had therefore been cast aside by historians; these facts required further on-the-spot enquiry, followed by the collection of practices found mostly in folklore and oral traditions and customary laws.[22] Furthermore, there was the evolutionist idea, current in the 19th century, whereby it was held that European customs were survivals, relics of former stages of evolution, which could still be found flourishing and preserved among non-Western peoples; in this way two fields abandoned by historians were taken over by anthropologists. Only they could provide the missing links by studying European customs and their exotic practices (or the other way round if necessary). Thus, they achieved their theoretical task – considered as a duty – of reconstructing a complete and faithful picture of the first stages of mankind, at least from those of its representatives who had left no written record.[23]

But if anthropology grew up from the convergence of two bodies of material ignored or discarded by historians, this does not mean that history itself, as a scientific discipline, was founded on any strict theoretical principles: in fact there is the same absence of any strict basis for the development of history's sphere of enquiry. On the one hand, for a long time it remained totally oriented toward western realities, if only for practical reasons. On the other hand, historians – since most aspects of popular or village life hardly appeared in written documents – had little choice but to view western reality through the testimonies of those people who, in the West as elsewhere, have always used and controlled writing processes, namely the cultured dominant classes and the various state administrations.[24] There is therefore no idea of inferiority or superiority as far as the relations between anthropology and history are concerned; nor is one more or less scientifically objective. All attempts to get them apart from each other or to forget the history of their development or their respective content, can only turn them into fetishist domains, into theoretical fetishes from which scientific enquiry is debarred.

This reminder of how history and anthropology were founded and developed is necessary for understanding two basic points: firstly, the enormous diversity of the modes of production and societies studied by anthropologists, a diversity which includes the last remaining bands of Bushmen hunters–gatherers of the Kalahari desert, farming tribes of New Guinea's high plateaux, agricultural tribes and opium producers, many of them mercenaries in the South-East Asian wars, the castes and sub-castes of India, African kingdoms and traditional Indonesian States, today integrated into modern nations, pre-Columbian empires which have disappeared and which modern ethno-history and archaeology are attempting to interpret, peasant communities of Mexico and Turkey, Macedonia and Wales. This is the vast extent of the realities studied in anthropology. They seem to be societies with little in common, results of the historical development of different economic and social systems; they have adapted at different speeds by processes of change which have gradually eliminated almost all archaic modes of production in favour of other systems, both more dynamic and more encroaching, of which the capitalist one is the most recent and most devastating example. We must not forget that, since the beginnings of the Neolithic Age (9000 BC), the economies and societies of hunter–gatherers have been gradually eliminated and driven back into ecological niches which are unsuitable for farming and herding; today they are near to complete extinction.[25] We should also remember that intensive farming methods now compete with the older extensive forms, a fact made necessary by increases in population and the need to produce goods for the market, etc.

Secondly, due to the logic and circumstances of its development, history has become the science and knowledge of civilisation (identified with the West and with some few exceptional cases such as China), and anthropology as the knowledge of barbarians, savages or backward, rural European populations at an inferior stage of civilisation. At the same time, the relationship between anthropology and history became a preferred means of expression; it was also a justification of ideological prejudices held in Western society by the dominant classes and about those societies which gradually fell under their control and exploitation. These included Western, rural populations which today have become an urban, industrial proletariat, or were forced to abandon their former way of life and adopt economic and social forms of organisation which allow them to produce, under the most favourable conditions, for a market where they confront organised competition following the criteria of capitalist economic 'rationality'.

For this reason we can now see why anthropology, among the social sciences, has always been one of the great sources – on the theoretical side – for the production and accumulation of ideological fetishes, ambiguities and

– on the practical side – for acute embarrassment. Fetishisation and ambiguity are, moreover, complementary products of an inherent contradiction in the anthropologist's profession; he must dedicate himself to the study and reconstruction of their societies' way of life which his own society is changing or destroying, and he cannot avoid either facilitating or contesting these changes, accepting or denouncing this destruction. This contradiction shows how the anthropologist, paradoxically, is more intimately and more dramatically linked to the contradictions in history's development – that is of living history – than the historian himself who studies the history of things past, a past where the outcome, already known in advance, is less disturbing since we are already beyond it. The anthropologist, on the contrary is inevitably involved and must take part in history; he must justify or criticise changes in those societies he studies and through them justify or criticise his own society which, for the main part, has imposed these changes. For the most part the anthropologist justifies these changes as progress, with some reservations, or denounces them as irremediably decadent. These two attitudes, in fact, presuppose the same ideological postulate; the assumption of the existence of a 'veritable' human essence which is being lost for ever (shades of Rousseau) or which will triumph finally and for ever (an attitude adopted by the philosophers of the enlightenment or English Victorians). Now, no such thing as the 'veritable' essence of man exists, which can be placed in any past, future or present time and which would accord with everyone's ideological involvement or with every epoch; this means the devaluation of societies and periods in human history where one or other of these two choices has not been given a special manifestation, an exceptional moment of the existence of this 'real' essence of man. And since there is no 'real human nature', the anthropologist cannot be given the sublime and privileged task of disclosing this secret. An Amazonian Indian, victim of genocide and the white man's 'peace', is no nearer to the true essence of man than a worker at Renault's or a Vietnamese peasant fighting imperialism. It is not through any normative ideology about the essence of man that we must analyse reasons for a given historical situation and the exploitation of human groups, or that we should suggest a means of ending them or abandoning them to fate. For this, one needs to have not an ideology but rather a true 'science' of history and its needs, which are neither 'natural' nor 'eternal'. History has placed as its starting point, 'man', as the evolution of matter has made him: a new nature not ready-made or prefabricated within Nature.

In order to grow and expand, the 'science' of history – since this is a developing science – demands, among other things, a new understanding and articulation between anthropology and history; a combination which cannot be effected without radical criticism of their ideological content and without a new progression, a hitherto unknown enrichment of their scientific content. We have already had an inkling how Marxism can furnish the means for such a radical criticism, we must now show more precisely how it may also provide a means for a new development of scientific matter in anthropology and history. In our view, the central problem in a science of history is to explain the circumstances behind the appearance of different social structures, articulated in a determined and specific manner with the circumstances of reproduction, for change and for the disappearance of these structures and their articulation. At the same time this is the problem of analysing the specific causality of overlying structures, of their particular role and different meanings in the processes of the appearance, reproduction and disappearance of the various articulated entities, called social relations, which are the content of History and, indeed, Man.

In order to resolve these problems, a method is required which allows an analysis of structures and the discovery of reciprocal laws of compatibility or incompatibility and their concrete, historic effectiveness. Such a method seems to have been elaborated and applied for the first time by Marx in his efforts to analyse the modes of capitalist production and bourgeois society. Marx's answer to the problem of the differential causality of various instances of social life – in other words 'the mode of production of material life conditions, in the last analysis, the process of social, political and intellectual life in general' – seems to us to be the essential hypothesis to be taken up and systematically explored in order to renew the scientific content of history and anthropology.

For a Marxist such a method and general hypothesis act as a *unique* problematic theory as much for the study of so-called 'primitive' societies as for other types of society, ancient or modern; is it not wise for Marxism to use anthropology in its relation to history or vice versa, and do not oppositions of this kind have their place? There is only one science now[26] and this covers both the *comparative* theory of *social* relations and the explanation of *concrete societies* during the irreversible course of history. This science combines history and anthropology, political economy, sociology and psychology and will replace what historians call universal history and what anthropologists try to aim at in their studies of general anthropology.[27]

With this kind of analysis we hope to explain and clear up a fundamental paradox in Marxist anthropology – a complex practice which systematically tries to develop and broaden the analysis of the modes of production in societies left to anthropologists so that they might develop their theories of kinship, politics and religion. This paradox results from the practices whereby Marxists appear as specialists in economic anthropology who, at the same time as they are radically contesting the possibility and rationality of such a narrow specialisation, are also striving to produce conditions for a general renewal of the different fields of anthropological science, reanalysed and reconstructed in their reciprocal interconnections with the structures of the different modes of production – a theory which has to be constructed. This complex theoretical situation determines the critical relationships which the Marxist approach has with anthropology along with two other trends which attempt to create conditions for a general renewal of this scientific discipline, i.e., the neo-functionalism of 'cultural ecology' and the structuralist approach of Claude Lévi-Strauss. Both use a materialistic approach. The first studies societies afresh, considering them as parts of larger wholes, different ecosystems of nature. Like Marxism it pays particular attention to the material bases of society's functioning. The second, again like Marxism, rejects the methods of positivist empiricism and endeavours to take into account the social realities in terms of structure. This dual confrontation permits us to elaborate further the concept of structural causality in economics.

In the meantime let us take a last look at the content and limits of the traditional scope of anthropology – a scope derived from two fragments of human history, those of non-western societies, usually non-literate and colonised by Europe, and rural Europeans with a backward mode of production and precapitalist and preindustrial types of social organisation. This is why the anthropologist is considered a specialist of primitive and peasant societies although there are radical differences. Let us look at the remarkable 'Memorandum' as to the use of the term 'primitive' in anthropology drawn up by Lois Mednick in 1960 and commented on subsequently by Francis Hsu in 1964 in *Current Anthropology*.[28] Two sets of characteristic features, negative and positive, are designated by the term primitive. The negative traits include the absence of positive traits found in Western societies (*non-literate, uncivilised, arrested in development, moneyless, non-industrialised, non-urban, lacking economic specialisation*), or the presence of these traits to a lesser degree (*less civilised, low level of technical achievement, traditional, simple tools, small scale*). In both cases, 'primitive' societies are understood to be 'inferior'. Their positive features, on the other hand, are considered to be those absent from civilised societies (*societies in which social relations are based primarily on kinship, with all-pervasive religion, in which cooperation for common goals is frequent*, etc.). The absence of these traits in modern Western and capitalist societies, far from being interpreted as a sign of inferiority, is more often considered, in prevailing Western ideology, as a further proof of their superiority. However, we are now faced not with ideological phantasms, but with realities. This presents a problem since the anthropologist must now explain what he understands by the dominant role of kinship and the reasons for the appearance or disappearance of this dominance. Anthropologists like Marshall

Sahlins, Morton Fried, Eric Wolf, have made great efforts to define primitive and peasant societies, avoiding the usual ideological implications of these terms. For them, primitive societies are those lacking exploiting classes, and organised in social forms, such as bands or tribes. On the other hand, so-called 'peasant' societies are class societies within which the peasantry constitutes an exploited class, dominated economically, politically and culturally by a class which no longer participates directly in production.

In primitive society producers control the means of production, including their own labor, and exchange their own labor and its products for the culturally defined equivalent goods and services of others...Peasants, however, are rural cultivators whose surpluses are transferred to a dominant group of rulers that uses the surpluses both to underwrite its own standard of living and to distribute the remainder to groups in society that do not farm but must be fed for their specific goods and services in turn.[29]

Peasants then, do not form a 'society', nor even a 'subsociety', a subculture (in Redfield's terminology), but a 'dominated class', and the nature and role of this class differs according to specific relations of production which make them dependent on the ruling class. One has, therefore, to characterise these relations of production each time and that is exactly what Eric Wolf has tried to do when, following on from Maine, Max Weber and Polanyi, he distinguishes the feudal domain, the prebendal domain (i.e., the domain conceded by a centralised State, as in China or in Persia at the time of the Sassanides, to functionaries who levy a revenue in the name of services rendered to the State) and the 'mercantile' domain which is based upon the private ownership of land for buying or selling on the market. The distinctions are far from corresponding to what Marx called the 'feudal mode of production', the 'Asiatic mode of production' and the 'mode of production founded on private property, independent landowning and the means of production'. Eric Wolf adds the 'administrative domain',[30] of the twentieth century, such as Russian kolkhozes or sovkhozes and Chinese communes or the *ejidos* established after the Mexican revolution, which resemble the 'prebendal domain', but are not organised as institutions to levy ground rent. They constitute forms, directly maintained by the State, of the organisation of agricultural processes. We can easily see that Eric Wolf has taken as his own Marx's analysis of the various precapitalist and capitalist forms of large-scale and small-scale land tenure, but the Marxist concept of 'modes of production', has disappeared along with the theoretical attempt to discover and reconstruct the structures of the mode of production within which the peasantry is an exploited class. This applies even more to George Dalton[31] and especially Daniel Thorner,[32] both of whom have tried to define a concept of 'peasant economy', but succeeded only in assembling a few common determining factors of all societies, where production is based on agriculture and where there is opposition between town and country and submission to an 'organised political power'. Such 'common' factors do not constitute any real understanding; they are at best, as Marx emphasised, apropos general categories in political economy, abstractions which are not brought up again in the discussion.[33] We must also stress the danger – avoided by Marshall Sahlins, but not Eric Wolf – of presenting producers in classless societies as all equal controllers of the means of production. In 1877, Engels warned against those who hoped to find in earlier communities the exact image of social equality: 'In the oldest primitive communities equality of rights existed at most for members of the community; women, slaves and strangers were excluded from this equality as a matter of course.'[34]

The whole of modern ethnology has confirmed this view, providing much information on economic and political inequalities to be found in classless societies – between older and younger siblings, men and women, 'big-men' and commoners,[35] founder lineages and stranger lineages, etc. Faced with the enormity of anthropology's theoretical task, due to the accumulation of valuable information on the multiple forms of social relations, one feels obliged to construct a theory of this multiplicity and to provide the reasons for differential evolution. At the same time, we have the huge problem of the circumstances and gradual changeover from classless societies to class societies, the question of the origins of rank, caste, class, the different types of State. It is also clear that any solution of such problems demands a radical redefinition of methods and concepts in anthropology, and above all, a rigorous elaboration of notions of causality and structural correspondences and – in the Marxist perspective we have defined – the elaboration of the concept of causality in economics, of social norms as engendered by the functioning of a mode of production. It is to this theme we shall dedicate the last part of our essay, primarily devoted to the epistemological problems of the knowledge of the economics of societies studied by anthropology.

ECONOMIES AND SOCIETIES: FUNCTIONALIST, STRUCTURALIST AND MARXIST APPROACHES

How is one to analyse the conditions surrounding the appearance of societies, the effects on the deeper logic, the functioning and evolution of these societies, the relations which men set up in order to produce the material conditions of life? We are back to the main theme of the first part of this exposition, but now we know what field of theoretical analysis is involved: that of an anthropology developed as a poorly knit and isolated study of two fragments of human history – classless societies and 'peasant' societies. We have seen how the concept of structural causality in economics is at the heart of the matter. Let us look at this briefly, recalling the ways which the functionalists, structuralists and Marxists have tackled it.

Although Malinowski, Firth, Evans-Pritchard, Nadel have done masterly and pioneer work in the study of the economies of Oceanic and African societies, most functionalists have not followed Firth's insistent recommendation, that the economic bases of these societies should be closely studied because 'the social structure...was clearly dependent on specific economic relationships arising out of the system of control of resources'...and thus making possible 'a deeper understanding of social conditions and structures in the communities the anthropologist studies.'[36] On the other hand, Robert McC. Netting, for the functionalists, stresses: 'The key to the complex and beautiful unity of society was conceived by its structure based on kin, marital and political relations...Here were hidden elaborate networks and subtle symmetries to be discovered, whereas subsistence activities were considered simple, undifferentiated, and boringly repetitive wherever one found them.'[37]

In practice, this theoretical attitude had the effect of producing minute and often profound analyses of kinship or politico-ideological relations, while the economies of numerous societies are studied in an 'eclectic'[38] fashion – illustrated perfectly in the compilation, rather than synthesis, of Melville Herskovits' *The Economic Life of Primitive Peoples* (1940).[39] But one should understand that this eclecticism or disdain for theoretical consequences, might to a certain extent, be justified by the facts, since it is true that in a great many precapitalist societies, kinship relations or politico-religious relations seem to 'dominate' in their functioning, and control the reproduction of their modes of production – this is the case with the Nuer (kinship) and the Aztecs or Incas (politico-religious).

Many saw in these 'dominating' influences, the proof that economics could hardly determine the functioning and development of non-Western, precapitalist societies and had only played a minor role in the history of mankind. Taking this to an extreme, some, like Warner on the Murngin of Australia, maintained that these kinds of society seemed to lack any kind of economic structure, since they could not discover one that existed *separately* from kinship relations, which functioned as 'general institutions' in Evans-Pritchard's happy phrase. In fact, here lies the crux of the problem: functionalist anthropologists and, often, would-be Marxists, imagine, in a glib and non-scientific way, that relations of production exist only when they can be distinguished and separated from other social relations, as in the case of relations of production within the capitalist mode of production.

We should no longer be surprised if, inspired by such an unscientific and *a priori* notion of the relations of production, many anthropologists analyse so clumsily and inadequately the economic bases of the societies they study. Economics, in fact, for them is reduced to what is obviously 'economic'. Now, given that one part of the relations of production often becomes hidden in the functioning of kinship and politico-religious relations, the study of an economy becomes little more than the study of the organisation of labour in subsistence production, property rights and, for good measure, the study of material culture, which *stricto sensu* does not belong to economics.

The missing pieces of the mode of production – the invisible part – can only be studied indirectly when the anthropologist analyses the various functions of kinship and politico-religious relations, so long as his analysis of kinship is not confined to a study of kinship terminology and marriage laws, residence and descent. This shows that the ideological and empiricist conceptions of relations of production are impoverished; analyses of the economy become falsified; at the same time and for the same reasons, the analyses of kinship, politics and religion are also falsified. Theoretical practice, in its totality and on all levels, becomes imbued and subverted by the effects of such empirical, ideological suppositions. When economics was faced with kinship, religion or types of political power or other external variables, it was not surprising that statistical enquiry into positive correlations between economics and social structure or between the evolution of the mode of production and the evolution of societies, came to a standstill, nor that G. P. Murdock should declare 'against the evolutionists, that there is no inevitable sequence of social forms nor any necessary association between particular rules of residence or descent or particular types of kin groups or kinship terms and levels of culture, types of economy, or forms of government or class structure.'[40]

Some of Murdock's disciples today, with over 577 specimen societies (rather than 250) and using a multifactorial analysis, are discovering significant correlations between the evolution of the mode of production and the appearance of certain types of kinship systems.[41] Despite this, the empirical results of anthropological studies have consolidated the idea – popular since the beginning of the twentieth century – that history is 'but a succession of *accidental* happenings which make a society what it is'. The extravagance of this supposition has made men like Evans-Pritchard speak out against it, while still accepting, however, the essence of functionalist principles.[42]

In fact, functionalism should be seen as complementary and, up to a certain point, contradictory to empiricism, since empirically the social structures merge into visible social relations. If these visible relations are seen as independent external variables without any statistically relevant link, how can any society exist as a whole and reproduce itself as such? Functionalism presupposes that the different surface social relationships within a society form a system, that is that they have a functional interdependence which permits them to exist as an 'integrated' whole, and which tends to reproduce itself as such – as a society. And it is because *certain* sections of this whole serve to 'integrate' the other sections into a single entity that the 'particular' subsystems (kinship, religion, economics) play roles as 'general institutions' in each society.

No one will deny that this is an advance on abstract and associationist empiricism, rejecting the study of social relations as separate parts and considering them as a whole or according to their reciprocal relationships, that is, as a form of a relationship system. But apart from these principles – now necessary conditions of any scientific advance – functionalism suffers from radical theoretical defects. We have already shown that by confusing social structure with external social relations, functionalist analysis is condemned to remain a prisoner of appearances within the social system studied and there is no possibility of uncovering any below-surface logic, not evident in the system itself, still less the structural and consequential circumstances of their historical appearance and disappearance. Our analysis must go deeper.

In fact, saying that kinship or politico-religious factors play a dominant role in certain societies, merely because they 'integrate' all other social relations, is an 'explanation' which falls far short of the mark and tends to obscure rather than clarify the facts. A social factor can only 'integrate' others if it assumes, within itself, *several* distinct functions, linked with each other by some kind of *hierarchy*; these functions in capitalist society are performed by distinct social relations which appear as so many specific subsystems within the social system. Kinship dominates social organisation when it regulates relations of descent and alliance between groups and individuals, when it controls their respective rights to sources of production and the products of labour, when it defines the relations of authority and obedience (political relations) within or between groups and, finally, when it serves as a code, a symbolic language to express man's relation to man and to Nature. This is not the case among Mbuti hunter–gatherers of Zaire where intergenerational relations prevail over kinship relations, nor was it the case among the Incas where politico-religious factors functioned as relations of production since, for better or for worse, Indian tribes handed over part of their labour to support the gods, the dead and the living members of the ruling class personified by Inca Shinti, the son of the Sun. One must therefore explain why and under what conditions such and such a social factor assumes such and such a function and what modifications of its form and internal mechanism are brought about by functional changes. In our opinion, this is the major problem in the social sciences today, whether it be anthropology, sociology or history. But one may object that the solution of this problem depends most on the possibility of analysing the structural causality of economics; briefly, even if one cannot explain it, the simple fact of the predominance of kinship, of politico-ideology is sufficient to contradict and eliminate Marx's hypothesis on the determining role, in the last analysis, of economics in history. This is a frequent objection made by functionalists and is the theme of Louis Dumont's last and important work on the social organisation of traditional India – and Dumont is a declared structuralist as well.

The objection no longer holds if we can show that it is not enough for a single social factor to assume *several* functions or any one function in order to be dominant but that it must necessarily take on the function of relations of production, that is to say not necessarily the role of 'an organisational scheme' for some specific and concrete work process, but the control of access to the means of production and to the fruits of social labour, a control involving both authority and social sanctions, therefore political relations. It is the relations of production which are the determinants in the dominance of any one element. They have a general determining effect on the organisation of society, since they determine both this predominance and through it, the general organisation of society.

It is not enough to say then that social relations must be functionally interdependent for a society to exist, nor even that this interdependence consists of several requisite, therefore complementary, functions. To get away from these themes, which soon become banalities, the essential point concerns the causality, therefore the specific efficacity, of each function (and therefore of the social relations involved) on the form and content of the social organisation. Now if, in reality, the various social factors are graded according to the functions they assume and if the function of the relations of production is the first principle in this grading, then a strict formulation of the problem for social sciences reads: *Under what circumstances and for what reasons does a certain factor assume the functions of relations of production and does it control the reproduction of these relations and, as a result, social relations in their entirety?*

One immediately sees that this problem was also Marx's and that it again assumes his hypothesis about the final determination of the process of social and intellectual life by the means of production in material life. It is also clear that this hypothesis is not contradicted by analyses of classless societies or non-capitalist class societies and that here there is no opposition between anthropology and history. Above all it is obviously necessary in answering such a question to take into account not only the economics of a society, but all levels of its social structure; such an undertaking does not result in the development of an economic anthropology conceived as an autonomous and fetishised discipline, but in a general and systematically rigorous renewal of the theoretical scope of anthropology.

These are the main points in our criticism of classic empirical functionalism. But the criticism does not stop there. The hypothesis concerning functional interdependence of all the parts of a social system and the supplementary hypothesis that the whole social system is in equilibrium or tends to remain so, have often made it difficult or impossible for functionalists to admit, or discover within the system they are studying, the existence of contradictions whether in the social structure or between several structures, and this has forced them to look beyond these systems for causes of their evolution and their disappearance. This evolution did not seem to have an internal cause, but was rather the result of contingent circumstances which were related to an inner logic within the systems. All human history appeared to be the contingent sum of all such accidental events.

There is obviously no question of denying the existence of external causes in the transformation and evolution of economic and social systems nor of denying that any system as a whole, in its functioning, necessitates the reproduction of the social relations which are its constituents, but it must be emphasised that whether the causes are external or internal they only have an effect because they bring into play (and are made to act as final causes) the structural properties of systems and that these properties are always, in the final count, immanent in this system, explaining the unintentional role of its functioning. It must also be stressed that to say that two terms or two relationships between terms – or two structures – oppose each other, is not to deny their complementary nature, but simply to affirm that the former exists within certain limits and that beyond these limits the development of the antithesis no longer permits the maintenance of complementarity. This fact has become almost banal since cybernetics and systems analysis formulated it mathematically and made it operative. Nevertheless, it is only another formulation of the old principle of the unity of opposites found in the dialectics of Hegel and Marx. Now, we have no reason at all to confuse this principle of the unity of opposites – a scientific principle – with the basic principles of Hegelian dialectics, that of the identity of opposites, which has no scientific basis. The principle of the identity of opposites is merely, as it happens, the necessary condition for constructing a closed metaphysical system, such as absolute idealism which derives from the unproven postulate that the 'Spirit' is the only existing reality, which while contradicting itself still remains true to itself in spite of the contradictions; matter is thought, which does not think or contradict itself in so far as it is thought, while logos is thought for itself which contradicts the thought in itself, and the matter: the unity of thought in itself and thought for itself is in their identity as forms of Absolute Spirit.

It should be emphasised that, if the principle of the identity of opposites implies *a fortiori* the unity of opposites, the reverse cannot be said to be true. Therefore there is no reason to concern ourselves with the first or to defend it, while defending or considering the second. Unfortunately, the frequent confusion made by Marxists between these two principles sanctions and reinforces the functionalists' refusal to look for contradictions in the systems they analyse. Is this also true of the neo-functionalists, who declare themselves supporters of a cybernetic approach to social factors?

In opposition to traditional American 'cultural anthropology', the idealism and psychologism of which was criticised, a number of anthropologists and archaeologists in the United States in the fifties, openly supported a new theoretical approach which they called, by contrast, 'cultural ecology'. Quoting early works by Leslie White and particularly Julian Steward, they emphasised the urgent need to study the material basis of society very carefully and reinterpret all human cultural activity as specific processes of adaptation to specific environments. Methodologically, they reaffirmed that each society must be analysed as a whole, but also as a subsystem within a larger totality, the particular ecosystem within which human, animal and vegetable populations coexist in an interrelationship based on biology and energy. In order to analyse the conditions of the functioning and reproduction of these ecosystems and reconstitute structures of energy flow, autoregulation mechanisms, feedback, etc., they called upon systems and communication theory. Functionalism as a whole seemed to have been given a new orientation – from now on, explicitly materialist and not simply empirical – new methods, using systems theory, and theoretical possibilities, which it seemed would mean tackling with greater certainty the problem of comparing societies (a problem which the functionalists only attempted to study uneasily or disdainfully) and by trying to construct a new scheme, this time multi-linear, of the evolution of societies (a question completely discarded since the attacks made by Boas, Goldenweiser and Malinowski on evolutionism). Are we not now in the theoretical universe, if not of Marx himself, at least of Marxism as it is generally understood and practised?

No, this is not the case as we shall show. First we must try to reveal the wealth of provisional attempts the nature and meaning of which we can only suggest. However, the limits of such undertakings are perfectly clear and result from the narrow materialism of these researches and particularly – since this is the core of their efforts – from the serious inadequacy of their perception of economic relations, and therefore the effect of economics on the organisation of society. More frequently it is a case of 'reductionist' materialism since it reduces economics to technology and to man's biological and energetical interaction with the environment; it also reduces the meaning of kinship and politico-ideological relations to one of resources which are functionally necessary for this biological–ecological adaptation and which offer various selective advantages. We shall return to these points, but first, we must briefly enumerate the positive advances made *rapidly* as soon as *detailed* studies of the *essential* aspects of the functioning of primitive or ancient societies were looked at; apart from some brilliant exceptions – Malinowski, Firth, Evans-Pritchard – most of these studies had been dogmatically neglected or maltreated.

Concentrated efforts were made to study in detail the ecological environment, the basic features of production, diet and the energy outputs of certain groups of hunters and gatherers (Richard Lee, De Vore, Steward), North-West coast Indians (Suttles) pastoral societies of East Africa (Gulliver, Deshler, Dyson-Hudson) and swidden farmers of Oceania and South-East Asia (Roy Rappaport, Vayda, Geertz[43]). Gradually data was accumulated which led to a collapse of the classic themes in cultural anthropology which had formerly been approved both in students' texts as well as reading matter for the educated public. It was found that productive members of the hunter–gatherer societies of the Kalahari desert or the Congo forest needed no more than four hours' work a day to produce enough to satisfy all the socially recognised needs of their group. With these facts, the idea of primitive hunters on a near-starvation level, lacking time to invent a complex culture and progress toward civilisation began to disintegrate fast. Marshall Sahlins, reversing former views, maintained that, on the contrary, they were the only societies of plenty ever known, since all social needs were satisfied and the means for satisfying them were never scarce. A stubborn prejudice about societies as far back as the neolithic and which originated from an ideological need to justify the expansion of farmers to the detriment of hunter–gatherers was thus 'unmasked'.

The potlatch of the North-West coast Indians therefore is not merely an 'excessive' form of competition deriving from a cultural tendency towards 'megalomania',[44] helped by a multiplicity of resources furnished by a prodigious environment. Suttles has shown that the environment was exceedingly diversified and that the resources were very unequally distributed between groups. He also demonstrated that further North this inequality became greater – local groups tended to claim with greater tenacity property rights on productive sites and practise potlatch. Suttles also emphasised the fact that where the resources were most strongly concentrated, as for instance among the Haida, Tsimshian and Tlingit, economic cooperation within the groups became more intense, the chiefs directing the process of production and distribution more closely; their authority was strictly linked to the functioning of kinship groups within which descent ties were more strongly unilineal than elsewhere.

The analysis of the potlatch is far from complete and Suttles has been severely criticised for not having shown clearly that the latent function of the potlatch is to redistribute a group's excess subsistence resources among groups which have a conspicuous lack. The potlatch does not 'reduce' itself to a complicated and disguised mechanism in order to insure against risks of crises in subsistence resulting from exceptional fluctuations in the production of natural resources. Such fluctuations were quite normal, but they could have catastrophic effects for hunter–gatherers or fishermen not producing their own resources. Suttles' and Vayda's theses have given rise to new works which now take into account all the information accumulated since Boas' time (Barnet, Murdock, Helen Codere, Piddocke, etc.). We have seen the publication of valuable studies such as *Making my Name Good* by Drucker and Heizer, and *Feasting with my Enemy* by Rosman and Rubel. It is now quite clear that potlatch rivalries and their famous practices of ostentatious destruction were not only an example of an original 'culture' putting honour and prestigious behaviour very high on their list of values. They were also a public expression both of a well-administered economy, capable of producing abundant and regular surpluses and a politico-ideological custom in order to oblige – through a ceremonial redistribution of this surplus – neighbouring groups or potentially hostile allies to recognise publicly and peacefully the legitimacy and continuity of the groups' rights over territory and resources. The potlatch facts therefore are multifunctional as Piddocke stresses; they are the 'total social facts' of Mauss, facts of 'political economy' in the full sense of the word. A scientific explanation demands the recognition of the economic functions of kinship and politico-ideological relations; facts have to be reconstructed in thought to show the exact configuration of the mode of production which allows the production and control of a vast surplus of subsistence and prestige goods. There is every chance that such a reconstruction will eliminate any 'culturalist' or idealist interpretation of the potlatch; but it also fails to confirm the hypothesis that the latent meaning, the hidden rationality of the potlatch assures selective advantages to groups practising it.

It is equally hard to uphold the idea, made famous by Herskovits, that African cattleherders are afflicted with a 'cattle complex', which expresses above all a 'cultural choice', rather than ecologico-economic constraints. The anthropologist has to explain, in effect, an ensemble of well known facts, which to Europeans often seem profoundly irrational. Cattle seem to be wealth accumulated in order to acquire prestige and social status rather than to assure the possessor's subsistence or financial enrichment through market exchange. When exchanged it is often not for market purposes but to seal matrimonial alliances and descent obligations. Cattle are usually accumulated in large herds and the meat is consumed on certain ceremonial occasions; the animals are not used as work beasts and provide, at the very most, a meagre milk supply. The animal far from being a utilitarian asset to man is primarily associated with those rituals accompanying his own birth, marriage and death and he is attached to it in an emotional, even mystical way.

With the works of Gulliver, Deshler, Dyson-Hudson, Jacobs, etc., these cultural 'traits' gradually became further illuminated. It was soon noticed that we had been too hasty in turning livestock into purely prestige goods; on many occasions cattle were used not only for ceremonial purposes but in exchange for agricultural and craft products of sedentary peoples. It was found that there were practical reasons for the killing and consumption of cattle even when it was on rare ceremonial occasions. The fact that a single unit of domestic production could not possibly preserve and consume the quantity of meat represented by one beast, necessitated its sharing with other units in the group; this division creates or reinforces reciprocal networks of obligations, which confer on the killing and consumption of the beast a ceremonial and symbolic value, stemming from social functions. Moreover, the fact that cattle killing is rare for each unit of production does not mean that the group as a whole does not consume meat quite regularly when ceremonial killing and the division of meat occur regularly in all families. Further, while herds are often vast and cause the excessive use of limited grasslands and harm to vegetation and soil, this is not only due to the owner's pride or emotional attachment to the older beasts, which they cannot bring themselves to sacrifice.

We know now that cattle losses due to water shortage can amount to 10 to 15 per cent of the herd per year among the Dodoth of Uganda for example; that death particularly hits young animals and that they take six or seven years to reach their prime when they produce twenty times less milk than a European dairy cow; it is not surprising therefore that a high value is placed on the numbers of livestock and that there is a complex and parsimonious strategy worked out to dispose of meat, milk, even the blood of the animals among herdsmen. The owner of sixty cows has many more chances of being able to deal with epizootic diseases, excessive drought and of reproducing his social conditions of existence (material and political), than one who starts with a herd of only six cows.

We have no space to treat in detail the remarkable studies made by Geertz, Conklin and Rappaport, of the functioning of those societies practising slash and burn cultivation in South-East Asia and Oceania, and the outstanding discoveries of archaeologists such as Flannery, McNeish, etc., who, following Braidwood and Adams, have been trying since the fifties to reconstitute minutely the ecological and economic conditions of existence among the peoples of Mesopotamia, Anatolia, Meso-America or the Andes. These are peoples who domesticated plants and animals and inaugurated fundamental material and social changes which in turn led to the appearance of new types of society based on new modes of production which resulted both in the progressive disappearance of palaeolithic societies of the hunter–gatherer type and to the appearance of class and state societies. Here again the discoveries were going to question and force a profound revision of such glorious ideas as Childe's 'neolithic revolution'.

Nevertheless, we must be aware of the limits and origin of neo-functionalism and those works which claim affinity with 'cultural ecology'. They derive solely from the basic inadequacy of their materialism, which has made them perceive complex relations between economics and society in a 'reductionist' way. The diversity of kinship relations, the complexity of ideological practices and ritual have never been accorded their proper significance.[45] R. and N. Dyson-Hudson (who produced some valuable work on the Karimonjong cattleherders of Uganda) have stated with reference to boys' initiation rites and their identification with the animal presented to them on this occasion: that here are the cultural manifestations of a fact of central importance: the fact that cattle are the principal source of their livelihood. The role of cattle in the life of the Karimonjong is always to transform the energy in the grass and scrub of the tribal territory into a form of energy readily available to man. They thus align themselves with the polemical statements of Marvin Harris, the willing and aggressive leader of this 'cultural neo-materialism'. Having undertaken to 'desacralise' the sacred cows of India, he states:

> I have written this paper because I believe the irrational, non-economic, and exotic aspects of the Indian cattle complex are greatly overemphasized at the expense of rational, economic and mundane interpretations...Insofar as the beef-eating taboo helps discourage growth of beef-producing industries, it is part of an ecological adjustment which maximizes rather than minimizes the calorie and protein output of the productive process.[46]

Here we recognise vulgar materialism, 'economism', which reduces all social relations to the status of an epiphenomenon associated with economic relations which are themselves reduced to a technique of adaptation to the natural and biological environment. The secret rationality of social relations is reduced to advantages of adaptation whose content, as already pointed out by Lévi-Strauss in respect of Malinowski's functionalism, resolves itself often into simple truisms.[47] Once a society exists it functions and it is a banality to say that a variable is adaptive, because it has a necessary function in a system. Even Marshall Sahlins says:

> Proof that a certain trait or cultural arrangement has positive economic value is not an adequate explanation of its existence or even of its presence. The *problematique* of adaptive advantage does not specify a uniquely correct answer. As principle of causality in general and economic performance in particular, 'adaptive advantage' is

indeterminate, stipulating grossly what is impossible but rendering suitable anything that is possible.[48]

This line of thought makes it impossible to analyse the reasons for the dominance of kinship or politico-religious relations, or for the specific interconnections in social structures. The structural causality of economics is reduced to a 'probabilist' correlation, and history, in empirical fashion to a series of events of greater or lesser frequency.[49]

Empirical scepticism can now take up the cudgels; the weakness in some neo-materialist analyses concerning kinship, religion, etc., serves to keep alive and reinforce idealist theories of society and history which partisans of 'cultural ecology' criticise and fight against. Empirical materialism and simplistic functionalism can never explain reasons why things exist, why for example history and the content of societies are never completely 'integrated' wholes, but entities whose unity results from the *provisionally stable* effect of a structural compatibility allowing different structures to reproduce themselves to the point where the internal and external dynamics of these systems prohibit these entities from existing again as such.[50] This failure, however, does not mean that the results of the work of anthropologists and archaeologists professing an ecological and materialistic approach are not on the whole positive ones. Knowledge of the functioning mechanisms of economies which rely on hunting and gathering, large-scale cattleherding or slash and burn agriculture has been considerably enlarged and made more explicit from the time they undertook a systematic and detailed study of *constraints* which the social environment and techniques exercise or were exercising on the material and social life of these societies, and from the time they began *measuring* those real relations existing between social needs and the means for satisfying them. A certain amount of wrong information reveals both ignorance of the real circumstances and those ideological prejudices of which anthropologists and economists are the conscious or unconscious vectors. They have now been recognised as such and their expulsion from the field of scientific knowledge is under way. Such a critical method arrives at an ideological postulate (and this is outside the field of anthropology), which vitiates at its source all bourgeois economic thinking and severely limits for all time the scientific worth of its researches and discoveries. We now have the metaphysical assumption that men are condemned by nature to not satisfying their needs, and are constrained therefore to calculate the optimal employment of their resources; herein lies the object and basis of economic science. H. Guitton states this with some conviction:

Man experiences a need of the infinite and is ceaselessly tormented by the finite in the universe. This antithesis is first expressed in the idea of scarcity. The needs appear to be countless and the means for expressing them limited. It may also happen that the means are sufficient, even over-sufficient. Then another notion intervenes – the notion of inadaptibility. The goods are not necesssarily there when or where the need arises. If too plentiful, they must be reduced and when insufficient they have to be produced.

We shall not linger long on an illogical thesis which at one and the same time postulates the insurmountable finiteness of resources, yet recognises that sometimes they are overplentiful. It is enough to stress that concrete and detailed analyses show up such ideological phantasma for what they are – theoretical puppets pretending to be real and not appearing to have their strings pulled; this *homo oeconomicus* puppet is the victim of an ontological fate and he is not permitted the choice between a non-satisfaction derived from the infinity of his needs and an inadaptability derived from the occasional overplenitude of his resources.

We can now see the epistemological conditions of a scientific analysis of the various means of production and the relations between economics and society gradually being defined and restored. An analysis of this kind is only possible when real structures are taken into account, remembering not to confuse, as empiricism does, the real with the visible; we also need a materialist approach without reducing the various structures and examples of social reality to the epiphenomena of man's material relations with his environment. If anthropology must be structural and materialist in order to be thoroughly scientific, should it not be inspired by the works of Claude Lévi-Strauss as much if not more than those of Marx? Though Lévi-Strauss devotes little space to the study of economics, it is vital to make a very close analysis of the main points of his methods of structural analysis and his study of both the relations between economics and society and society in relation to history, in order to evaluate the theoretical significance and limits of his materialist structuralism and to understand the difference between the thought of Lévi-Strauss and Marx.

There are two methodological principles, recognised by functionalism, structuralism and Marxism alike, which are basic to the scientific study of social facts. The first stipulates that analyses of social relations must not be analysed in isolation, but considered in their reciprocal relationships – as entities forming 'systems'. The second stipulates that these systems must be analysed in their internal logic prior to analysing their genesis and evolution. In a way these two principles mean that modern scientific thought has to confront 19th-century evolutionism, historicism and diffusionism, in so far as these doctrines – in spite of differing concepts as to the evolution of societies – were often content with a superficial analysis of the real functioning of customs and institutions within the societies studied and the bulk of their efforts were devoted to unearthing their origins and retracing their history through earlier stages of this purely conjectural evolution of mankind. But, apart from this agreement which only concerns the abstract formulation of these two principles and not the concrete facts of putting them into practice, there is a total opposition between functionalism, as against structuralism, and Marxism when it comes to understanding the term 'social structure'. For Radcliffe-Brown and Nadel, a social structure is the 'order, the arrangement' of man's apparent relationships, an arrangement derived from the reciprocal complementarity of these relationships.[51] For functionalists, therefore, 'structure' is one 'aspect' of the real; they maintain that this reality exists outside the human mind. For Leach, on the other hand, structure is an ideal order which the mind brings to things converting the multiform flux of the real to simplified representations which allow reality to be grasped; it has pragmatic value and permits action and social practice.[52]

For Lévi-Strauss, structures are part of reality, are reality in fact, and here he is in agreement with Radcliffe-Brown and in opposition to the idealist empiricism of Leach. However, for Lévi-Strauss, as well as for Marx, structures are not directly visible or observable realities, but levels of reality which exist beyond man's visible relations and whose functioning constitutes the deeper logic of a social system – the underlying order by which the apparent order must be explained. This is the meaning of Lévi-Strauss's famous formula, which Leach and some structuralists have insisted on interpreting in an idealist and formalist sense. They prefer the first to the second phrase: 'The term 'social structure' has nothing to do with empirical reality but with models which are built up after it...social relations consist of the raw materials out of which the models making up the social structure are built.'

In replying to Maybury-Lewis, Lévi-Strauss had already insisted on the fact that: 'Ultimate proof of the molecular structure is provided by the electron microscope which enables us to see the *actual* molecules. This feat does not mean that in the future the molecule will become more visible to the naked eye. Similarly, it is pointless to expect that structural analysis will change the *perception* of concrete social relations. It will only explain them better.' And in his introduction to *From Honey to Ashes*, he again asserts in categorical terms: 'I have thus completed my demonstration of the fact that, whereas in the public mind there is frequently confusion between structuralism, idealism and formalism, structuralism has only to be confronted with true manifestations of idealism and formalism for its own deterministic and realistic inspiration to become clearly manifest'.

In order to analyse structures whose reality, he claims, lies outside the human mind beyond the superficial aspect of social relations, Lévi-Strauss puts forward three methodological principles. He considers that:

a. all structure is a determined ensemble of relations all connected according to internal laws of change which have yet to be discovered;

b. all structure combines specific elements, which are its proper components and that for this reason it is useless to insist on 'reducing' one structure to another or 'deducing' one structure from another;

c. among different structures belonging to the same system, there is a relationship of compatibility whose laws must be discovered, but this compatibility should not be regarded as the effect of essential selection mechanisms for the success of a biological process of environmental adaptation.

It is obvious that Marx was working along the same lines when, after showing that economic categories of wages, profit and income are defined and dealt with in daily life by agents of the capitalist mode of production, he declares that these things express the visible relations between owners of labour, owners of capital and owners of land; they have a pragmatic value in this sense, as Leach would say, since they permit the organisation and direction of these visible relations without having any scientific value; they conceal the fundamental fact that profit and income for one person is the unpaid labour of others:

The *final pattern* of economic relations as seen *on the surface*, in their real existence and consequently in the conceptions by which the bearers and agents of these relations *seek to understand* them, is very much different from, and indeed quite the reverse of, their *inner but concealed essential pattern* and the *conception corresponding* to it.[53]

It must also be remembered that Marx's theoretical greatness was in demonstrating that industrial and commercial profits, financial interest and income from land – which seem to come from totally different sources and actions – are so many *distinct* yet *changed* forms of surplus value. They are forms of distribution among the different social groups which form the capitalist class, distinct forms of the global process of capitalist exploitation of wage-earning producers.

We know in fact that Marx was the first to formulate a hypothesis about the presence of essential relations of correspondence and structural compatibility between the forces of production and relations of production, as also between the mode of production and superstructures, without any intention of reducing the former to being merely epiphenomena of the latter. Does Lévi-Strauss's structuralism merge into Marx's historical materialism? It would seem so. But in order to answer this question, it is essential to get nearer to what Lévi-Strauss understands by history and to understand his ideas on causality in economics, as well as seeing how he has applied them in theoretical practice.

For Claude Lévi-Strauss, it is 'tedious as well as useless, in this connection, to amass arguments to prove that all societies are in history and change: that this is so is patent.[54] History is not only 'histoire "froide"', where 'societies which create the minimum of disorder...tend to remain indefinitely in their initial state.'[55] It is also made from 'non-recurrent chains of events whose effects accumulate to produce economic and social upheavals'.[56] To explain these changes, Claude Lévi-Strauss accepts 'the incontestable primacy of infrastructures' as 'a law of order'.[57]

'I do not at all mean to suggest that ideological transformations give rise to social ones. Only the reverse is in fact true. Men's conception of the relations between nature and culture is a function of modifications of their own social relations...We are merely studying the shadows on the wall of the Cave'.[58]

And Lévi-Strauss himself claims that, with his studies on myths and the 'savage mind', he wants 'to contribute' to a theory of superstructures hinted at by Marx.[59] We can only note that these theoretical principles are contradicted in *From Honey to Ashes*, where he discourses on the fundamental historical turmoil in ancient Greek society, 'when mythology gave way to philosophy and the latter emerged as the necessary pre-condition of scientific thought'. Here we see 'one historical occurrence, which can have no meaning beyond its actual happening at that place and in that time'.[60] History, however, subject to a law of order by which the whole of society is organised, remains deprived of all necessity and the origins of western philosophy and science are explained away as simple accidents. 'I am not rejecting history. On the contrary, structural analysis accords history a paramount place, the place that rightfully belongs to that irreducible contingency without which necessity would be inconceivable.'[61] And Claude Lévi-Strauss quoted Tylor's phrase of 1871 for his epigraph to *Elementary Structures of Kinship*: 'The tendency of modern inquiry is more and more towards the conclusion that if law is anywhere, it is everywhere; with this he finally finds himself in agreement with empiricism which sees in history a mere succession of accidental events. 'To return to ethnology, it was one of us – E. R. Leach – who remarked somewhere that "the evolutionists never discussed in detail – still less observed – what actually happened when a society in Stage A changed into a society at Stage B; it was merely argued that all Stage B societies must somehow have evolved out of Stage A societies"'.[62]

Now we have come back to the same standpoint as the functionalist empiricist.[63] 'The historian has changes, the anthropologist structures,' and this is because the changes, 'the processes are not analytical objects, but the particular way in which temporality is experienced by a subject:'[64] a thesis in radical opposition to the thesis of the law of order in social structure and their changes, which Lévi-Strauss took from Marx.

How does he arrive at this point? How can he obliterate, *annul* in his *practice*, those theoretical principles to which he refers, but which evidently remain largely inoperative? Here we are not going to make an internal analysis of Lévi-Strauss's work and we make no claims to estimate their scientific value. But let us admit straight away that his work has made an impact in two domains, those of kinship theory and ideological theory and that all progress now has to be made with the help of his successes as well as his failures. Fundamental questions such as the incest prohibition, exogamy and endogamy, cross-cousin marriage, dual organisations which were formerly treated separately and inadequately have all been linked together and explained as deriving from the basic fact of marriage as an exchange, the exchange of women; and that kinship relations are primarily relations between groups rather than relations between individuals. In distinguishing two possible mechanisms of exchange, restricted exchange and generalised exchange, Lévi-Strauss discovered an *order* in a vast ensemble of kinship systems which before seemed to have little in common and which were part of societies which had had no historical contact. And this order is an order of transformation. A huge Mendelian tableau of 'types' of kinship systems was gradually constructed. This tableau does not cover the 'complex' kinship structures, which only define a limited circle of kin, leaving other mechanisms, such as economics or psychology, the process of determining the interconnection.[65]

Nevertheless, structural analysis, while not denying history, cannot go hand in hand with it, since it has separated the analysis of 'types' of kinship relations from the analysis of their 'functions'. These functions are neither ignored nor denied, but they are never explored for what they are. And so the question of any *real articulation* between kinship relations and other social structures which characterise historically determined, concrete societies, is never analysed: Lévi-Strauss confines himself to extracting from concrete facts a 'formal system' of kinship relations, a system which he then studies in its internal logic and compares with other types, either similar or different, but belonging even in their differences, to the same group of transformations.

In this connection, it could be said that Lévi-Strauss, unlike the functionalists, never studies real societies and does not try to account for their diversity or internal complexity. Of course, it is not that he is unaware of these problems, but he has never treated them systematically. Thus, concerning Murdock's correlation of patrilineal institutions and 'highest levels of culture', Lévi-Strauss declares: 'It is true that in societies where political power takes precedence over other forms of organisation, the duality which would result from the masculinity of political authority and the matrilineal character of descent could not subsist. Consequently, societies attaining this level of political organisation tend to generalise the paternal right.'[66]

In spite of the woolly notion 'stage of political organisation', Lévi-Strauss is here confronting the fact of the emergence, historically, of societies within which kinship relations are no longer playing a dominant role, and instead politico-ideological relations are beginning to take over. Why and under what circumstances did it become so? Why are patrilineal rights more compatible with this new type of social structure? Lévi-Strauss does not answer these questions, nor does he even explain under what circumstances such societies appear – societies in which kinship systems and marriage have little or nothing to say about the kind of person one may marry. Allusion is made to the fact that in these societies, wealth, money, bridewealth and social hierarchy play a determining role in the choice of marriage partners; but how is this so, and where does history come into it? Not that history, for a Marxist, is a category which explains; on the contrary, it is a category that has to be explained. Historical materialism is not another 'model' of history, nor another 'philosophy' of history. It is primarily a theory of society, a hypothesis about the articulation of its inner levels and about the specific hierarchical causality of each of these levels. And when it is able to discover the types and mechanisms of this causality and articulation, Marxism will show its ability to be a true instrument of historical science.[67]

To have more understanding on this point, we have to go beyond a structural analysis of kinship forms and the uncovering of formal codes and a grammar of Amerindian myths. These structural analyses may be indispensable, but they are not sufficient in themselves. Lévi-Strauss recognises this himself when he criticises with justification the principle of looking solely at the accidental events of history and at the diffusion of exogenous causes, for the *raisons d'être* of a kinship system: 'A *functional* system e.g., a kinship system, can never be interpreted in an integral fashion by diffusionist hypotheses. The system is bound up with the *total structure* of the society employing it and consequently its nature depends more on the *intrinsic* characteristics of such a society than on cultural contacts and migrations.'[68]

In order to go beyond a structural analysis of the types of social relations or modes of thought, we must practise this kind of morphological analysis in such a way as to discover the intrinsic connection between *form, function, mode of articulation and conditions* for the appearance and transformation of these social relations and the ways of thinking in specific societies studied by historians and anthropologists. In our opinion, it is only by a resolute involvement along these lines that we may hope to make any progress in a scientific analysis of a field usually neglected or maltreated by materialists, and where idealism, whether it derives from functionalism or structuralism, for this very reason has a privileged role. In the same way this is how we shall make progress in the field of ideology and, as a result, as far as symbolic forms of social relations and practice are concerned.

Elsewhere,[69] we have shown how Lévi-Strauss has made enormous advances in a theory of ideologies, which he has tried to develop along Marxist lines; using Amerindian myths, he revealed in precise detail that all those elements of ecological, economic and social reality are transposed into the myths, showing that they are the thoughts of men living in specific social and material relations. At the same time, he also reveals that at the core of this mode of social thought, there is present and functioning a formal logic of analogy, i.e., the activity of human thought which reasons about the world and organises the content of experience in nature and society into symbolic forms of metaphor and metonym. In fact, Lévi-Strauss, even should he take exception to the interpretation, has brought together under his unique phrase 'la pensée sauvage', a dual content; one refers to nature, that is to say to formal capacities of the mind whereby reasoning is done by analogy, and by equivalence, more generally, to 'pensée à l'état sauvage', 'a direct expression of the structure of the mind (and behind the mind, probably, of the brain)'.[70] The other element refers to 'la pensée des sauvages', to the way men think while they are actually hunting, fishing, or gathering honey, growing cassava or maize and living in bands or tribes. But what is neglected and missing from this gigantic theoretical exercise is an analysis of the articulation of form and content, of thought in its 'savage' state and the thought of 'savages', the social functioning of these representations and the symbolic practices which accompany them, the transformation of these functions and their content, the circumstances of their transformation. Finally, that which exists as a *void* in thought, which is like keeping an object of thought outside thought itself, is an analysis of forms and fundamentals in the 'fetishisation' of social relations, an analysis which few Marxists have attempted; and on which depends not only a scientific explanation of political and religious elements in general, but also and foremost an explanation of the circumstances and stages of development of rank, caste or class societies, and even an explanation for the disappearance from history of former classless societies. It is precisely in order to achieve this complex task, a task which presupposes a combination of multiple theoretical practices, that Marx's hypothesis on the determination of types of society and their evolution and modes of thought by the conditions of production and *reproduction* in material life, must be used as the central hypothesis: 'The history of religion itself, without its material basis, lacks criteria. Indeed, by analysis, it is easier to discover the content, the terrestrial nucleus of religion's mist-enveloped conceptions than, conversely, it is to reveal how the actual conditions of life gradually assume an ethereal form.'[71] We hope we have shown, despite appearances and contradictory statements, that it is to this central hypothesis that functionalism and structuralism must necessarily lead, as soon as they start penetrating more deeply into the logic of the societies under analysis.[72]

We may now conclude our criticisms and take a new direction, based on a theoretical position beyond and outside the boundaries of functionalism and structuralism. In this way we may be able to bring to light and study 'the action of social structures' on each other, and to understand the relations of structural causality between the different modes of production which have appeared in history and different forms of social organisation. However, we shall not merely hint at the direction to take but shall try to give a clearer idea of the type of results which may be arrived at. To do this we shall look at a few points taken from my unpublished study of the modes of production and social organisation of the Mbuti Pygmies of Zaïre, using Colin Turnbull's remarkable and detailed material. Such a résumé cannot do justice to the wealth and complexity of facts, but for our purposes it is enough to give an idea of the results which can be achieved. These results were shown to Turnbull at each stage and he agreed fully with them.[73]

The Mbuti Pygmies inhabit a generalised ecosystem of a simple type,[74] the equatorial forest of Zaïre. They are hunter–gatherers. They use the bow and net for hunting game, consisting mainly of different varieties of antelope and occasionally elephant. The women collect mushrooms, tubers and other wild plants as well as molluscs and thus contribute more than half the food resources. Honey is collected once a year and its harvest is the occasion for the division of each band into smaller groups, which come together again at the end of the honey season. Hunting is done collectively. Married men in a semicircle hold their individual nets (about thirty metres in length) end to end, while unmarried women and children head the game back toward the nets. These activities are repeated every, or nearly every, day and in the evening the produce from hunting and gathering is divided and consumed by all members of the camp. Each month, if game becomes scarce round the camp, the band moves to another site, but always within the same territory, which is known and respected by neighbouring bands. Kinship and family relations, such as they are, play a secondary role in production because work is divided according to sex and generation. Individuals frequently leave the band where they were born and go to live in neighbouring bands, sometimes for good. Wife exchange is practised and the spouse is sought preferably in a distant band; never in the mother's or paternal grandmother's band. Bands do not have chiefs and authority is divided according to generation and sex; old and renowned hunters do, however, enjoy greater authority than other members of the band. War does not occur between bands but murder and severe punishment are very rare within the band. The death of all adults, men and women, and girls' puberty are accompanied by ritual and festivity; *molimo* in the former case and *elima* in the second. In these, the forest becomes the object of intense worship and 'makes its voice heard' through the intermediary of sacred flutes. Bands number between seven and thirty hunters and their families; hunting with less than seven nets is ineffective; while with more than thirty hunters there would not be sufficient game to provide regular supplies for the group; and the organisation of hunting with nets, normally performed without a real leader, would have to be modified in order to remain effective.

When these economic and social relations are analysed closely, we see that the conditions of production determine three internal constraints on the modes of production and that these constraints express the conditions of reproduction for these modes of production together with the restricted possibilities of this reproduction.

– Constraint No. 1 is a 'dispersion' constraint on hunting groups and on the minimal and maximal numbers limiting each group.

– Constraint No. 2 is a 'cooperation' constraint on individuals according to sex and age in the process of production and in the practice of hunting with nets.

– Constraint No. 3 is a 'fluidity' constraint, a 'non-closure', or as Turnbull puts it, the maintenance of a state of permanent 'flux' within the bands; this flux is expressed by the frequent and rapid variation of their strength and social composition.

These three constraints express the *social* conditions of the reproduction of the process of production, given the existing nature of the productive forces (special techniques for hunting and gathering) and the nature of the biological conditions for reproduction of animal and plant species which go to make up the generalised ecosystem of the equatorial forest of Zaïre. These constraints create a system, that is to say each intervenes along with the others. Constraint No. 2 for example, the 'cooperation' constraint on individuals according to sex and age, which assures their own existence and reproduction as well as that of the band, assumes a form determined by the action of constraint No. 1, since the size of the band must be kept within certain limits, and by the action of constraint No. 3, since the necessity to keep bands in a state of flux, constantly modifies a group's size and social composition, that is to say, ties of kinship, affinity or friendship between those called upon to cooperate each day in the process of production and redistribution of hunting and gathering produce. Equally, one could show – and this should be done – the effects of constraints 1 and 2 on 3, and constraints 2 and 3 on 1. We should also note that these constraints (particularly those of 'dispersion' and 'flux') are such that both the individual and band's social conditions of reproduction are equally and immediately conditions of reproduction in Mbuti *society* as a whole and are always present in all parts of it. They are, therefore, internal conditions for each band and at the same time *common* conditions for *all* the bands; this makes for the reproduction of the socioeconomic system in its entirety.

These three constraints, therefore, make for a system. This system is born from the very process of production whereby it expresses the material and social conditions of reproduction. And the system itself is at the basis of a number of simultaneous structural effects on *all* the other instances of Mbuti social organisation, effects which we can only list, since a full demonstration would take too long. All these effects consist in the determination of the *elements of content and form* of instances which are *compatible* with these constraints, therefore assuring the reproduction of the Mbuti mode of production. Thus, these constraints, *internal* to the mode of production, are at the same time channels by which the mode of production determines, in the final analysis, the nature of the different instances of Mbuti society and, since the effects of these constraints are *simultaneously* active on all instances, by the action of the system of constraints, the mode of production determines the *relation* and *articulation* of all the instances among them and in relation to itself, that is, determines the general *structure* of the society as it is, the specific form and function of each of these instances which go to compose it. To search and find the system of constraints determined by a social process of production, is to proceed epistemologically in such a way that one can show the structural causality of the economy on society and, at the same time, the general specific structure of this society, its logical ensemble, even though this economic causality, this general structure of society and this specific logical ensemble are never directly observable phenomena as such, but facts which have to be reconstructed by thought and scientific practice. Proof of the 'truth' of this reconstruction can only be that it offers to explain *all* observed facts and poses new questions to the student in the field,[75] questions which require fresh research and new ways of finding answers; this is the very process and progress of scientific knowledge.

Having demonstrated and analysed this system of constraints, we are now ready to take account and reveal the *necessity* of all *major* facts observed and recorded in the works of Schebesta and Turnbull.

The idea of *distinct* territories[76] is explained by the dispersion constraint; using the flux constraints, the 'non-closure' of bands can be explained by the inexistence of *exclusive* rights of bands to their territory.[77] What is invariable is not the internal composition of bands, but the existence of *stable* relationships *between* bands, therefore a relationship which reproduces and permits the reproduction of all bands. Now we can explain the reason for the *form* and *content* of the social relations of ownership and the employment of this basic resource which is the hunter's and gatherer's territory – that part of nature which constitutes 'a store of primitive goods' or a 'laboratory for the means of production' (Marx). What we wish to reveal here is the origin of rules and the customary laws of appropriation in the very process of production and the use to which nature is put. Now a revelation of the origins, outside consciousness, of the system of conscious norms of the social practices of production agents, operating within determined means of production, is a fundamental step ahead in the use of Marx's methods, but it is generally neglected or caricatured by Marxists. Here we should like to express our agreement with C. Bettelheim in his critical analysis of the confusion reigning in the theory and practice of both economists and rulers in socialist countries as far as the juridical aspect and the real content of relations of production is concerned.[78]

The 'juridical' sphere also penetrates to norms of action of individuals and groups regarding their territory for hunting and gathering and their production resources; we cannot, however, elaborate this point; instead we shall make a rapid analysis of the structural effects of the mode of production on Mbuti kinship relations. Here again, the facts and norms coincide with the structure of the mode of production and with the constraints imposed, particularly constraint No. 3, the 'non-closure' of bands, which maintains a structure of flux between them. Kinship terminology mainly stresses generational and sex differences, reproducing forms of cooperation in the process of production (constraint No. 2). When relations of affinity are analysed, we find a preference for marrying into distant bands and the prohibition of marrying within your mother's or paternal grandmother's band. These are positive and negative norms which accord with constraint No. 3, because they prevent 'closure' of groups and their constitution as *closed* units exchanging women in a *regular* and *directed fashion*; since in taking a woman from his mother's or grandmother's band, he would be *reproducing* the marriage of his father and/or his grandfather, therefore reproducing former and older relations which would make relations between bands *permanent* – each generation would be linked apropos the exchange of women necessary for the reproduction of society and each individual band.

Moreover, by *simultaneously* prohibiting marriage between neighbouring bands on adjacent territories, the formation of closed bands (constraint No. 3) is made even more impossible.

Thus, constraints 1 and 3 affect forms of affinity and at the same time explain the fact that marriage is primarily an exchange between individuals and nuclear families;[79] all this preserves the fluid structure of bands. It also explains why the band as such only interferes in order to regulate the new couple's place of residence; this is of great importance since a young man only receives a net ('made by his mother and maternal uncle') and shares fully and individually in hunting activities after marriage, thereby becoming a full agent of production in the reproduction of the band.[80] Then again, the relative weakness of any collective control over the individual (constraint No. 3) and over the couple explains the relative *precariousness* of marriage among the Mbuti.[81]

The structural effects of the mode of production on descent are perfectly complementary with those on affinity. The Mbuti, as Turnbull has shown admirably, do not have a true lineage organisation and when we refer to lineage 'segments' in order to indicate groups of brothers living in the same band, this is awkward and a misuse of terminology. The fact they there are no regular or directed matrimonial exchanges between bands, which would mean each generation following its ancestors' example, prohibits continuity and the formation of consanguinal groups of any high genealogical degree or groups which could control their continuity by an essential segmentation. At the same time, in order for society to reproduce itself through matrimonial exchanges, there must be at least four bands in order for these matrimonial relations to exist. Band A (of self), band B (the mother's band), band C (the paternal grandmother's band) and band C (the spouse's band, which as we know must not be a neighbouring one).

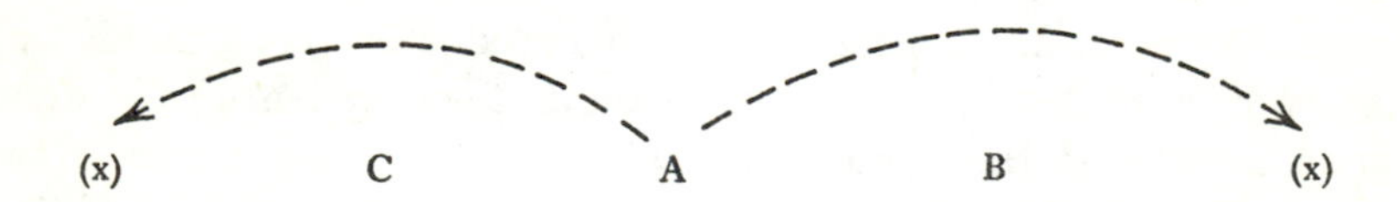

From a methodological point of view, it is clear that it would be a mistake to imagine that a logical study of the functioning of a society can be made by analysing only one band or a single local unit.

Other effects of the constraints imposed by the mode of production appear when we analyse the political relations existing between and within bands. These effects are different in their content because they have an effect on a different aspect, irreducible to elements of the process of production, but they are *isomorphic* to the effects produced on other instances of Mbuti society. This isomorphy derives from the fact that all the different effects come from the *same* cause acting simultaneously on all levels of society. This method of carrying out a structural analysis within a Marxist framework, as distinct from ordinary cultural materialism or some people's so-called Marxism, does not *reduce* the various instances of a society to economics nor does it represent economics as the only true reality, whereby all other features reflect differing and phantasmic effects. Our way of using Marxist theory takes fully and strictly into account the specificity (and their relative autonomy) of all things.

Two features characterise political rule and practice among Mbuti Pygmies: *a*. lack of any significant inequality in political status or authority between individuals, men and women, or between generations, the old, the adult and the young. Inequality does exist, favouring adult men in relation to women; old men in relation to individuals; and men over women in younger generations; *b*. a systematic refusal of all kinds of violence or any collective repression in the regulation of conflicts between individuals or bands.

In the first case, should inequality threaten to develop – for example if a great elephant hunter wishes to convert his prestige as a hunter to one of authority over the group, the institutional response is one of mockery, public gibes; in brief a systematic erosion of all attempts to develop inequality over and beyond certain limits compatible with the voluntary (constraint No. 2) and always provisional (constraint No. 3) cooperation between individuals and within a band. In the second case, the response to all conflict which may *seriously* threaten the unity of the band or relations between bands results in a systematic recourse to compromise or diversion. In each band one person plays the role of buffoon (Colin Turnbull, in the first months of his stay among the Mbuti, played this role unawares), and this person is responsible for avoiding all serious conflicts which could lead to a dramatic event such as murder or the band's fission, thus threatening the internal goodwill and understanding necessary for cooperation and reproduction (constraint No. 2). To avoid conflict getting out of hand, the buffoon systematically draws attention away from them. Say, two individuals, *a* and *b* are in serious conflict because one has committed adultery with the other's wife, and their confrontation threatens to lead to physical violence or murder, the buffoon (who may be male or female) using artifice, exaggerates the importance of a minor tiff which other individuals, *c* and *d*, for example, are having; after several hours of shouting and quarrelling *a* and *b* will find themselves on the same side against *d*. All this tends to diminish the intensity of their own particular quarrel. In two instances only does the band practise repressive violence: first, if a hunter secretly places his personal net in front of all the other nets which are placed end to end, and thus improperly appropriates a greater share of game. This means that he is transforming communal effort of the band, hunters and beaters (women and children), to his own personal advantage; secondly, if, during a *molimo* festival in the forest's honour, a man goes to sleep and forgets to sing the sacred songs in unison when the forest is replying to the men's call (the voice of the forest being heard through the intermediary of the sacred flutes carried by the young men of the camp).

In both these cases, the thief and the man who goes to sleep, the internal solidarity of the group is disturbed and the real or imaginary conditions for reproduction are threatened (constraint No. 2). In both cases the guilty one is abandoned, left alone and defenceless in the forest, where he will soon die unless the band who exiled him, comes to find him again. It is the forest therefore which is entrusted with the task of sanctioning ultimately the major violations of the band's rules regarding social reproduction. Although it is, in fact, the band who has in practice condemned a guilty man, it is as though the forest were punishing him. Here, we find ourselves in the presence of a process of fetishisation of social relations, a process we shall return to when we analyse the religious practice of the Mbuti forest cult.

In interband conflict, violence is also avoided and all observers have pointed out, as a remarkable fact, the absence of war among the Pygmies. When a band captures game on another's territory, it sends a portion of the slaughtered game to this band; the conflict is thus regulated by compromise and sharing. Why is it that war is eliminated from Mbuti political experience? Because it would bring about oppositions which would crystallise groups and create rigid frontiers, excluding other groups from the use of certain territories and resources, increasing or decreasing the numbers of victorious or vanquished groups respectively and breaking the delicate equilibrium necessary for the reproduction of each band and for society as a whole. War is therefore incompatible with constraints Nos. 1, 2 and 3 of the mode of production, taken separately or in their reciprocal relationships. The absence of witchcraft among the Mbuti can be explained by the same reasons, because witchcraft presupposes suspicion, fear and hate between individuals and groups, preventing a good understanding or collective and continued cooperation between members of a band. If it did not lead us so far way from our theme, we should make a comparison between Mbuti hunters and Bantu farmers – their neighbours – who practise witchcraft avidly.

We might extend these different analyses further; for example, we could account for *all* the reasons why the existence of personal authority, such as 'big-men' or the existence of a permanent and centralised political hierarchy are incompatible with the conditions of reproduction or the mode of production. The possibility that individuals may, at any moment, leave one band and join another, the non-existence of lineal kinship relations, of continuity in the marriage alliance, are converging factors which make it impossible for authority to remain in the hands of a single individual who would eventually pass it on to his descendants – thus resulting in the formation of a hierarchy of political power in favour of closed groups, kinship, lineage or any other kind of group. At this theoretical stage, our aim is to show the specific action of each instance, combined with the action of internal constraints of the mode of production, as for example, the effect of the content and form of Mbuti kinship relations (non-lineal) on social forms of authority combined with the direct effects the mode of production can have on all political relations (absence of war, fluidity in a band's membership, etc.). We are now faced with a complex epistemological question concerning the analysis of *reciprocal* effects, convergent or divergent, which increase or limit themselves reciprocally, and analysis of the mutual effect of all instances on the basis of their specific relationships, their *general articulation* determined finally by the mode of production. Such an analysis is absolutely necessary in order to explain the content, form and function of Mbuti religion, a religion which dominates their ideology and symbolic actions.

Let us now consider those data which are almost impossible to decipher – religious facts. Among the Mbuti, religious practice takes the form of a forest cult. It is observed every day and in all their actions: in the morning, before leaving for the hunt, in the evening when they return and prior to dividing the game, etc. The more exceptional circumstances in the life of individuals or bands – birth, girls' puberty, death – are occasions for ritual. The most important are the *elima* festival for girls and the great *molimo* festival for the death of a respected adult. In case of epidemics, a succession of poor hunts, serious accidents, the band carries out 'little *molimos*'. In all everyday or more exceptional events in the life of both the individual or the community, the Mbuti turn to the forest and worship it, that is to say, they dance and, especially, sing in its honour.

The forest, for the Mbuti, is 'Everything'.[82] It is the ensemble of all inanimate and animate beings; it is a higher reality which exists as a person, a divinity to whom one speaks as to a father, mother, friend, even lover. The forest insulates and protects them from their Bantu neighbours; it is bountiful with gifts of game and honey; it scares away illness, punishes the guilty. It is Life. Death overtakes men and other living things because the forest goes to sleep and therefore it must be awakened[83] to persuade it to carry on providing nourishment, health, goodwill – in short, happiness and social harmony for the Mbuti in whatever band they may happen to live. Mbuti affirmation of dependence on, and trust in, the forest culminates in the great *molimo* ritual. Over a period of as long as a month, the band spends every day hunting with extra special ardour. There is an abundance of captured game; and it is shared out and eaten at a feast which is followed by dancing and singing lasting almost till dawn and, in the morning, the voice of the forest summons the Mbuti to fresh hunts and more dancing. Woe betide anyone whose tiredness from the night's activities prevents him from waking when the forest voice is heard and the sacred trumpets enter the camp on the shoulders of strong excited young men. The guilty person who has spoiled this communion, this unison, with the forest, may immediately be put to death or banished to the forest which punishes him by letting him die. One finds here an isomorphism involving two violations of the law which provoke punishment. To refuse to hunt with everybody or to sing with everyone, is to disrupt the vital cooperation and unity of the band for the reproduction of its real and imaginary conditions of existence (constraint No. 2).

What the forest represents then is both a supralocal reality – the natural ecosystem within which the Pygmies reproduce themselves as a society – and the totality of the material and social conditions for the reproduction of their society (the forest, as a god, provides game, health, social harmony, etc.). Mbuti religion therefore is an ideological instance where the conditions of reproduction of their mode of production and their society are represented; but they are represented *upside-down*, as 'fetishised', 'mythical'. It is not the hunters who catch game, it is the forest which provides them with a certain quantity for them to subsist and reproduce. Everything takes place as if a reciprocal relationship existed between persons of different power and status, since as distinct from men, the forest is omnipresent, omniscient and omnipotent. Toward it, men adopt attitudes of gratitude, love, respectful affection. When they forbid the needless killing of animals, the destruction of animal and plant species, it is the forest they are respecting (representation of the consciousness of constraint No. 1 and the conditions of renewal in the process of hunting and gathering natural, determined species).

But Mbuti religion is not just a system of representations, it is also social practice and plays a fundamental role in the very reproduction of society.

Can we use this method to construct a 'theory of the process of fetishisation' in social relations and – going further than different kinds of ideological, religious or political fetishism – tackle, in scientific manner, the domain of symbolic practice? These different realities have been badly mishandled by materialists, who appeal to a cultural ecology[84] or to Marxism,[85] even passing over these realities without a word.[86] These studies are usually pursued from an idealistic point of view, associated with functionalism (as in Turner's work) or structuralism. From this point of view, relations between a society's symbolic actions and its mode of production are practically never explored, since idealism is powerless to reveal or reconstruct them, even if it does not dogmatically deny them. Yet this is one of our major theoretical problems and its solution would contribute to an explanation of the conditions and reasons for the origins of class and state societies, and, as a result, the historical reasons for the disappearance of most classless societies. We shall try to show with the help of an example, how to tackle an analysis of the relationship between symbolic practice and the mode of production, thereby revealing the function of these symbolic practices in the reproduction of social relations as a whole.

The example is the great Mbuti *molimo* rite. Religious activity here implies an intensification of the process of production, extra work permitting an increase in the quantity of game to be shared out. Each person receives more and the result is an exceptionally large consumption of food which transforms an evening meal into a banquet and ordinary life into a day of celebration ending with dancing and unison singing. In this the Mbuti communicate with the forest, 'rejoicing' in it and calling for its blessing, its watchful presence, which brings with it game in plenty, good health and preservation from epidemics, want, dissension, death. The *molimo* rite, therefore, is a form of *symbolic labour*, which aims, according to Turnbull, at '*recreating* life and society, combatting the forces of hunger, dissension, immorality,' and which expresses 'the dominant preoccupation of the Mbuti which is, not to perpetuate individuals or lineages, but the band and the Mbuti *as such*'. As a result of this strenuous hunting and the plentiful supply of game shared out, cooperation and reciprocity are intensified and exalted, group tensions diminish almost to nothing or are pushed into the background for the time being, while dancing and polyphonic singing imply, respectively, the participation and union of all individuals. In short, with all its material, political, ideological, emotional and aesthetic aspects, religious activity broadens and exalts all positive aspects of social relations and at the same time allows the maximum attenuation, the temporary putting aside, of all the contradictions contained within these social relations. Religious activity therefore is a form of genuine *labour* involving contradictions determined by the structure of the mode of production and other social relations, such labour constituting one of the essential conditions for the reproduction of these relations – the relations of production as well as other social instances. Far from having nothing to do with material culture and the mode of production, as some idealists would wish, religious observance is both a material and political function and is at the core of the process of reproduction of this mode of production. Here again, social activity is presented 'topsy-turvy', present in a 'fetishised' way, since the restored harmony, the exceptional goodwill, abundance, happiness all result from the intenser cooperation, reciprocity, the deeper emotional fellowship which have come about in the relations between men because of these exceptional circumstances. They are represented and subsist as the effect and proof of the forest's closer presence and the greater generosity of this imaginary being, the personification of the group's unity and the very condition of its reproduction.

Mbuti religion, then, is not the domain of fantastic shadows projected into the depths of their consciousness by a reality existing in itself – solid and material – a reality which is their social relations in the production of the material sources of their existence. Far from being a ghostly reflection – both passive and derisory – of a reality which might move off elsewhere, these representations and religious observances draw their content, the very weight of their existence and the efficacy of their presence from the central join, from the hidden articulation of their mode of production and the instances corresponding to it. Though they seem to involve imaginary beings and relationships on the edge of human society, they in fact penetrate the furthest depths, the most secret inner parts of their society, to the invisible join which welds their different social relations into a whole, capable of reproducing itself. What the Mbuti are conscious of and what appears as elements or attributes of the forest, is in fact this invisible join in the inner parts, close and distant at the same time, of their society. When the Mbuti hide as far as possible and attenuate their contradictions and tensions (perforce engendered by the very structure of their social relations) by uniting together to carry out rites, hunting, feasts, dancing and singing in order to extol the forest – maternal dispenser of all that is good, and paternal protector from all evil, the watchful guardian over their behaviour, their children, their future – they are acting on this join, that is on themselves and the political and ideological conditions for the reproduction of their society.

Theory and practice are both directed towards the spot where their social relations become welded into a whole – a whole which must be reproduced as such; their religion is both a form of presentation and of presence of this dual suture and of a form of action of it. Representation and action that are such that at the time that this suture becomes known it offers the possibility of action; it becomes theoretically unknown when it is the illusory objective of practical action. Both present and latent in its manner of presentation, this invisible articulation of social relations (in their inherent basis) is both seen and unseen; it is the spot where man becomes estranged from himself, where real relations between men and things appear upside-down and fetishised.

At this point, which might be considered the beginning of a Marxist theory of religion and symbolic practice, we shall conclude by demonstrating the theoretical possibilities offered by a systematic analysis of the methods we suggest in order to explore the relations between economics, society and history. In this way we shall reconstruct the bases, the forms and direction of causality and, in the final analysis, of the determining influence exercised in the past or present of the various modes of production which have been developed or are in the process of development in history – through a system of constraints which condition their reproduction.

At this point all distinctions and oppositions between anthropology and history disappear; we can no longer analyse the relations and systems of economics as if they were one fetishised and autonomous domain.[87] It is impossible to find a place in this theoretical Marxist perspective for the study of what is generally called economic anthropology – whether it be a 'formalist' or 'substantivist' one. Discovering and reconstructing, in thought, the modes of production – both past and present – is something far different from setting up a discipline called economic anthropology or whatever similar term. This is a task which requires a new look[88] at those theoretical questions imposed by a knowledge of societies and their history, that is to say the question of discovering laws, not of 'History' in general, but of the different economic and social forms which the historian, the anthropologist, the sociologist or economist analyse. Such laws do exist and express the unintentional structural properties of social relations, their proper hierarchy and their articulation on the basis of determined modes of production. It is because they express the objective conditions of *reproduction*, and therefore of the *non-reproduction* of these modes of production and their articulation with other instances in society, that these laws are laws of function and laws of transformation at one and the same time. In this way contradiction between the synchronic and diachronic are overcome. Up to now neither functionalism nor structuralism have been able to do this.

Only a theory and method which enables us to think and analyse the form, function, the hierarchy and the articulation, the conditions for the appearance and transformation of social relations can hope to take over in a radical way from the impotence of functionalism and structuralism, putting an end to the state of helpless vacillation existing in the human sciences. As distinct from the Marxism normally practised, a Marxism which can very quickly become vulgar materialism, we maintain that Marx, when he distinguishes between infrastructure and superstructure (presupposing that the deeper logic of societies and their history depends, in the final analysis, on transformations to the infrastructure), reveals for the first time a hierarchy of functional distinctions without any prejudice to the *nature* of the structures which perform these functions (kinship, religion, politics, etc.), nor the *number of functions* which such a structure may perform.

We can now grasp why such a theoretical step – free from all bias – can be both a tool for theoretical analyses as well as a model for social revolution. We shall finish, as we began, by quoting Engels, a quotation little known to those Marxists who distrust anthropology or to anthropologists who distrust Engels:

> In order to carry out this critique of bourgeois economy completely an acquaintance with the capitalist form of production, exchange and distribution did not suffice. The forms which had preceded it or those which still exist alongside it in less developed countries had also, at least in their main features, to be examined and compared.[89]

2
The concept of 'social and economic formation': the Inca example†

The notion 'social and economic formation' seems useful, above all, in the analysis of *concrete* historical realities, found at some actual irrevocable point in time and at *one* fixed period in history. We shall thus try and determine the 'social and economic formation' characterising the Inca Empire in the 16th century, on the eve of the Spanish conquest. In determining a social and economic formation we shall be able to produce a *synthetic definition* of the exact nature of the particular diversity and unity of economic and social relations which characterise a society during a specific epoch. In order to obtain this synthetic definition, a Marxist perspective requires a number of scientific steps, for example:

(1) identify the number and nature of the different modes of production combined in a specific way in a specific society and which constitute the economic basis of that particular epoch;

(2) identify the different elements in the social and ideological superstructure which in origin and function correspond to the different modes of production;

(3) determine the exact form and content of the articulation, that is the combination of different modes of production found in a hierarchical relationship (one in relation to another) when one of the modes of production dominates the others, obliges them in some way to adapt to the needs and logic of its own functioning system and integrates them more or less into the mechanism of its own reproduction;

(4) determine the proper functions of all elements in both the superstructure and the ideology which, in spite of different origins due to different modes of production, are combined in a specific manner according to the way the different modes of production are articulated; whatever their origins, these features of the superstructure are, to some degree, redefined and recharged.

Let us look at the example of the Incas without any further discussion. We know that the numerous tribes subjugated by the Incas in the middle of the 15th century and integrated into their empire and economy, had a system of production based on the *ayllu*, local village communities of kinship groups of lineage type. Ownership of land was communal, periodically distributed among a specific number of families in such a way that they could never transform this right of usufruct into one of sale, and therefore a form of private property, different from common ownership. Work also had a communal form, based on mutual cooperation between villagers in their different productive tasks. The village chief, the *kuraka*, was the main beneficiary of village cooperation; and common land was specially cultivated to maintain the tombs and local divinities. So, we have a mode of production requiring the cooperation of direct producers, all linked by what Blas Valera, the Spanish chronicler, described as 'the law of fraternity', which is to say the reciprocal obligations between kin and neighbours. There was a degree of social inequality between chiefs and commoners, but it was not very pronounced. When they came under the yoke of the Inca state, these communities, or at least the ethnic and tribal groups organised in communities of this type, underwent profound changes. A portion of their land was expropriated and became the property of the State or Church. On the land they still retained, the communities lost some of their former communal rights, since the Inca state claimed primary rights to all land in the kingdom, a right to control land; this meant the end of the communities' former autonomy; on the lands they farmed, the land tenure remained the same as it was before the Inca conquest, and production continued to assume a communal form. Nevertheless a new mode of production had been set up.

The lands appropriated by the State were now worked *on behalf* of the State by peasants subjected to a régime of forced labour. This did not merely apply to individuals; whole villages participated as family units; the Inca State provided food and drink in the same way as during the traditional *ayllu* system when the beneficiary of the community's cooperative work had fed those who helped him. The State provided tools and seed and forced the people to come to work in their holiday clothes and with music and song. In this way, older forms of economic reciprocity corresponding to the traditional forms of ideology and ritual, were used in the functioning of direct relations of economic exploitation and servitude, which characterised a new form of the mode of production, similar or derived from an 'Asiatic mode of production'.

Taking the analysis further, we find that the Inca State, in order to organise its own economy and ensure a stable form of reproduction, needed to check on all lands, people, animals and other products. This required creating an administrative machinery which would cover the population and control it both directly or indirectly; they also popularised the cult of the Inca, son of the Sun, and maintained an army to suppress uprisings, etc. These institutions, as a whole, corresponded to the new mode of production, which in 1532 was fully operative, the State having been obliged to transfer entire populations in order to establish military colonies to control unruly local peoples. Traditional tribal links with the land were partly destroyed and the development of a type of slavery, called *yanacona*, created a new social stratum, the *yana*; these were people completely cut off from their home communities and attached to the person of their master. And so, these third-type relations of production were no longer based on a general dependence of local communities in relation to a higher community merged with the State, but on personal ties between aristocratic families and peasant families or subject cattleherders. A new way of evolution was opened, linked to the development of new forms of property ownership and exploitation, which became more and more separated from the former community relations.

Of these three types of relations of production, corresponding to different epochs in the evolution of Indian societies in the Andes, the second, in the 16th century, played a *dominant* role in the economic and social formation that constituted the Inca Empire. This economic and social formation had thus its own contradictions, oriented in a certain direction (the development of the *yana*, *mitma*, etc.), which was brutally interrupted by the Spanish conquest. The Spaniards, in turn, destroyed the specific economic, political and ideological institutions of the Asiatic mode of production, which was the primary mode of production in the economic and social formation of the Inca Empire. Vast stretches of land were taken over by the Spanish colonists and the Indian communities were subjected to a régime of exploitation *of a new type*, the *encomienda*, based primarily on the Indians', and their communities', *personal* dependence on their Spanish masters who were responsible for converting them to Christianity, or else ties of dependence on the Spanish crown.

These feudal-type forms of dependence developed within the historical context of the birth of capitalism in feudal Europe and they were useful principally for, what has been called, the primitive accumulation of capital (development in the production of gold, silver, exotic products, etc.).

Deprived of their traditional social hierarchies, expropriated, impoverished, enslaved to masters having a foreign language and culture, the Indian communities either disappeared or retired into themselves. In response to this foreign-imposed exploitation, an exploitation which made the Indians' main problem more one of *survival* than merely accepting a state of slavery, the communities could not even *reproduce* themselves, or ensure the *common* survival of their members, except by maintaining within *determined bounds* that economic inequality and social competition which had developed spontaneously and inevitably and which could have led to their destruction in favour of a minority of fellow Indians. Taking into account the content and forms of domination exercised by the exploiting classes of the new colonial society, it was inevitable that these mechanisms of competition and redistribution would *assume a form* corresponding to the Catholic ideology of the new dominant classes and would be converted into forms tolerated by these rulers. We now have operating what has been called 'a prestige economy', with competition for office and municipal or religious responsibilities (*los cargos*) within the community.

Some people have seen in these institutions merely a survival of pre-colonial, 'archaic' forms of reciprocity and competition, a custom close to the potlatch of the Kwakiutl Indians, whereas in fact they corresponded to a new system of social relations, those of a colonial society created at the dawn of capitalism.

I have presented this sketch of the history of Andean societies from the end of the 15th to the beginning of the 17th centuries merely to point out the modes of production and the elements in the superstructure which followed each other during this period (Theoretical operations 1 and 2). It has shown the existence, and the succession, of *two* economic and social formations, one precolonial, dominated by a mode of production established after the Spanish conquest and dependent, within its internal structure and functioning, on the mode of production in feudal Spain at the time of the origin of capitalism, a period which according to classical economists was one of the 'primitive accumulation of capital'.

One can therefore say that the succession, one after the other, of these two economic and social formations is not the result of an *internal* evolution within the Indian society of the Andes. The Inca conquest had already upset the internal evolution of the Andean tribes and communities. Later, the Spanish conquest was to modify, for a second time, the new developments resulting from the Inca conquest. Of course, for over a thousand years or more, many states and empires had grown up on the high plateaux and coastal valleys of Peru and collapsed after a certain period. The Inca State was but the last of these and the rise and fall of empires testifies to the fact that, in this ecological and cultural zone, decisive economic changes, linked with the spread and perfecting of maize and cotton production on the coast, and potatoes and other tubers on the plateaux, had revealed profound social inequalities between tribes and the dominant classes and the centralised forms of power which exercised this domination. However for tribes which had not yet reached this stage of economic and social development, and this appears to be the case for the numerous tribes in the Cuzco region, their integration into a conquering and centralised empire resulted in an upheaval imposed from outside. This is even truer of the effects of the Spanish conquest.

Therefore, in order to explain the unique history of Andean societies, the play of both internal and external causes has to be analysed. What seems at first sight a succession of accidental events which had upset the development of Indian communities is in fact a result of historical necessity which has to be explained. In order to do this we must try and grasp the relationship between events and social structures and more particularly the causality between structures. We are then faced with problems of types 3 and 4 concerning the articulation of the *modes* of production and elements of the superstructures within the economic and social formations.

In an Indian community, prior to the Inca conquest, production was based on the common ownership of land and assumed a communal form founded on the cooperation of relatives and/or neighbours. This cooperation was the result of technological necessity and the obligation for reciprocal mutual aid which kinship relations and neighbourliness imposed on individuals. There was profound social inequality between lineages and some even had hereditary chiefs, however the mode of production was still, as Marx puts it 'the direct association of producers...such as we find on the threshold of the history of all civilised races'.[1]

Within the households to whom the community's land was periodically redistributed, the division of labour was by sex and age. A great deal of work was done by the community as a whole 'acting' as one and the same 'social' labour force.[2] In 1571 the chronicler, Polo de Ondegardo, emphasised that the Indians, 'when they have to accomplish a task never begin before estimating and measuring what each person's share is to be', or rather, each family's share.

It is clear that in order to carry out an analysis of this type of social relations of production corresponding to the old, prestate mode of production in Andean societies, we must get rid of doctrines, which in an abstract or dogmatic way, only see in the kinship and/or neighbourly relations of many primitive societies, elements of the superstructure of these societies in a relationship of correspondence, which are more or less external to their economic infrastructure. Labour, as an activity which is *simply* and solely economic (as Marx understood perfectly) does not exist in these ancient modes of production. Kinship relations assume political and ideological as well as educational functions (thus the transmission of traditions and values associated with religion and ancestor worship) but they also function as elements of the relations of production and so, as elements of the infrastructure. Kinship relations are therefore plurifunctional, and it is this plurality which confers on them their dominant role in social life. At the same time, there is an internal unity in this plurality of functions, involving an intimate fusion without, however, any confusion.

We should also consider the failure of all theorising about infrastructure–superstructure relations to make any attempt to grasp their close interconnection; instead we find vague metaphorical proposals about the superimposition of their relationships, one on top of another, thus making the built-up relationships finally become the foundation for a basis for construction.

A brief look at the two dominant and later modes of production, the Asiatic mode of production and the colonial mode of production, also provide an opportunity for some theoretical observations.

The striking fact about the mode of production which served as the economic basis for the Inca State, is that it depended on a régime of forced labour imposed by a conquering State; this time we are faced with relations of production which *no longer depend directly on kinship relations or those of neighbourliness*. According to the chronicler, Cobo, 'It is only from the day of their marriage that men are required to take part in public works'.

The *old* kinship relations therefore took on a new function. According to John Murra's well-phrased formula: marriage, as a rite, within a local community became the means of access to a new status, and as a symbol of this status, subjects became liable to enforced labour for the Inca State; they therefore became members of a much wider community which was quite different from that of the ayllu or the local tribe.

This is an example of a multiple transformation of the former social relations caused by the enforced integration of Indian communities into the framework of a new mode of production; this transformation was destined to *reproduce the mode of production automatically*. Let us try to determine the nature of these transformations.

When the Incas obliged the peasants to come dressed in their holiday clothes to work on the State lands and the lands of the Sun God, and gave them food and drink, they were using an earlier form of production based on reciprocal obligations between members of local communities, a form 'known and understood by all' (John Murra, p. 32), in order to organise the new relations of production founded on oppression and domination. As a result the producers lost control over their work, now forced labour, and also over the products of their labour.

In addition, while permitting the cult of local divinities, the Incas added their own Sun God and his son, the Great Inca, in honour of whom the peasants supplied their labour as they already did traditionally to the local divinities.

In general, therefore, the new mode of production took *advantage* of the existing relations of production together with the social and ideological institutions already present in order, eventually to overthrow them. Here, therefore, we have a mechanism by which relationships are extended beyond their original sphere and their original functions.

The characteristic feature of this mechanism is that the mode of production positively *maintains* some of the former communal relations, takes advantage of them and utilises them for its *own* mode of reproduction; this results in the partial *destruction* of the former communal relations.

In practice, therefore, both economically and politically, the Asiatic mode of production *prolongs and contradicts* former communal relations. On the ideological level, this inferior deformation of former communal relations *hides* the oppression and domination inherent in the Asiatic mode of production, because the old ideological forms, which now serve different ends, correspond to former, more egalitarian relations of production.

In so far as subjects and oppressors shared the same ideology (politico-economic reciprocity and religious displays), real oppression was concealed from both groups; it was therefore fully justified in the eyes of the latter and passively borne, if not accepted, by the former.

We might also look at the mode of production set up at the Spanish conquest and find that the Indians had no other choice but to survive by eliminating all social inequalities which appeared among them and which threatened the solidarity and unity of their community. They were able to do this only by making use of municipal and religious institutions which the Spaniards had introduced by force for the functioning of their communities. We also find an economy based on prestige and competition for *los cargos*, which was tolerated by the Spanish rulers because it had its roots in their own political and catholic ideology and was therefore a justification for continuing it. The exploitation of the Indians in fact, was *officially* justified by the Spaniards because their first duty was to christianise them, subsequently to civilise them.[3]

The preceding theoretical observations aim to illustrate what we understand by the phrase 'defining an economic and social formation' and to give an inkling of some of the steps required for a *synthetic* definition of the exact nature of the particular diversity and unity in economic and social relations which go to characterise a given society at a particular period in time. It goes without saying that in producing this synthesis we are presenting history and anthropology as complementary fields in historical materialism.[4]

3

The concept of the 'Tribe': a crisis involving merely a concept or the empirical foundations of anthropology itself?†

> The analytical method which is the beginning of criticism and understanding...is not concerned to develop the various forms genetically but to unify them through analysis starting from given preconditions. Analysis is the necessary condition for genetic exposition and for the true understanding of the process of forms in their different stages of constitution.
>
> Karl Marx, *Hist.Doct.Ec.*, VIII, 185.

TWO REALITIES: A SINGLE TERM

Anthropologists, when using the term 'tribe', refer to two realities, two fields of facts which are different, yet linked. Almost everyone uses it to distinguish a *type of society* from others, one specific mode of social organisation which can be compared to other modes of organisation in society – 'bands', 'states', etc. This, however, does not mean that there is any unanimity among them, owing to the vagueness of the criteria which have been selected to define and isolate these different types of society. But there is even more disagreement over the other use of the term tribe, when it serves to designate a *stage of evolution* in human society.

The link between the two uses of the term tribe, seen as a *type of society* and as a *stage of evolution*, is very clear since, according to the evolutionist's viewpoint, each stage of evolution is characterised by a specific mode of social organisation. But the majority of anthropologists have failed to arrive at any decision regarding the existence of a mode of social organisation or the existence of a necessary stage in the evolution of humanity. Some even disagree on the theoretical possibility of analysing scientifically the evolution of human societies (Leach), or they disclaim any interest in their history. With the notable exception of Evans-Pritchard and Raymond Firth, this is the case with most functionalist or structuralist anthropologists. More complications arise from the fact that among those who defend attempts to construct a scientific theory of social evolution, some, like Herbert Lewis, do not accept that the tribal mode of organisation in society is a *necessary and general* stage in this evolution; while others, like Morton Fried, go further still and see it merely as a secondary effect of the appearance of state-type societies and a veritable blind alley in the evolution of mankind.

Disturbance, dispute, the crisis of a concept

Thus, the term 'tribe' while literally obtruding in all the writings and discussion of anthropologists seems not to have entered the most bitter theoretical combat zones. For a decade now, doubt, concern, criticism and sometimes outright rejection have gradually been creeping in with regard to the term; and today we are faced with a conflict of opinion. Neiva, after Leach, has cried out against 'the scandalous imprecision of the concept'; Julian Steward, himself an evolutionist, appeals for the greatest prudence before what he calls a 'holdall' concept; others, like Swartz, Turner, Toden systematically choose to ignore it, keeping silent about its very existence even though they are exploring fields in political anthropology where the concept of 'tribe' has traditionally played a key role. This is only half the trouble; along with these criticisms of a theoretical nature there is real consternation and violent attacks have been made against the ideological use of the concept in its secondary form and the related concept of 'tribalism'. The existence of tribal organisations in Africa, America, Oceania, Asia appears, in fact, to be the reason for the difficulties encountered by young nation states in their economic and political development and in achieving independence. The continuing presence of precolonial tribal organisation appears to have been the cause for such dramatic events as the Biafran war and the Mau-Mau revolt, along with the dissensions among the Tuaregs or 'pagan' tribes of Southern Sudan and the decadence of the South-American Indians, etc.

Here, as Jomo Kenyatta showed in his book *Facing Mount Kenya*, we not only have to interpret the world but to use its contradictions, transforming it by way of an exact analysis. Now, there are many anthropologists and politicians who challenge, as theoretically false and politically harmful, the use of concepts such as 'tribe' and 'tribalism' in order to determine modern contradictions found in 'underdeveloped' countries. They see in the contradictions attributed to tribalism not so much a relic of precolonial structures (tribal organisations believed to have been destroyed but which flower again, even violently), as a legacy of the colonial period and the new relations involved in neocolonial domination. Eliott Skinner, anthropologist and US ambassador for the Upper Volta Republic in 1967, wrote:

> It is unfortunate that 'tribalism' with all its connotations of primitivity and traditionalism is the name given for the identity being used by groups competing for power and prestige in contemporary Africa. Some of the names which are now used as symbols for group identity do refer to distinct sociocultural entities in the past. However, many of the so-called 'tribal' groups were creations of the colonial period. But even those groups for which continuity with the past could be claimed have lost so many of their traditional characteristics that in fact they must be viewed as new entities.[1]

The concept 'tribe', therefore is 'in crisis'; and there is an urgent need, both theoretically and practically, to get to the root of the evil and redefine it in order to criticise and evaluate its real significance. To do this, it seems best to retrace briefly the history of the concept, from Morgan, the founder of anthropology, to the present day, with special reference to Marshall Sahlins, an anthropologist who has made the most sustained and brilliant attempts to redefine this concept and reinterpret all the ethnographic material which has accumulated over the past hundred years. At the end of this summary, we may discover that the root of the evil involves not only a concept but the very foundations and empirical methods of anthropology and the social sciences.

A BRIEF SURVEY OF THE INDO-EUROPEAN ORIGINS OF THE TERM

French 'tribu' and English 'tribe' come from the Latin *tribus*, Umbrian *trifú*, or the equivalent Greek *phule*, linguistic terms designating Indo-European institutions of great antiquity. (In this connection we should look at Emile Benvéniste's superb etymological and semantic analyses of these words.) From the outset, these concepts were empirical ones and as a result, have taken on different meanings in the course of these peoples' history; in their most ancient form, however, they designated a particular kind of social and political organization existing in all these societies. An Indo-European tribe referred to the largest kind of social and political community which existed before the appearance of the city state. More elementary social units were included in it, from the smallest, the Greek *genos* and the *phratra* and the Latin *gens* and *curia*. It is important to establish here that all these terms (apart from *curia*) belonged *both* to kinship and political terminology; this means there was an internal relationship, real or implied, between kinship and political organisation. In fact, as Benvéniste points out, the principal Indo-European languages all agree in giving 'birth' as the main criteria for membership in a social group.[2] In this context, the concept of tribe, as perceived in the language and thought of Indo-Europeans, was a fact of their experience and an observable one.

But this internal relationship between kinship and politics – and therefore an understanding of the exact nature of the social groups designated by the terms clan, phratry, tribe – has been largely hidden over the centuries, once the ancient Indo-European institutions had disappeared. As Morgan observed in the mid-nineteenth century, at a time when anthropology was becoming a scientific discipline, these terms had for a long time been used indiscriminately by missionaries, administrators, geographers and travellers alike; and this was the situation when Morgan himself undertook the scientific analysis of the type of social organisation found among the Iroquois, and later, other Indian peoples of North and South America.

The starting point: Morgan (1877)

To understand Morgan's ideas about the 'tribal' forms of social organisation, we must briefly look at his great discovery first stated in *Systems of Consanguinity and Affinity of the Human Family* (Washington, 1871). Morgan demonstrated that the kind of social relations which dominate the organisation of most primitive societies are kinship relations. He then showed that these kinship relations had an internal *logic* which had to be discovered through detailed studies of marriage rules and kinship terminologies, rules and terms which seemed to lack all sense in the eyes of Europeans who were dumbfounded by such institutions as the 'classificatory' kinship systems found in Africa, Asia, Oceania, America. He assumed that these kinship systems had a *historical* sequence man evolving from animal groups and sexually promiscuous primitive hordes, and that gradually the incest prohibition had been introduced and marriage between blood relations in wider and wider categories became tabooed. The 'human family' evolved from a primitive form of 'group marriage' (today, completely disappeared) to the monogamy of European nuclear families. Morgan also supposed that matrilineal kinship systems had preceded patrilineal ones.

From this, we can understand Morgan's definition of tribal organisation. A tribe is a '*completely* organised society' (p. 122), therefore a form of social organisation capable of *reproducing itself*. 'It *illustrates* humanity's condition in a *barbarian state*', i.e., humanity no longer primitive and savage but not yet civilised, not a 'political' society, nor a state. Nevertheless, if a tribe is 'a completely organised society', we shall never understand how it functions without first understanding the 'structure and functions' of the elementary groups in it, the clans. A clan is a consanguineal group of relatives, descendants of a common ancestor, distinguished by a *gens* name and linked by blood relationships. Having discovered 'the identity of structures and function' in the Amerindian clan and in the *genos* or gens of ancient Greeks and Latins, Morgan used the term *gens* in preference to clan and spoke of 'gentilitius' society instead of 'tribal society'. A tribe is a collection of clans. 'Each tribe is individualised by a name, by a separate dialect, by a supreme government and by the possession of some territory which it occupies and defends as its very own.' By 'supreme government', Morgan meant a council of sachems and chiefs elected by the *gentes*, and in some case, a 'supreme chief' of the tribe. Two further 'functions and attributes' of tribal organisation should be mentioned: 'the possession of a common religious faith and cult' and (as is strongly stressed in his polemic against McLennan's thesis in *Primitive Marriage*) the tribe is an endogamous group while the clan is exogamous (pp. 518–24). Clans and tribes have constantly multiplied and become differentiated through migrations as a result of population increases and the limits imposed by subsistence resources.

> In course of time the emigrants would become distinct in interests, strangers in feeling, and last of all, divergent in speech. Separation and independence would follow, although their territories were contiguous. A new tribe was thus created...(which) must be regarded as an inevitable result of the gentile organisation, united with the necessities of their condition (p. 105).

Differentiation in their modes of life and linguistic stock was due therefore to this 'constant tendency to disintegration...followed by a complete segmentation' (pp. 104, 107) which characterises tribal organisation. Tribal multiplication was accompanied by a state of permanent war among them since each tribe considered itself at war with all those with whom there was no formally signed peace treaty and these were provisional (pp. 111 and 119). Constant segmentation and war was a powerful obstacle in the progress of savage and barbarous tribes.

There were, however, some tribal societies who reached the 'civilised' stage, but at the price of the dissolution and disappearance of their clan and tribal organisation. For Morgan, civilisation came with the State and was based on the control of territory and the people living on this territory; they were no longer organised solely into kinship groups but into territorial ones, cities for example. The reforms of Solon and Cleisthenes in ancient Greece, for Morgan, were the result of the radical impossibility of 'founding a political society or state upon gentes' (p. 123), and showed the necessity of transforming these former kinship groups into territorial groups.

The paramount chief of some Indian tribes was not a king so much as a war chief provisionally elected in the same way as the Greek Basileus. For Morgan, the alleged kingdoms of the Aztecs, the Incas, etc., were only 'military democracies' (see his famous article on 'The Banquet of Montezuma'). 'All the members of an Iroquois gens were personally free, and they were bound to defend each other's freedom; they were equal in privileges and in personal rights, the sachem and chiefs claiming no superiority;... Liberty, equality and fraternity, though never formulated, were cardinal principles of the gens'. The appearance of the State demanded a 'fundamental change'; it is the necessary result of the disintegration of society based upon gentes as a consequence of the advent and development of private ownership of herds, land and the unequal accumulation of private wealth, along with the consolidation of the monogamous family. This leads us to Morgan's last, basic point. The general evolution of humanity and the determination and succession of different stages are due to the fact that man was educated to civilisation 'working on himself'. The mechanism of this transformation is a twofold one. In inventing new subsistence techniques, man developed the seeds of his thought; ideas germinated in his brain which were part of God's 'Supreme Intelligence' scheme. This explains how Morgan could declare simultaneously that 'it is probable that the successive arts of subsistence afforded the most satisfactory bases for divisions' (in the evolution of mankind as seen by ethnic stages), his book being constructed by analysing in succession the *parallel* development of three ideas: government, family and property, temporarily leaving out the development of religious ideas, a difficult and little known field of customs 'grotesque and to some extent unintelligible' (p. 5).

This, in the main, is what Morgan meant by the concepts of clan and tribe. It is clear that they are not unimportant concepts in his work and that they involve crucial problems in anthropology and history. It should be noted that Morgan established an order of priority, structural, functional and historical, between these two concepts of tribe and clan. The concept of tribe can only be *rigorously* defined after we have a concept designating 'the primary fact' of tribal social organisation, that of lineal and segmentary descent groups, the concept of clan (p. 518). Even if subsequent discoveries in anthropology have invalidated his thesis about the universality of unilineal kinship groups by revealing the existence of non-lineal groups (cognatic descent), the concept of tribe has continued to cover a reality of a secondary level, integrating the elementary and segmentary units (whatever they may be) into a greater social unit, thereby constituting, as Morgan said with regard to clans, 'the fundamental basis of the social and governmental system in ancient societies'.

One can see why Morgan's work, through this composite blend of materialistic and idealistic documentation, gave rise to contradictory interpretations, the most famous being that of Marx and Engels regarding his ideas about materialism, whilst in our time, Opler has attempted an idealistic rereading.

The fundamental point, in evaluating Morgan's work, is not just to praise and accept the depth and boldness of his general hypothesis (as Marx and Engels did) nor to ridicule or reject them by harping on unproved extrapolations or interpolated proofs (Goldenweiser, Murdock, etc.), but to go back to a theoretical reasoning which can reveal why his methods cannot produce any proofs for his own hypotheses. It is the analysis of the fundamental deficiencies in Morgan's method in relation to his hypotheses which is absent in E. Terray's book on Morgan, and this greatly reduces the significance of the comparison he made between Marx and Morgan. For Marx in *The German*

Ideology, had arrived at the same general hypothesis as Morgan, in *Ancient Society* (1877); that is to say, that the social conditions of production of material life determine, in the final analysis, the content, form and evolution of society. Marx's theoretical significance lies in the fact that on the basis of this hypothesis, he undertook the study in depth of one form of society, bourgeois society, and the material basis peculiar to it, 'the capitalist mode of production'. In this study he dismissed empiricism and going beyond a system's superficial appearance, sought those deeper structures which can reveal a logic both hidden and obscure. He aimed at unveiling the *mechanism* for this mode of production showing how its reproduction transformed the society as a whole. A unique and pioneer step, left unfinished, which must be followed up in the study of precapitalist societies and modes of production; something which Marx left for others to work out. It is the absence of the analysis of the exact mechanisms in the structural causality of economics which prevents Morgan's methods from producing any proof of his own hypotheses. 'It is probable that the successive arts of subsistence which arose at long intervals will ultimately, from the great influence they must have exercised upon the condition of mankind, afford the most satisfactory bases for these divisions. But investigation has not been carried far enough in this direction to yield the necessary information' (p. 9).

After this, all Morgan could do was to draw a *parallel* in a largely speculative and hypothetic way, between series of material inventions and stages of social evolution (p. 12), without showing their internal and necessary interrelationships, i.e., reconstructing the mechanism of causality within these structures.

Where are we today? What have we kept, developed or thrown away with regard to Morgan's analysis of the concept of tribe?

A century later: functionalists and neoevolutionists

If we look at John J. Honigmann's article on 'Tribe' for the *Dictionary of the Social Sciences*, 1964, published under the auspices of UNESCO, Morgan's definition has been retained as far as his descriptive idea of a *type* of society is concerned; but it has been completely rejected when it comes to any reference about the *stages of evolution* corresponding to a type of society: 'In general anthropologists agree on the criteria by which a tribe may be described (as a system of social organisation): common territory, a tradition of common descent, common language, common culture, and a common name – all these forming the basis of the joining of smaller groups such as villages, bands, districts, or lineages.'[3] This rejecting can be partly explained by the collapse, at the beginning of this century of evolutionist theories and the development of current principles of functionalism which followed naturally in anthropology. To functionalists with the exception of Evans-Pritchard and certain other brilliant field workers a social system is a total whole, sections of which are necessarily interlinked; but, according to them, even the history of a system can tell us nothing of the necessary linking of parts, because history belongs to the order of consequential and accidental events and not to necessity. Laws of functioning exist but there are no laws of their evolution or necessary transformations.

Even amputated, rid of its evolutionist content, the concept of tribe shows further fissures which leave little left. Some are of little importance. It has been shown that linguistic, cultural and 'tribal' unity are are not always the same things (see articles by M. Fried, G. Dole and the works of such linguists as Dell Hymes, John Gumperz, Paul Friedrich, C. Voegelin, and statisticians like Driver, Naroll. The inspiration behind these researches comes mainly from the work of Boas, Morgan's critic). We now know that the names of 'tribes' were often terms used by outside or foreign groups, or that they simply meant 'the people' (Leach, Fried), and that the common descent of tribal members from founding ancestors was mere fiction (Malinowski, Leach). Finally, it has been shown that the existence of group sentiment and common ideology did not very often mean that this ethnic community was a tribe, whereas for Linton this was the 'test' of tribal unity (cf. Moerman on the Lué of Thailand, and Naroll's reply, and also Bessac's article on the Mongours and Yögur): more seriously it has been pointed out that the chronological precedence of matrilineal descent groups over patrilineal ones has never been proved; that structures of hunting and gathering bands are sometimes very complex; that real aristocracies and hereditary chiefdoms existed among primitive tribes (Morgan denied the theoretical possibility of this, p. 259); and that the Incas and Aztecs were neither 'military democracies' nor simple chiefdoms, but proper states where the ruling class merged with the state and where tribal organisation had not disappeared, etc. It is perhaps here, on the question of the nature of political relations that tribal organisation may be found. Honigmann, moreover, stresses this with the greatest clarity: 'While there is general agreement on the characteristics already stated, difficulties arise when the political characteristics of the tribe are discussed.'

Honigmann then cites a classification, widely used among anthropologists, which distinguishes three types of tribes by referring to their form of political organisation: non-segmentary acephalous tribes, segmentary acephalous tribes, and the centralised tribes. This leads him to define as 'tribes', Eskimo bands of hunters and fishermen, African Ibo farmers (simple, non-segmentary tribes), Nuer cattleherders of the Sudan or the matrilineal farmers and fishermen of Dobu in Oceania (segmentary, acephalous tribes) as well as the former Polynesian chiefdoms of Hawaii, Tonga, the Mongol Khanats and the Mossi kingdoms (centralised tribes).

This pinpoints the major difficulty in any concept of tribe, a difficulty which Honigmann's very reserve expresses eloquently; he abstains from adding political criteria to other 'already established' criteria used to define this concept. Any primitive society, therefore, (or at least all which have no clearcut forms of class relations or state power) can be characterised as a tribal society. And even this reservation does not absolutely hold true since many African or Asiatic kingdoms are genuine state societies. One may quite legitimately question the advantage of such an ungainly concept, a nocturnal concept in the Hegelian sense when he speaks in *The Philosophy of Law* of all cats being grey at night.

This is the concept, inherited from Morgan – one element of its content amputated by the functionalists and subjected to a harping criticism – that Marshall Sahlins, Service and other neoevolutionists have attempted to redefine in a scrupulous manner and to use again with all its original applications: to characterise a type of society within the framework of comparative anthropology as well as a stage of social evolution within a theory of history.

Sahlins, in 1961, and Service, in 1962, proposed a scheme of social evolution in four stages: the band, the tribe, the chiefdom and finally the state, whereby 'civilisation' made its entry into history. 'A band is only an association, more or less residential of nuclear families.'[4] A tribe 'is of the order of a large collection of bands but it is not simply a collection of bands'.[5] A kingdom is 'particularly distinguished from tribes by the presence of centers which coordinate economic, social and religious activities',[6] and redistributes a large part of the production of local communities'. Then the state appears, reinforcing this centralisation and constituting a political structure definitely superior and exterior to the local social groups, transforming social inequality of rank into class privileges.

Broadly speaking, this is also Morgan's scheme, rearranged to take into account new ethnological data. We shall look at only two of these new concepts. Firstly, the concept of the 'band' has taken the place of the 'Primitive horde' to describe 'the dominant type in palaeolithic society';[7] secondly, the existence of 'chiefdoms', societies, which in Morgan's work had no very firm theoretical status, is now recognised.

What are the hypotheses underlying the setting-up of such a scheme? The evolution of societies is supposed to have developed like a living organism, from the undifferentiated to the differentiated, from the simple to the complex, and each distinct stage therefore corresponds to an ever more complex level of structural differentiation and integration.[8] For the causes of this evolution,

Sahlins considered the changes in the economy, the 'neolithic revolution', which permitted, not exactly the birth, but the general expansion and domination of tribal societies over hunting and gathering societies of the palaeolithic. Using these hypotheses, Sahlins and Service constructed a 'probable' representation of these processes, selecting the functioning 'traits' of some present-day societies which appear to correspond to each of these levels and then placing this evidence into the corresponding slots of their scheme. The very fact of placing these actual societies into slots automatically *metamorphosed* them into 'typical' representatives of the organisation of human society at such and such a stage of their development; at the same time they lost their unique evolution, their history – History itself. Moreover the societies are made to illustrate a stage that they have not yet historically passed through; they therefore acquire an imaginary future at the very moment that their past is disappearing.

In 1968, Marshall Sahlins in his *Tribesmen*, made significant changes to this scheme, reducing it to a succession of three stages, instead of four – band, tribe, state. He provides no justification for the change and presents no doctrinal modification concerning the principles and origins of the social evolution which preceded or accompanied this change. The reasons, which in 1961 caused the 'chiefdoms' of the tribal stage to be excluded – that is to say the presence of 'hereditary functions', of a 'permanent political structure' in the hands of certain segments of society – seem no longer valid in 1968. Tribal societies and chiefly societies are now placed together as 'two developments' of the *same type* of 'segmentary' society, like two permutations of the same general model, which leads one to an extreme decentralisation of these segmentary social relations, the other to their integration into higher levels of social organisation than local segments. The first permutation engenders 'segmentary tribes proper';[9] the second engenders 'chiefdoms', wherein 'tribal culture anticipates statehood in its complexities'.[10] Between these two opposing types stretches a multitude of intermediary combinations (including almost all known primitive societies), which Sahlins regroups under the concept of 'tribal society'. This extreme diversity for him is the result of multiple structural variations imposed by the adaptation of 'neolithic' economies to extremely diverse ecological niches in the course of an expansion involving the whole world, a movement which began around 9000 years BC, in the Near-East and around 5000 BC, in the New World, and included the first forms of plant and animal domestication. Then came the progressive disappearance of palaeolithic hunters and gatherers who were slowly driven back into marginal ecological zones which were unsuitable for neolithic farming and cattlerearing techniques. Under the concept of neolithic economies and tribal society we have the slash and burn farmers of the Amazon,

Oceania, Equatorial Africa; nomadic herders who roamed the dry belts of Asia and Africa; hunters and fishermen of the north-west coast of North America, who, thanks to the abundance of food resources in their environment, had already reached the tribal level even before the appearance of neolithic agriculture; the hunters of America who had rapidly transformed their culture with the redomestication of the horse introduced by the Whites; and societies practising intensive agriculture, often with irrigation, like the Pueblos, the Polynesians of Hawaii, etc.

Such an inventory of societies and the innumerable economic systems is too heteroclitic and to justify it, we should have to prove that we are in fact faced with as many mutations of the *same* basic *type* of 'neolithic' economic relations. Sahlins follows up this first hypothesis with another, proposing that this ecological and economic diversity explains the diversity of social relations encountered in 'tribal' societies and the diversity of kinship relations in particular – lineal, cognatic, etc.

It would be absurd to reproach him for not having solved 'the deeper mysteries of cultural anthropology',[11] and presented us with a complete theory of the social evolution of humanity. The point is of an epistemological nature and turns on the fact that Sahlins, like Lewis Morgan long before him, *resorts to a method which does not allow his own hypotheses to be verified* and which consists primarily in comparing a great number of stateless, classless, primitive societies by *isolating* their common features and provisionally *leaving aside* their differences. This is an empirical step which contradicts the desired result. In order to show that the various economic systems and different types of social relations listed are necessary and controlled transformations in social structures, and which must be reconstructed in thought since they are not directly observable as such, Sahlins has to use a method whereby at the same time and *by the action of the same principles*, both similarities *and* differences between these economic and social systems can be taken into account; a method which does not rule out differences or find them merely an embarassing residue left over from the similarities. Now, it is this pendular motion between similarities and differences that we find with Sahlins.

The first characteristic common to all 'tribal' societies, which he isolates, is the fact that all elementary social units are multifamilial groups which collectively exploit an area of common resources and form a residential unit the whole year round, or the major part of it. He names these elementary units 'primary segments', from which the term 'segmentary societies' indiscriminately used instead of 'tribal societies' appears. Sahlin proceeds by intentionally 'abstracting' the inner features of these social segments, i.e., the exact nature of the kinship relations shaping these multifamilial groups and by showing that these segments are of patrilineal descent (Tiv), or matrilineal

(Iroquois), cognatic (the Iban from Borneo, the Lapps) etc. In this way what is isolated is more a characteristic of the 'general form' of a large number of primitive societies than their specific content.

The second common element is the multifunctional character of the kinship relations organising these primary segments. By this he wants to show that kinship relations, apart from their patrilineal, matrilineal, bilineal or non-lineal characteristics, function *simultaneously* with economic relations, political relations, ideological relations, etc.; in short, they have the property of being 'functionally generalised', as Evans-Pritchard puts it. This recognition of the multifunctional characteristic of kinship relations is of great critical significance in the theoretical scheme, since we can no longer see kinship as a mere element in the social superstructure, distinct and separate from the economic infrastructure and the mode of production. From this Sahlins concludes that the different economic systems of 'tribal' societies are so many varieties of the same basic mode of production, 'the familial mode of production'. This expression is not synonymous with the mode of familial production, since production within tribal societies often implies the cooperation of several families, or, going beyond family productive forces, the cooperation of non-familial social groups (by age, etc.). It merely means that production and consumption are *in the final analysis*, regulated, stimulated and limited by the needs and resources of familial groups.[12]

Up till now, the expression 'tribal societies' has been used for all primitive societies which have two visible functioning features in common: the existence of elementary social units – primary segments possessing the form of multi-familial local groups; the multifunctionality of kinship relations which shape these familial groups. However, once beyond this common denominator, you find differences of a primary order between tribal societies which must be listed and explained. Now, while some simply lead us to distinguish subdivisions within tribal society, others are of such a nature that they question the very unit of this division and it is here that all difficulties involved in a comparative, empirical approach are concentrated. To prove this, one need only look at Sahlins' contradictory statements when he attempts to include a third element in the definition of tribal societies: 'structural equivalence' of primary segments in tribal societies. Here we are touching on fundamental problems in anthropology.

By 'structural equivalence' of primary segments we mean the fact that they are functionally equivalent, i.e., economically, politically, culturally and ideologically identical and equal. Each segment, each local community is like another and does for itself what another does. For Sahlins, the best illustration of this principle of the structural equivalence of segments is Tiv society in Nigeria. All Tiv local communities are segments of lineages claiming descent from a common ancestor and occupying adjoining territories. Higher levels of social organisation in these local communities do not function except, temporarily, where there is internal conflict. If community *a* attacks community *b*, then the whole of lineage I affirms its solidarity and mobilises to confront lineage II. If lineage segment *d* attacks the local neighbouring community *e*, all descendants of ancestor A mobilise against the whole of lineage B. The higher levels of kinship and social organisation on the local segmentary level, therefore, do not exist, becoming complementary only by 'opposition', to use Evans-Pritchard's phrase when he speaks of the Nuer.[13]

Let us compare this scheme with the model scaled for the Polynesian chiefdoms, 'integrated' into the shape of a vast 'conical clan' (cf. Kirschoff) and on which Sahlins makes special comments.

It is soon clear that in the case of the Polynesian chiefdoms, the principle of the structural equivalence of primary segments is absent; and this is the principle existing for the Nuer and Tiv, which, according to Sahlins should characterise all tribal societies. All the segments and individuals which constitute the chiefdom are now ranged in order of hierarchical descent, beginning with the chief *a*, the eldest son of the clan founder's eldest son's descendants (Among the Kachin of Burma, on the other hand, authority is traced back through the last son of the founder ancestor's last son's descendants. Cf. Leach). We are faced, certainly, with a segmentary society, but showing a

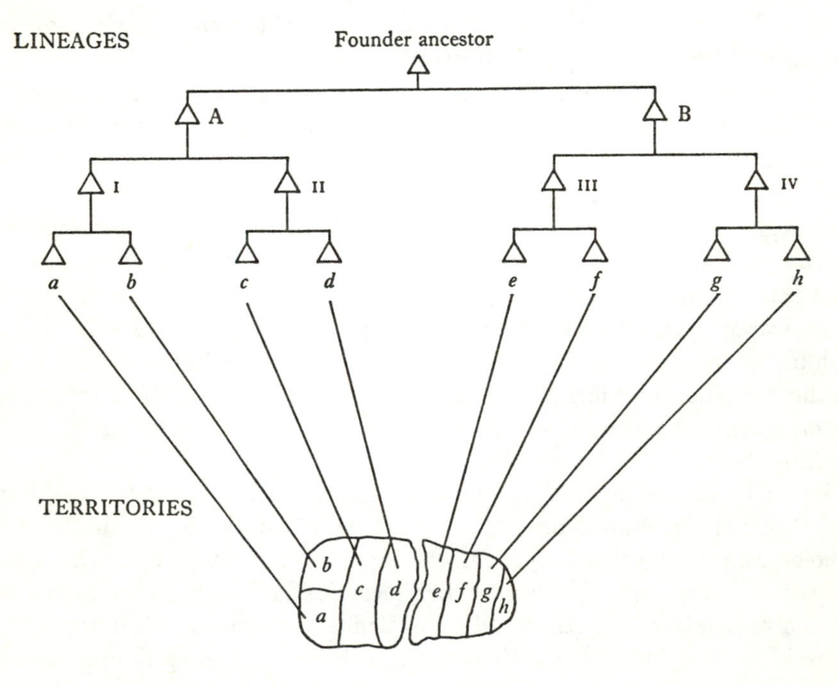

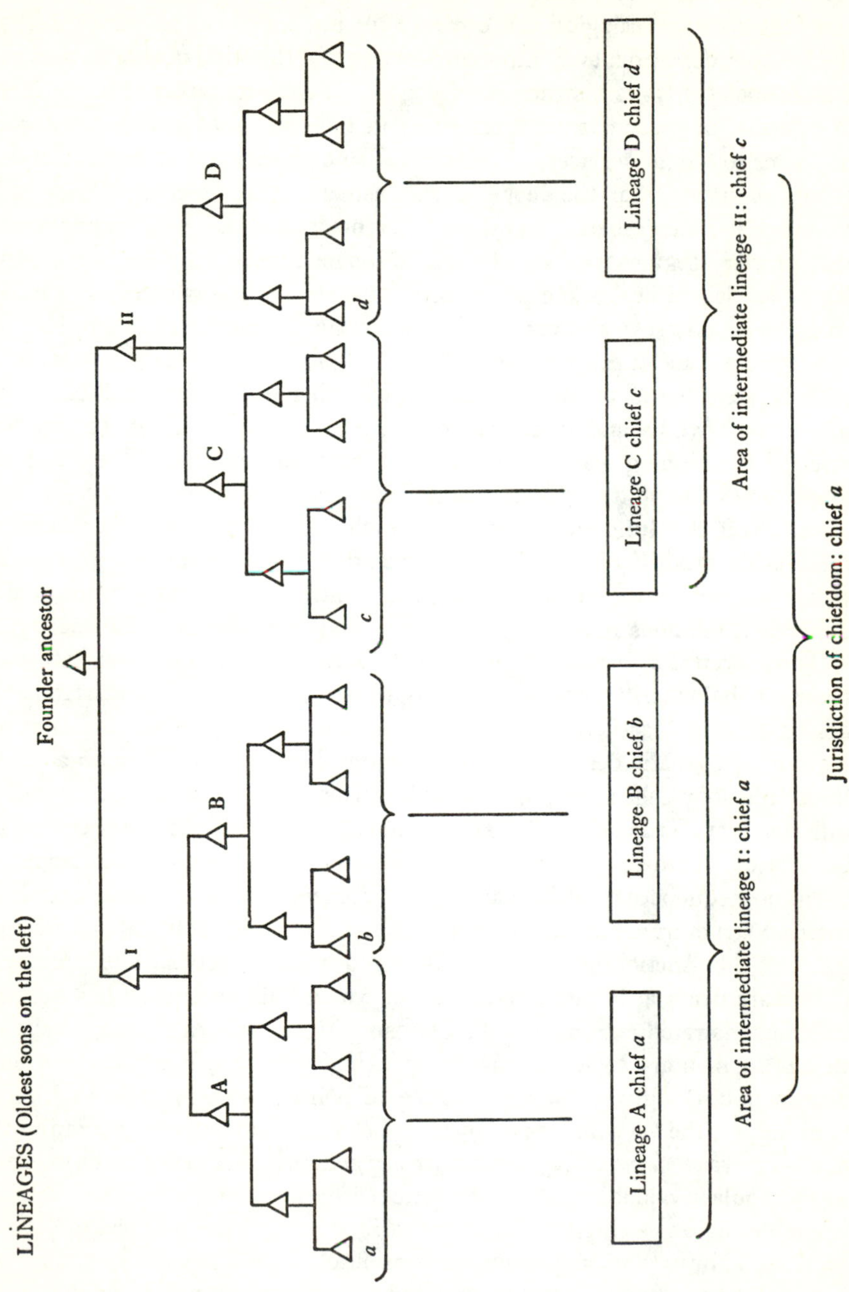
LINEAGES (Oldest sons on the left)
Founder ancestor
I
II
A
B
C
D
a
b
c
d
Lineage A chief *a*
Lineage B chief *b*
Lineage C chief *c*
Lineage D chief *d*
Area of intermediate lineage I: chief *a*
Area of intermediate lineage II: chief *c*
Jurisdiction of chiefdom: chief *a*

hierarchy of ranks and unequal social status which is emphasised the more you follow the genealogical line down to the juniors of junior branches from the founder descendants. Sahlins emphasises that this kind of chiefdom is not a class society: 'It is a structure of degrees of interest rather than conflicts of interest: of graded familial priorities in the control of wealth and force, in claims to others' services, in access to divine power, and in material styles of life, such that, if all the people were kinsmen and members of society, still some are more members than others.'[14] Henceforth and for the *same* reasons that primary segments of society are no longer functionally equivalent, the *higher* levels of lineal organisation with local segments – which have merely an episodic existence and very limited social significance in the reproduction of acephalous societies – exist in the shape of *permanent institutions*, endowed with *different functions* complementing each other in the reproduction of the society as a whole and therefore controlling, effectively if differently, the internal functioning and reproduction of local communities. These last no longer enjoy the political, economic and ideological autonomy of 'acephalous tribes'. It is this functional hierarchy which makes the paramount chief and the kinship group from which he is descended, the focus and summit of the whole society, since he personifies and controls the totality of mutually dependent relations in all the groups and of all individuals in the society.

Thus, even if a *formal* similarity exists between the lineal organisation of some acephalous tribes and the lineal organisation of some chiefdoms (remembering that in Marshall Sahlins' own opinion the Polynesian clan is more a group of cognatic descendants, non-unilineal in fact, though with a patrilineal 'ideology', the main point is that lineal descent functions in a completely different way. True, kinship relations are segmentary and multifunctional in both cases, but these 'formal' similarities are of limited importance compared to the consequences resulting from the differences in their functions and their internal structure which affect every aspect, economic, political and ideological, of the functioning and reproduction of these societies. The structural effects are necessarily interrelated; a fact which Sahlins himself has defined and demonstrated extremely well. Choosing Melanesian examples, he shows that in segmentary societies 'strictly speaking' (this very limitation reveals a certain doubt) – given the high degree of political autonomy in each local community, the very intense *competition* between each and every community and their *economic capability* to produce a regular surplus to exchange in order to accumulate valuable goods not produced by themselves, such as shellfish – some individuals emerge who temporarily dominate the political life of the local community and neighbouring communities, and ensure for their own community an equally temporary period of prestige and political superiority over other neighbouring communities which are related or allied, friendly or hostile. In order to become a 'big-man', one must show exceptional economic and political ability, set up many matrimonial alliances, increase the production of subsistence goods and pigs, establish a vast network of commercial partners with whom to exchange pigs for shellfish, feathers, etc., and finally contribute more than any other member of the community toward the gifts and counter-gifts accompanying marriage, war, peace, etc. The 'big-man', thus, becomes a symbol – 'glorious and glorified' (Malinowski) – of the wealth and prestige of his group, the most active agent of the group's political superiority and the personification of its common interests. But such a social promotion is precarious for the same reasons which bring it about. The 'big-man' is not only helping his community, he is also using it and thereby stirs up jealousies, oppositions, factions which threaten his own authority, while rivals in neighbouring communities accumulate goods making him lose face by overwhelming him with gifts he will be unable to return. In the long term, as Strathern[15] has pointed out, these economic and political mechanisms (of gift and counter-gift) balance inequalities between local groups and recreate and reproduce their 'structural equivalence'. In the sphere of economic exchanges, the multi-centred character of the accumulation of material wealth and political power leads to and favours intense exchanges between local communities and encourages the existence and circulation of many and varied forms of 'primitive' currency. In the ideological field and especially the field of religious representations, local cults are more intense and are addressed to ancestors and supernatural powers very close to men (for good and for evil), while the highest divinities – the great gods responsible for the ultimate ordering of the Universe – seem, if not indifferent, at least rather unconcerned by man's day to day affairs (cf. Meggitt on the religion of the Mae-Enga, Evans-Pritchard on the Nuer, etc.). There would be an advantage to be gained in finding a structural correspondence between the weak economic and political significance of the higher levels of lineal organisation, compared to that of local segments, and the lack of importance given to the cult of the higher divinities in the indigenous pantheons; yet, here the suggestions are too hasty and lack a theoretical analysis which would explain why, for example, the worship of the Forest among the Mbuti hunters and gatherers of the Congo, or the cult of the Sun and Moon, supreme deities for the Baruya farmers of New Guinea, play an essential role in the political and ideological spheres, while their social organisation is far more highly segmented than those of the Nuer or the Mae-Enga.

In spite of theoretical deficiencies of this kind, which Sahlins is aware of and humourously puts down to his method of 'unverified comparison',[16] the main point is that Sahlins' analyses do demonstrate the existence of a radical structural difference between acephalous societies and an 'ideal' chiefdom in precolonial Polynesia. Within the latter, a pyramid of public functions, of titles and social strata, exists independently of the personal capabilities and merits of individuals who fill them and profit from others by virtue of birth, functions, titles and status being attached to ranks; and the rank of an individual depends on his genealogical distance from the founding ancestor in the chiefdom. The 'general form' of social relations then, always depends on kinship relations and kinship relations always function hand in hand with political relations, economic relations and ideological systems; however, the content of these political, economic and ideological relations is totally different.

In the economic scheme, except for the 'big-men' of Melanesia, the chiefs – at least, from all the big chiefdoms like Hawaii, Tonga, Samoa, Tahiti – do not directly participate in the material process of production. They guide it, however, and direct it by controlling labour, the use of natural resources and the products of local communities through the mediation of local chiefs and a kind of 'administration' consisting of the relatives and hangers-on of the big chiefs.

A considerable portion of each local community's products is regularly set apart and dispatched to the paramount chief, providing him with the material sources of his livelihood, a prop for his rank and the wherewithal to support his relatives, friends, followers, etc. Thanks to the great mass of accumulated products, controlled by him and his ability to mobilise a labour force among the commoners, the chief is the only person who can bring together sufficient people for great communal enterprises of collective interest: wars, religious ceremonies, public works such as temples and even, as in Hawaii, an irrigation network, all undertakings beyond the capacity of any one local community. The sum total of mobilised labour and the quantity of redistributed products on these occasion is beyond the wildest dreams of the richest of the Melanesian 'big-men'. Moreover, a large part of the local products, including the most valuable, circulate between communities through the mediation of chiefs who collect and redistribute them; this means that *direct* exchanges between local communities are far more infrequent than in segmentary acephalous societies.

In the political and ideological scheme the power of the chief and high dignitaries is justified by their being direct descendants of the founding ancestor of the chiefdom, himself descended directly from a supreme deity. As a divine being, the chief's person is sacred and has to be protected by numerous prohibitions and taboos. Supreme deities are the object of intense worship; ceremonies mobilise all local communities and integrate them into a single ideological community dominated by the high priest and the chief who *alone* have access to supernatural powers ensuring material prosperity, victory in war, etc. And to punish those who infringe his decisions or offend him, the supreme chief has powers of coercion at his disposal, the punishments varying according to the status of the criminal.

This résumé clearly shows that, even if the general form of social relations here still involves multifunctional kinship relations, we have as far as segmentary acephalous societies and the great Polynesian chiefdoms are concerned, two different modes of production. The *difference is not that of two varieties of the same kind*: Sahlins' 'familial mode of production'. What first and foremost characterises and determines relations of production in Polynesian chiefdoms, are the relations between an aristocracy – men who *do not work* and who enjoy a *monopoly* of political, ideological and religious power and who have at their disposal the labour, the products and material resources from direct producers – and the mass of the common people who live in local communities. Certainly it is important to note and explain that aristocrats and commoners are, or consider themselves to be, distant relatives and treat each other as such. It is equally important, but less so, that their kinship relations are patrilineal in form. What is decisive, however, is the fact that the mode of production and the interrelated political and ideological structures are of quite a different order from those found among lineal societies such as the Nuer or Tiv. Sahlins is not the only one to blame; anthropologists like P. P. Rey, C. Dupré, etc., who call themselves Marxists, have suggested 'the notion of a lineage mode of production' in order to designate 'the' mode of production for most primitive societies with or without chiefdoms. It is not by coupling Marx's concept of 'the modes of production' to the concept of 'lineage' that we can create a 'new' Marxist concept. And since these authors also consider that the opposition between young and old is 'class' opposition, we have even more problems than those of functionalist empiricism. The appearance of true social classes specifically presupposes not the disappearance of kinship relations but their capacity to act as a general form of social relations: there would have to be very special circumstances for the political and ideological relations as well as relations of production between the aristocracy and the common people to develop outside kinship relations. Sahlins is certainly not unaware of this basic problem concerning the appearance of class, but he mentions it only in passing.

AN ATTEMPT AT AN EVALUATION: THE CRISIS OF A CONCEPT OR A CRISIS IN THE EMPIRICAL FOUNDATIONS OF ANTHROPOLOGY

After an unusually sustained effort to redefine and effectively use the concept of 'tribe', we arrive at a largely negative result. The classification 'tribal society' is split in two and on each side of a dividing line (the nature and origin of which remains obscure); on one side are the acephalous segmentary societies and on the other chiefdoms. Structural differences between these societies are more important than the similarities, both in quantity and quality, and in this sense Sahlins' 1968 attempt to regroup, in a single category, these two societal groups which he distinguished and contrasted in 1961, is a failure. This failure confirms the results of the statistical studies of Cohen and Schlegel; using Fisher's mathematical process of regressive analysis for the co-variance of multiple variables, they concluded in 1967, that 'there was no solid support for the idea of the existence of a unified social stage between the bands of hunters and gatherers and state societies'. Cohen and Schlegel also stressed that in each of these groups there are great differences in social structure and that this diversity is greatest among non-migratory agricultural and acephalous societies. This leads one to suppose that farming creates greater structural differentiation than cattleherding or other production techniques (gathering, hunting, fishing, etc.). It is possible that detailed structural analyses of the economic systems of all these societies would reveal the existence of more than two modes of production within these two types of society, and therefore upset this over-summary classification. This does not mean that we would discover as many modes of production as there are forms of *technical* capacity in social labour, as Terray and other 'Marxists' do when they invent a mode of production each time they discover a distinct technical form of individual or cooperative labour, implying a collaboration of 2, 10 or *n* individuals. In fact, relations of production of similar type may involve different forms of the technical division of labour. This is a matter for future research and discussion, but in the meantime, we may conjecture the existence of several different modes of production among the different societies we call chiefdoms. Grouped under this concept, we have pastoral nomads, Turks or Mongols of Central Asia, some slash-and-burn farmers of South-East Asia, Indian hunters and fishers of the north-west coast of America, farmers from West or Central Africa and, finally, the former Chinese and Scottish 'clans', the Israelite 'tribes', etc. Perhaps what counts more in the formation of chiefdoms is less the nature of these *techniques* of production than the importance of the 'surplus' they produce. Sahlins is content to affirm that the appearance of chiefdoms and their typical economic form, linked to the practice of concentrating material wealth in the hands of the chiefs and subsequent redistribution is 'a classic example of evolutionary progress – the ability to organise greater economic and environmental diversity within a single cultural scheme, indeed within a single political group.'[17] This is a classic example of functionalist evolutionism, which takes effect for cause and cause for functional ends.

Split down the middle, the category of 'tribal' societies is hardly distinct from two other categories of society opposing each other: the 'bands' of hunter–gatherers on the one side, 'state' societies on the other. Herbert Lewis and Morton Fried have shown that both Sahlins and Service in defining segmentary tribal societies *do not distinguish* them from societies called 'bands' from which they are supposed to be distinguished. Segmentation, kinship multifunctionality, the alternation and complementarity of independent activities and forms of mutual dependence for the reproduction of their kinship relations, their ideological and political unity, perfectly characterise bands of hunter–gatherers: the Mbuti Pygmies of Zaïre (Turnbull), Bushmen of the Kalahari (Marshall), Australian aborigines (Elkin, Berndt), not to forget the Grand Basin Shoshone of North America, which Steward, toward the end of his life, gave up considering as typical examples of the simplest level of social integration, the family level.[18] It is enough to think of the internal complexity and multiplicity of the ways of life among the Murngin of Australia, the existence of patrilineal descent among the Ona of Tierra del Fuega or the Puelche and the Charrua of Patagonia, to find we are confronted by the usual collapse of empirical classifications when exceptions are more numerous than the rule. Moreover it would be wearisome to enumerate cases where the internal composition of segmentary tribes and their boundaries are as unstable as those of hunter–gatherer bands. The boundary is equally vague, though perhaps a little less so, between tribal societies 'with chiefs' and state societies. There are numerous examples of state societies in pre-colonial Africa and America, societies composed of a multitude of local 'tribes' subject to a ruling tribe, the chiefs of whom composed both the state and the dominant class.[19] Far from being radically and totally incompatible with the existence of tribal societies, the state very often only existed through the consolidating of chiefdoms and dominated tribes; sometimes created from nothing, without needing (like Fried or Colson) to infer from this process (verified recently by the practice of European colonial powers) that tribes and chiefdoms are exclusively *secondary* social formations, by-products of the process whereby state societies are formed.

In short, it seems that the concept of 'tribal society' covers a group of external features found in the functioning of many 'primitive' societies, the 'segmentary' character of elementary socioeconomic units, the real or apparent nature of 'kinship groups' in these socioeconomic units and the 'multifunctional' nature of these kinship relations. The vagueness of these criteria is such that we could apply this concept to a vast number of primitive societies juxtaposed in large congeries without clear boundaries. The most surprising thing in the history of this concept is that it has varied little in basic meaning since Lewis H. Morgan (1877). The innumerable discoveries in the field since then have only aggravated and accentuated the imprecision and difficulties without leading to any radical critique, still less to its expulsion from the field of theoretical anthropology. Content-wise, there has disappeared, through some sort of melting away, the element which was directly linked to Morgan's speculative notions, the idea of a necessary sequence of matrilineal kinship systems, followed by patrilineal ones; these notions are now out of date even for neoevolutionists who still side with Morgan.

This shows *a contrario* that the quarrel between partisans and adversaries of an evolutionist theory of forms of social organisation is being played out in a theoretical field *largely* dominated by empiricist methods; no one has ever really questioned the merits of these methods. It is not enough, like Swartz or Turner, to ignore the concept of tribe by referring no longer to it; to appeal to prudence, like Steward; or to criticise its scandalous imprecision (Neiva), its theoretical sterility and fallacies (Fried) its ideological manipulation as a tool in the hands of colonial powers (Colson, Southall, Valakazi). The evil does not spring from an isolated concept but has roots in a problem which will necessarily produce similar theoretical effects as dictated by the scientific work put into it. In Sahlins' case, the method is one of contemporary neoevolutionists empiricism: add the limitations of one to the weakness of the other. All empiricism has a tendency to reduce the analysis of societies to a demonstration of their visible functioning traits, then regrouping the societies under various concepts, according to the presence or absence of some of these traits chosen as points of comparison. In this way we get 'abstract' concepts made up of descriptive résumés of traits abstracted from the whole to which they belong. Such concepts are neither completely empty nor useless (as Marx said apropos of concepts of 'production in general' or 'consumption in general') in that they avoid useless repetition, but they do not constitute scientific concepts.[20] They are simply legal currency for rational thought. They only become truly negative on another level when invested with an 'explanatory' value, that is, a demonstrative value, within the framework of the theoretical analysis of a precise problem, for example, the evolution of forms of society. It is at this point that neoevolutionism adds its own impotence to the limitations of empiricism. Neoevolutionism, in fact, utilises abstract results, thought processes produced by the empirical operation of classing and naming societies in order to construct a hypothetical scheme of the evolution of human society. Such a scheme is not constructed from the results of analysing the *actual* evolution of societies, but is built logically from conclusions drawn from studying the evolution of nature and, in particular, the evolution of human beings. Conclusions borrowed from the natural sciences may be summed up in a few general principles: a tendency towards a greater *internal complexity* of organisms and a greater differentiation of specialised features to integrate this complexity and reproduce it. These principles have been transferred from the field of natural sciences, particularly from biology, to the field of anthropology, sociology and history, where they serve to define in advance, and in the abstract, general tendencies and the direction and principal stages of the evolution of society.

It is enough then, to select from the material furnished by anthropologists (the overwhelming majority of whom cling to empirical functionalism, and ignoring the historical analysis of the societies they describe) and, without questioning the significance of this material, to choose those particular societies best able to illustrate the sociological features of a stage, a period through which humanity logically had to pass in order to arrive at the great state-type societies, beginning with small segmentary societies little differentiated from palaeolithic hunter–gatherers. The chosen societies automatically become paradigms, lodged in the different divisions of a transformational scheme going from the simple to the complex, from the undifferentiated to the differentiated. In this way 'descriptive' material becomes explanatory by becoming 'illustrative'.

Let us recall the criticism such a problematique has aroused. Empiricism, in all its aspects, has been reproached for its tendency to reduce the functioning of a society to a collection of manifest or latent characteristics, then (when comparing different societies) to land in the endless dilemma of the exception and the rule. To these general criticisms we can add others particularly applicable to neoevolutionist empiricism. This approach never seriously analyses the phenomena of reversibility, even less the phenomena of devolution, which are found in the evolution of societies; they envisage this evolution almost exclusively as a *general, one-way* movement, a march forward in general stages – apart from Julian Steward and some others who see in evolution a multilineal phenomenon. Now, many hunter–gatherer societies of South America, according to C. Lévi-Strauss, constitute 'false-archaisms', because, far from being the last representatives of the primitive stage of hunting economies in tropical forests, they are vestiges of very advanced agricultural societies, who have been pushed back by other agricultural societies from the river banks toward the forest *hinterland* where they completely lost their ability to farm. P. Clastres has revealed such a phenomenon among the Guayaki Indians,[21] and Lathrap has generalised this hypothesis for the majority of hunting societies of the tropical forest zone of America, the Tukuna, the Cashibo, Siriono, etc.[22]

Leach, for his part, has shown, apropos the Kachin of Burma, that a rank society, ruled by a chief who is, or claims to be, the last born of the direct descendants of the last of the sons of the founding ancestor in his village, can become, in certain circumstances, a society of the 'gumlao' type, without internal hierarchy and no chief, and then again a 'gumsa' chiefdom, etc.

Although Leach's explanation of these reversible evolutions are not very convincing, since he sees in this primarily an ideological fact (the effect of successive choices by the Kachin for one or the other of two models of social organisation as suggested by their system of 'values'), the analysis of such examples of reversible evolutions and even the process of devolution, is of crucial importance if one is to discover the laws of change in social structure. Jonathan Friedman was even able to prove that the social organisations of the Naga, the Wa and other peoples living near the Kachin, but with very different organisations, were so many 'involuted' forms of the Kachin system under the effect of specific economic constraints. One sees why the demonstration of the existence of such a system of transformations makes it ludicrous to class all these societies as either segmentary tribal societies or societies with chiefs.

This example shows us something more than that there is no evolution without involution; no evolution in one direction without the possibility of it in another, or several directions. It shows us primarily that there is no evolution 'in general', nor is there a 'general evolution' of mankind. Mankind is not a subject any more than are societies and their histories; History is not the story of how a germ or organism develops. To go back to a phrase of Marx, 'world history did not always exist; history as world history is a result.'[23] Finally, it is difficult to apply to past history, ideas which express recent forms of a society's evolution. The notion of 'neolithic revolution', to which the archaeologist Gordon Childe attached so much importance giving it no little panache, today seems to obscure rather than illuminate. Its implicit and modern connotation suggests rapid, deep and brutal discontinuities, the process of animal and vegetable domestication demanding specific circumstances and several milleniums to arrive at a significant differentiation of the multiple forms (agricultural, pastoral and mixed farming) of production assuring the subsistence of the overwhelming majority of primitive or 'tribal' societies.

To deal with facts such as these, which require a grasp of both the continuities and the ruptures, formal similarities and functional and structural differences, a method is needed which avoids reducing observed social and historical reality to increasingly fine abstractions, a method which can represent, in thought, their internal structures and discover their laws of reproduction, non-reproduction and change. Conditions for structural reproduction change, but the changes are made according to laws expressing the particular characteristics of systems and are, therefore, constants. Our method must be capable of elucidating structures, i.e., functioning mechanisms and principles which are not directly observable. It must also be able to discover the characteristics of structural change and determine the origins and causes of such changes. To do this we must pursue our researches until we can determine the specific causality of each structure or structural level. However, this requires that we first recognise the relative autonomy of each level, exploring the connection between the form and content of the structures. If we are able to show that lineage organisation constitutes the general form of social relations in two (or more) types of societies characterised by different modes of production, it is of extreme importance because it demonstrates both the relative autonomy of structural levels and emphasises the need to go beyond a structural analysis of forms, the kind of structural morphology used by Lévi-Strauss, and utilise a structural theory of the functions and modes of articulation in social structures. The ultimate problem lies in determining the hierarchy of these functions within societies, the differential causal effects of each structure on other structures and on the reproduction of their functions and their interconnections.

If a *differential* structural causality does exist, the *decisive* problem in the comparative theory of societies, of structures as well as their histories, is to establish the cause; the determining cause in the final analysis and, therefore, the prior one in reality, even if it is not the unique or exclusive one in these structural arrangements and their transformations. From Marx to Morgan, from Morgan to Firth, from Firth to Sahlins, despite these writers' differences, the initial differential causality has been sought in the material basis of societies (neolithic revolution, industrial revolution, etc.), and in their economic organisation. It is through analyses such as these that we shall be able to determine the scientific aspect of the concept of tribe, of 'tribal society', provided, of course, that we stop studying societies out of context, considering them as entities in relation to neighbouring tribes, working, as Herbert S. Lewis puts it, on *specific and limited phylogenes.* In this way, we shall gradually be able to reconstruct, not only a theory of the evolution of societies, but a theory of kinship, religion and politics within their specific structural connections and through a logic of different modes of production.

Changing the terms of the problem

'We are no longer thinking in terms of definitions in order to include things, but of determined functions expressed by determined categories.'

Karl Marx, *Le Capital* Vol. 4, p. 208

How can we be surprised that in explaining the concept of tribe and summarising its history, we have stirred up from the depths of anthropology's discourses and texts, a contradictory and theoretical dead end, involving habits of thought which are quietly accepted and reproduced; but which for the most part are roads leading absolutely nowhere. Yet the concept of tribe appears in profusion in the writings and thoughts of anthropologists, basic to the most delicate problems, the fiercest polemics in anthropology. The reality is, in fact, somewhat different. The concept of tribe continues to remain ill-defined, despite a few abstract definitions common to a large number of so-called 'primitive' societies. While its content and usefulness are obvious, they are limited; a repertoire of a few abstract definitions subsumed under the same term, providing an indication as to the evolution of societies collected together under this term, of certain *forms* created by their evolution, but remaining silent about the mechanisms and causes of this evolution. It is little else but a kind of hieroglyph in a dead language yet to be deciphered. In order to decipher it and develop a critical evaluation of the concept of tribe, we must do more than go on analysing the realities it covers. We must learn, in some way, to read from the very substance of the content, the distinct cleavages which correspond, not to the separate properties of these realities, but to the distinct 'effects of thought', that is to say to the effects of different ways of thinking of setting about work – working on the evidence of its representations. What is the evidence for the concept of tribe? It is the representation, elaborated by thought and language, of a 'general form' covering the social relations of a certain number, albeit very large, of modern and ancient societies. This 'general form', as E. Benveniste has shown with reference to Indo-European vocabularies, involves one of kinship relations; its 'generality' suggests that kinship relations play or played a dominant role in these societies. What the concept of tribe signifies, both in the mind and in language, is a spontaneous representation derived from experience, a fact of observation; as far as this goes, it presents no difficulties.

The difficulties involved in the empirical concept of tribe derive from elsewhere, from the fact that this 'general form' under which the typical social relations of certain societies appear, only reveals the *appearance* of these relations, while hinting at something regarding their essence, their nature or internal connections. Difficulties also stem from the fact that it reveals these social relations *only* as aspects of kinship and therefore prevents us from seeing social relations except as aspects of kinship. The very form under which social relations are described, some Anglo-Saxon anthropologists significantly call them 'kinship societies', already contains a kind of unasked for answer to the implicit question about the real nature of these social relations; the answer is already there before the question has been made explicit or formed in the abstract. Thus we can see how theoretical thought is engaged, consciously or unconsciously, in a direction already indicated by this 'form' of the appearance of social relations. This is the kind of thing which decides the destiny of the concept of tribe and its heuristic value. If it follows the direction suggested by appearances, which is a correct empirical approach, it is in danger of judging facts according to this unasked for and unquestioned answer – a thing understood, a *sous-entendu*, which guides one's thinking and limits it, even although we believe we are humbly following the factual outlines without prejudice. This *sous-entendu*, this presumed answer, quite simply leads thought toward a theoretical conclusion which, in abstract terms, we shall formulate as follows: If the 'general form' of social relations in these societies is that of kinship relations and if the kinship relations play a dominant role, this means that they *determine* all other social relations.

This is how the concept of tribe, elaborated by theoretical thought in this way, becomes an ideological concept, a concept which fails to recognise the reality it expresses. The concept itself is quite innocent of its own effects, just as spontaneous thought is when it expresses the manner in which reality appears. The problem concerns only abstract thought when it refuses or agrees to follow the spontaneous language of appearances.

For this reason 'difficulties' in concepts of 'tribe' and 'tribal society' are not isolated or unique. They are found in other guises as soon as adjacent or like concepts are made clear: concepts of 'band', of 'state society', concepts designating other forms under which the social relations of other societies appear and around which people build general schemes of the social evolution of mankind. For this reason we cannot hope to improve on the concept of tribe, cure it of its ills in isolation; we must consider other concepts and improve them all in turn. The truly theoretical revolution will be to abandon the world of appearances and change the terms of our problems before tiring ourselves in trying to resolve those *as they present themselves*. At the very least we should consider problems where solutions may be found. The new terms in which to formulate the question are: what determines the fact that, in certain societies, kinship relations play a dominant role and endow all social relations – society – with its general form? What determines the fact that in other societies (the Inca or Aztec theocracies, for example) politico-ideological relations play a dominant role, impregnating all social relations, endowing society with its general form, etc. This is the direction which Sahlins and other authors have taken. They seek answers to questions about the exact nature of 'tribal society' and its forms of appearance, about the 'forms of neolithic economy', the 'familial mode of production', or 'the mode of lineal production'. This is not their error. The fault is in not analysing the modes of production, in having continued to *describe them in the forms they appeared*, without trying to show and analyse their specific structural causality, that is to say, 'the action of ultimate determination' of the different modes of production on other levels of organisation in these societies and on their modes of appearances or their general forms.

For reasons such as these we shall not be able to get rid of the difficulties involved in the content of the concept of tribe; we cannot silently bury it with a mere death sentence, or stigmatise those who continue to use it with the epithet 'infamous' empiricism. In so far as new concepts will not appear to resolve our problem, this concept of the 'tribe' will continue to be used in more or less refined forms and will deliver the same goods and the same kind of bad service. Until *it loses its* object it will not lose its *place*, to exist like a shadow of a former mode of thought always open to spontaneous thinking, but which scientific thought will have learnt to suspect and do without.

And there is another good reason to hasten this process of scientific thought. We must continually attack the political and ideological manipulations by which the concepts of 'tribe' and 'tribalism' are used as a tool by the Powers who dominate and oppress the young nations of the Third World. These powers often make it seem that tribal conflicts are modern contradictions which have their origin in the functioning of pre-colonial structures: in fact, these conflicts are explainable primarily by reference to colonial domination. While we must not fall into this trap and, in the name of anthropology, become accomplices of such arrant nonsense, let us not forget that their value as evidence and political practicality derive from the structural characteristics of former societies of the Third World and from their development. A scientific analysis of these structural characteristics is therefore not a disinterested exercise of pure thought, it is an urgent task involving thought and practical reasoning.

PART II

Dead sections and living ideas in Marx's thinking on primitive society

4

An attempt at a critical evaluation†

The development of Marx's and Engels' thought concerning classless societies and the forms of appearance of the State and class relations may be broadly outlined.

In *The German Ideology*, written in 1853, a very simplified scheme of the evolution of society was constructed by Marx and Engels in order to illustrate their fundamental discovery: that social life has its ultimate origin in the forms and structures of different modes of production. Four stages are outlined: tribal communities corresponding to primitive forms of economy (hunting, fishing, cattleherding, the beginnings of agriculture), the Graeco-Latin commune in the form of a State, feudal society, bourgeois society. The reasons for passing from tribal communities to the ancient city-state are barely suggested. The transition from ancient to feudal society is depicted in broad outline; the part played by the Teutonic invasions is mentioned but receives no important treatment.

In 1853, India entered this scheme and with it the whole Orient whose typical features were summarised in India's history. The analysis of the patriarchal tribal stage, barely sketched in 1845, was considerably enriched. The problem of the birth of the State and its primitive forms is set out clearly and given an original solution. The existence of multiple agricultural communities, isolated and requiring extensive cooperation for works of collective interest is the basis upon which despotic forms of State are built. This structure, combining neighbouring communities and a central despotic State, constitutes a form of transition from primitive, barbarian society to civilisation. But where a community's isolation and archaic structure prohibits decisive progress in productive forces, then this transition remains incomplete and Asia is left to stagnate for a thousand years beside the great current which leads to capitalism. However, western evolution may only be reconstituted and understood when the Asiatic forms, considered as relics of the past, are taken as its point of departure.

In 1858, the secret of surplus-value and profit-making was discovered by Marx. Criticism of political economy finds its permanent basis. The problem of the historical conditions for the appearance of capitalism may now be set down scientifically. The singular nature of capitalist relations of production combining and opposing the owners of the means of production and the money paid to wage-earners (the owners of their labour force alone) is contrasted with a few precapitalist forms of production. A new scheme of historical evolution was constructed, a scheme into which were integrated the analyses, in 1853, on Asiatic forms of land ownership, the organisation of labour and its exploitation by despotic powers.

Since then, the common ownership of land and communal labour have been explicitly set down as the starting point for the evolution of economic formations in society, which has its origins in the form of a natural community based on the kinship of its members. Marx called this community a horde or tribe. Asia is made out to be the museum and cradle of primitive forms of land ownership among cattleherders and farmers. From these original forms, where the community is owner and the individual only possessor, many evolutions have taken shape.

One which does not change the *form* of social relations, but partially modifies their content, is the general development of oriental despotism, a kind of State found in Peru, Mexico, Russia as well as Asia, and which manages the exploitation of man by man without breaking the structure of former communities or transforming the age-old relationship of the individual *vis-à-vis* his community of origin. Another evolution, a more dynamic one, gives rise to forms of ownership which go against the most primitive forms but develop from the same basis as tribal organisation. The ancient community accords its members the right to private property alongside rights of communal possession of State lands. The Teutonic community is the association of private landowners who jointly use non-arable lands. These two forms, where private property acquires more and more significance and where the individual acquires more and more autonomy, are the starting point for forms of exploitation of man by man, forms which as they develop destroy the former community relations and are the origin for a new development of 'secondary' formation characterised by the existence of antagonistic classes and the State.

Two processes for the genesis of the State and a dominant class are suggested, one internal to the community, the other external – both capable of working together. The unity of the community may be embodied in the person of the head of a family or some imaginary, supernatural personage employing real people. A hierarchy is constituted within the community, which might give birth to a higher community dominating them, the State, personified by a despot. War and conquests likewise raise some victorious communities above others, and their domination necessitates new political and economic structures, States.

From 1858 to 1877, *Capital* and *Anti-Dühring* elaborated these themes: *Capital* by analysing income from property – a form of exploitation peculiar to societies where the State is the ultimate landowner – and *Anti-Dühring* by generalising the idea of functional power being transformed into oppressive power and by outlining two ways of arriving at the State – one leading to despotic forms of State, the other to western forms of class societies based on various forms of private ownership, ancient and feudal, and on slavery or serfdom.

In 1880, analyses of the Russian Commune (which had increased since 1870), the former Teutonic community reconstituted by Maurer and revealed to Marx in 1868, and knowledge of Kovalevksy's works, all led Marx to elaborate a new concept, the *rural commune*, and to incorporate a far more complex scheme: the position and significance of the Hindu, Russian, Teutonic, etc. communities.

Asia becomes 'rejuvenated' in this scheme and agricultural communities appear in a more dynamic light. The ancient community where private property had already made its appearance, the march association, formerly described as the Teutonic community, no longer belong to primary, tribal forms. Another Teutonic community, reconstituted by Maurer deriving from the march association takes the place of the latter within the primary form.

In 1883–4, the discovery of Morgan's work changed this scheme of primitive history again. The importance of kinship in primitive societies is definitively affirmed and several of its forms are distinguished. Clan organisation appears as the key to the primitive history of civilised peoples while tribal organisation appears only as a late development. With the discovery of the historic role of clan organisation, America and the hunting societies – previously barely mentioned in the evolutionary movement – take the place of Asia in the reconstruction of the early phases of history. Instead of the Hindu model we now have the Amerindian one. The genesis of the State among the Greeks and Germans acquires a new originality because the State seems to emerge directly from a former society based upon *gentes*. Previous analyses of the Asiatic mode of production are in no way repudiated, but they now refer more to a way of evolution distinct from that of the West, a transition to civilisation which was less rapid and did not lead to civilisation's most dynamic form, bourgeois society. The analysis of primitive forms of society remains incomplete, shelved for the time being and in 1884, Engels, in spite of his admiration for Morgan, can write: 'There would be no sense to the whole thing if I merely wanted to give an "objective" report on Morgan without treating him critically, without utilising the results newly achieved, without presenting them in connection with our views and the results already achieved. Our workers would gain nothing by this.'[1]

And in 1891, he was already modifying certain sections of his book. The lesson is clear. If you wish to take the works of Marx, Engels and Lenin seriously, it does not mean 'believing' in every word and transforming their provisional hypotheses into eternal dogmas.

What is interesting in this evolutionary scheme is primarily its continuity, its breadth and scope which is always capable of taking in new material and information. We have already seen its continuity. From 1845, the themes of tribal ownership, opposition between town and country, inequality in primitive societies are constantly set out and elaborated up to 1884. On India and the Orient, Marx's wealth of reflections is such that to this day, he, together with Maine, may be regarded as the first to have drawn Asia into the forefront of historical consideration. And Marx did it with such theoretical breadth that not only does he occupy a foremost position in the mainstream of 19th-century comparative history, but he dominates the scene with his breadth of vision and theoretical horizons.

This theoretical richness is explained by the fact that Marx and Engels were ready to receive with open arms all discoveries made by others, such as Maurer and Morgan, who founded new scientific disciplines. We have broadly reconstituted the configurations of the theoretical field within which Marx and Engels were operating and which was being shaped according to the problems and discoveries then arising in linguistics, political economy, comparative history, ethnology, archaeology, colonialism and biology – not forgetting that they were linked to concepts inherited from the 18th century. Their reflections accepted and enriched all these elements, because they analysed them in the light of principles borrowed from a revolutionary theory, historical materialism, and from a theoretical revolution in the field of political economy.

Conclusions which have been superseded or are a dead letter have become so because of the progress made in those sciences founded in the 19th century. Before listing briefly these 'dead parts', let us emphasise that the great leap forward in their studies on primitive history, the most dominant aspect, is their analysis of primitive agricultural communities, the Asiatic mode of production and the existence of several evolutionary paths from primitive communism toward class society and the State. It is with these studies that their thinking extended beyond the boundaries of their century and became, after so many years of dogmatism, part of contemporary thought and knowledge. And it was not Engels who gave birth to this dogmatism; it was its birth that made *Origins of the Family, private property and the State* a dogma.

Of course many conclusions advanced in the 19th century and accepted by Marx and Engels are old-hat today. Let us cite the most important. The theory that pastoral, nomadic economy had necessarily preceded agriculture has been refuted by archaeology and by the ecological and genetical analysis of diverse domesticated species. Now, three stages of domestication can be distinguished.[2] One preagricultural stage which saw the domestication of the dog (mesolithic), the reindeer, goat and sheep (these play an important role in the first agricultural settlements of 9000 BC, called 'natoufian'); an agricultural stage (between 6000 and 4000 BC) when 'harvest thieves', the cow, the buffalo, yak, pig and gaur are domesticated:[3] finally, we have animals used for transport and work, such as the elephant in the tropical forest zone, the horse, camel, donkey and onager. With the domestication of the horse and camel, purely nomadic, pastoral economies became possible.[4]

We have already pointed out that there was no published archaeology of ancient Greece or Rome at the time Marx and Engels were writing, that the archaeology of countries in the Near-East, except for Egypt, was just beginning, that the archaeology and knowledge of China's ancient history, Japan and the great pre-Columbian civilizations had not yet come to light. Only with the discovery of the Jarmo site in central Iraq and Braidwood's excavations (1948–51) did we get proof of the first village communities (5000 BC), contemporary with the first stages of non-migratory agriculture and the domestication of animals.[5] Since then there have been numerous discoveries which confirm that towns and states appeared well after the development of village communities. For example, in Southern Mesopotamia there was a village community in 9250 BC, while the first Sumerian city-states began to appear around 3500 BC. Another theme was still discussed only in rough outline in the 19th century: that of caste societies. Several explanations were put forward; that caste originated from the domination of indigenous peoples by foreign invaders or that it was like a borderline case of the division of labour combined with a limited type of kinship relations, endogamy.[6] We had to wait until the beginning of this century and the works of Bouglé and Hoccart for a better description of how caste systems function, showing the hierarchical and religious aspects of this functioning in a convincing manner.[7] The explanation for the phenomenon of caste assumes especial importance because the present and past history of countries like India have world-wide significance and because the combined existence of caste and State power suggests an original form of the appearance of the State; this compels a rigorous definition of the relationship between class and caste.

Even more out of date are some of Morgan's theses on the nature and causes of the evolution of kinship relations in primitive society. And with these the whole façade of Engels' *Origins of the Family* collapses.

Morgan took upon himself the task of explaining the origins of sexual and conjugal prohibitions, the appearance of which put an end to the animal nature of primitive sexual promiscuity and as these progressions progressively increased so did the evolution of kinship relations progress up to clan organisation. His proffered explanation for the origins of the incest prohibition and exogamy are reduced to the biological argument of natural selection. Now, until our times, genetics was unable to determine the positive, negative or neutral effects of repeated marriages between close kin, which was a thousand-year-old practice in some primitive societies and countless village communities. The biological argument seems like a rationalisation *a posteriori*. However, the study of sexual behaviour in primates, whose social life may present an image of an animal mode of existence from which man evolved, shows practically no case of pure sexual promiscuity.[8]

But this is not the real problem. It has been established that *any* kinship system presupposes some form of sexual and conjugal prohibition and this proves the *social* nature of kinship relations. In renouncing their rights to certain women (mothers, sisters, daughters), men make these women available, offering them to other groups and acquiring rights over other women. The incest prohibition not only forbids but ordains. It initiates, directly or indirectly, immediately or otherwise, an exchange between groups. Any form of marriage implies a form of conjugal prohibition because marriage is not a 'natural' relation, but a social relation involving the group such as it is, and it must be compatible with the demands of collective life, the survival of a community. There cannot be purely consanguineous kinship. A kinship relationship presupposes both consanguinity and alliance.[9] The explanations for incest prohibition and exogamy must therefore be sought in social and not biological life. The principle of natural selection cannot explain the origin or the foundation for the distinction so frequent in primitive societies between cross-cousins and parallel cousins, for the ban on marriage between the former, who are considered like brothers or sisters, and the possibility, even prescription, of marriage with the latter, when these cousins are biologically equivalent and equidistant from the person concerned. Finally, we must remember that in primitive society, woman is of decisive importance in the maintenance of communities through her reproductive and economic functions, and this importance makes access to women a necessary social control. But it is always *men* who exercise this control. The relationship between the sexes in primitive society is therefore fundamentally asymmetric and non-reciprocal. Reciprocity exists only between men. In matrilineal systems, authority reverts to the woman's brother and the maternal uncle, while in patrilineal systems it reverts to father and husband. For this reason the two systems are not just simple, mirror-image reflections of each other. In a patrilineal system it is the men's *wives* who reproduce the lineage, in a matrilineal system it is their sisters. The question is therefore whether to secure complete control over the wife and renounce control over the sister or vice versa.[10] There is no matriarchal state therefore, even if in matrilineal societies women enjoy a very high status, correlative to the fact that the husband has no rights over the children. Nor is it because the father's identity was uncertain in the primitive era[11] that matrilineal systems preceded patrilineal ones. It is because filiation is matrilineal that the father's identity does not have the same social importance as in patrilineal societies.

This questions the validity of Morgan's methods of reconstructing the evolution of kinship relations and family forms. That there was an evolution cannot be doubted, but our image differs profoundly from that of Morgan's and depends primarily on a further theoretical investigation of the nature of kinship relations. For Morgan's evolutionary scheme to be valid, there has to be binary correlation between kinship terminology and family structure. In fact, the whole of Morgan's reconstruction rests on the hypothesis that there *must* have existed, for each type of kinship terminology, a *state* and an epoch where a form of marriage corresponded directly, for example in the Hawaiian system, any man called 'father' could marry any women called 'mother'. And then in order to organise these fictitious states into a chronological and logical sequence, Morgan used the hypothesis according to which evolution consists in multiplying the number of conjugal prohibitions between consanguine relations. Hence all known kinship systems were to be ranged in inverse order from the number of conjugal prohibitions associated with them.

Now, such a correlation between terminology and marriage could not be verified,[12] and as we shall see, *cannot* be, since kinship relations in primitive society do not *only* relate to marriage rulings, but also to residence, property, inheritance, i.e., the entire social and economic relations. Establishing classificatory systems of kinship, and it is to Morgan's credit that he isolated them, has perhaps rested on the necessity, in primitive society 'to increase the size of the mutual-aid group, and on the other, it effectively promotes solidarity among the members of the group by making them close relatives.'[13]

Marxism therefore cannot be held responsible for 19th-century postulates about evolutionism, even if the fundamental fact of the evolution of nature and society is recognised. Evolutionary schemes outlined in the present century encounter an extra difficulty unknown to Morgan. Classifying kinship systems by patrilineal and matrilineal descent refer only to unilineal systems. Alongside them, modern ethnology has revealed the existence and frequence of bilineal and non-lineal (cognatic) systems.[14] If bilateral systems can often be interpreted as forms of transition[15] between unilineal systems, the discovery of cognatic systems has profoundly modified discussions on the evolution of kinship relations in primitive society.[16] In cognatic systems all descendants of a common ancestor belong to the same group regardless of sex. This group does not have the structure of a clan, a unilineal group, but that of 'ramage', an old medieval term reinstated by Firth and others. The dominant characteristics of these systems are their extreme flexibility, the wide scope open to individual initiative regarding the manipulation of economic resources and political alliances.

By a singular paradox, modern research has revealed that the Scottish 'clan', the Welsh 'clann' and the German 'sib', were not clans but different forms of cognatic descent groups[17] and that descent groups in the Malay–Polynesian area belonged, for the most part, to this type. We are far from Morgan's thesis on the 'primitiveness' of Hawaiian systems and further still from the belief that Hawaiian social structure was a centralised kingdom with already existing class distinctions.[18]

Faced with this new diversity and complexity in kinship relations, the task of reconstructing their evolution becomes very much more difficult. Patrilineal, bilateral and even matrilineal forms already exist in hunter–gatherer societies. The Australian systems, which Engels places very close to most primitive forms of kinship and which should have been matrilineal, are on the whole patrilineal; however one also finds matrilineal and matrilocal (Dieri) systems, matrilineal and patrilocal (Aluridja), alongside patrilineal and patrilocal (Mara) and patrilineal and matrilocal (Karadjeri).[19]

One of the most likely schemes of evolution developed in our time, suggests a succession of bilateral, matrilineal and patrilineal forms of filiation over the course of history. Murdock's factorial study of 577 societies selected globally, aims at showing that, for the world as a whole, lineage descent has slipped from matrilineal to patrilineal forms along with the appearance of complex forms of government and economy. Still more complex social structures tend to make the unilineal forms of descent disappear in favour of bilateral forms, which generally speaking also characterised the much older stage of hunter–gatherer economies.[20] Morgan's hypothesis would then be partially valid but for very different reasons than those he advanced. However, as we have seen, the correlation between complex political structures and kinship systems cannot be mechanical since in all primitive society, whatever the kinship system, political authority belongs to men. One should therefore not expect to find matrilineal kinship relations within less developed forms of complex societies, e.g., in State-less tribes. We may quote the example of the matrilineal Ashanti of Ghana, citizens of a kingdom.[21]

One of the fullest case studies in the structural evolution of kinship is that of the Shoshone Indians who were organised into patrilocal bands and drew their subsistence from hunting and gathering in the high desert plateau of Utah and Nevada. One section broke away and spread toward the South, thereby occupying a zone more favourable to small-scale agriculture. A new division of labour was created, the women devoting themselves to agriculture and the men to hunting and warring. The bands became matrilocal and organised themselves round a group of women (perhaps the grandmother, her daughters and granddaughters) cultivating plots of maize. Later these Shoshones were pushed further south, possibly by the Apaches, where they formed large agglomerations in the valleys of Arizona and became Hopi Indians. Matrilocal residence continued to hold good, the land and houses remained in the women's possession. A matrilineal organisation was created and with the increase in population, lineages became regrouped into clans, each claiming descent from a common ancestor, though unable to reconstitute exactly the stages of this descent. This evolution of a patrilocal society of hunters–gatherers toward a matrilineal society of farmers seems, then, to have been brought about by the combined effect of changing over to agriculture, matrilocal residence plus a greater density of population, together with the new facilities created as a result of their resettlement (the introduction of the horse by the Spaniards).[22]

The problems of evolution in kinship relations therefore still remain and will only be solved with new discoveries in archaeology and ethnology, together with theoretical progress in the analysis of kinship in archaic societies. But this analysis cannot be separated from the economic relations, forms of authority, ideological systems which characterise primitive societies. In these fields there has been much progress too.

The inventory of forms of ownership and production in primitive society has emphasised the diversity and complexity still further. On these points continuity with the great works of the 19th century is widespread. The simplistic interpretation, weakened by the notion of 'primitive communism' where everything is owned by everybody, was not held by Marx or Kovalevksy. From 1858, Marx insisted that multiple forms of common ownership existed, that is to say the multiple forms which the relationship between a community's right of ownership and the individual's right of possession and use might take. He also suggested that where a form of ownership existed, it did not often, nor necessarily, mean that forms of common labour also existed. The latter appeared to exist either at very archaic levels (cooperation among certain primitive hunters and farmers), or in special ecological conditions (semi-arid zones), or because of politico-religious reasons (work on behalf of the State or the gods) or historical reasons (conquered peoples' subjection to their victors). Rights of ownership in primitive society, according to Malinowsky,[23] form 'composite systems' of different rulings according to whether they involve land, cattle, the tools of production, planted trees, ritual observances. The Siane of New Guinea distinguish two types of ownership;[24] one concerns the appropriation of land, sacred flutes, ritual observance, protected goods which may not be transferred and with which the individual has a relationship resembling that of a father (*merafo*) to his children. The other concerns the tools of production and the goods produced: axes, needles, planted trees, pigs, clothes, harvests. These goods are appropriated individually and may be transferred. According to the natives, the individual has rights over these objects because they are like his shadow (*amfonka*). Between these two types of ruling there exists an ordered connection: if one has a *merafo* relationship with the soil, then only work which involves planting trees on this soil gives the right to personal appropriation (*amfonka*). The existence of this ordered connection between the two 'rights' shows that the basis for this system is in belonging to a clan and that the control the clan has over other dependent groups (lineages) and over individuals is the main guiding force of the system. The system as a whole protects the interest both of the individual and the group, striving to limit the opposition which might arise over the control of essential resources, by giving group priority over the individual.[25]

The analyses of the functioning of society based on a hierarchical system and primitive forms of State also confirm the existence of numerous ways in which tribal aristocracies gradually dispossessed lineages and local communities of part of their rights involving land and scarce resources.[26]

Nevertheless, the presentation of the economic function of primitive society was markedly changed in the 19th century. The image of primitive peoples obliged, through the slender level of their productive forces, to devote themselves almost entirely to subsistence activities and live in a state of quasi-autarky, became largely outmoded.

In fact, in both primitive and complex societies, there exist two areas of economic activity corresponding to a general division of goods into two distinct and hierarchical categories: subsistence goods and prestige goods, as Cora Dubois puts it.[27] Within each category, an article may easily be exchanged for another, but it is difficult, wellnigh impossible or unthinkable, to exchange an article from an inferior category for one from a superior category. For example, among the Siane, all goods, except land, were divided into three heterogenous categories; subsistence goods (agricultural, artisan and gathered products), luxury goods (tobacco, salt, palm oil, screw-pine nuts), and precious goods (shells, bird-of-paradise feathers, ceremonial axes, pigs), which circulated at times of marriage (kinship relations), peace treaties (political relations with neighbouring groups) initiation and religious ceremonies. There was, therefore no generalised exchange of goods and services as in a market economy, only limited and separate exchanges.

The hierarchy of goods therefore expresses the hierarchical value attached to different social activities and these values express the dominant role of certain social structures within the society (kinship relations, religion). In the category of most rare goods are those which permit the attainment of the most valued social roles, for which social rivalry is the strongest. The limited number of these dominant roles implies that social competition, from the economic aspect, is effected through the possession and distribution of goods which are difficult to obtain. From this we can understand why, in many primitive societies, there are objects whose rarity seems 'artificial', such as pigs' teeth spread out in spirals (Malekula), series of shells deliberately limited in number (Rossel Island), copper plaques (Kwakiutl Indians) each with its name and history. It is as if society had 'instituted' the rarity by choosing unusual objects, unwonted for certain exchanges; in other cases, scarcity and rarity value arise from the fact that these precious objects come from far away (shells) and are obtained only by a larger transfer of local products.

Competition within a group, therefore, belongs for the most part beyond the sphere of production and the ownership of subsistence goods; it does not involve loss of physical objects but of an individual's social *status*. In excluding from competition such problems as the access to the means of production (the land) and subsistence goods, the primitive community, while authorising competition around scarce commodities giving access to women and authority, guarantees its survival and ensures physical continuity and its own existence as a *society*. At the same time, because competition derives primarily from conspicuous consumption or through gifts, social inequality develops within relatively narrow limits and is not permanently institutionalised. This is true only for societies which have not yet developed a hierarchy of hereditary statuses, reducing the field of competition to rivalry between aristocratic lineages. The theoretical analysis of the development of social inequalities and the origins of class therefore boil down to the discovery of the reasons whereby the strategic centre for social competition shifts from the field of distribution of the most valued social products toward the field of distribution of the factors of production, without in any way implying that competition for the distribution of the social product ceases to play its role. This is a process which leads some tribal societies to new forms of society entailing an embryonic or developed class structure, where former principles of reciprocity and redistribution disappear or stop playing the same role; here all possible stages have to be distinguished. For example, a social minority may acquire *for good* an exceptional social position (religious power, polygamy) even if it does not directly control the factors of production or the redistribution of the bulk of the products to which its exceptional position gives it the right ('rank' or 'stratified' societies).

Before pursuing this direction which brings us to the problems of the Asiatic mode of production, let us pause to emphasise a few consequences of these analyses and consider how far we have come since the 19th century.

1 It seems obvious that the concept of 'subsistence economy'[28] or 'self-subsistence' – used frequently to characterise primitive economies – should be rejected since it masks the fact that these economies do not limit themselves to the production of subsistence goods, but produce a 'surplus' destined for the functioning of the social structures (kinship, religion, etc). It also masks the existence of many forms of exchange which accompany this functioning. Exogamy, war, imply positive or negative relations between communities and, accompanying these relations, a circulation of precious goods which could, in a different context, play the role of a primitive currency with a limited circulation, while at the same time assuming other functions.[29] Primitive man does not 'live by bread alone', nor is he condemned to spend most of his time battling with nature in order to survive.[30] Recent time-and-labour studies[31] in hunter–gatherer societies have shown that they have much greater time for leisure than agricultural societies do. It should be stressed that, with progress in agriculture and more recently in industrial societies, the hunting societies have been driven back to inhospitable or fringe zones, which do not correspond to the living conditions of palaeolithic hunters. The neolithic revolution therefore increased the number of socially necessary working hours and this calls for a fresh analysis of the common evolutionist viewpoint[32] that the great advance made by the neolithic in augmenting the amount of available leisure hours, paved the way for a general cultural progress. This progress does exist just as the great neolithic advance, but their relationship demands another type of explanation.

2 The existence of a 'surplus' does not automatically lead to an enlargement of the level of productive forces. The fact that subsistence goods often enter only *indirectly* into social competition in many primitive societies, means that their production has no need to be advanced beyond their socially necessary needs. Functioning in primitive society rarely demands *maximum* use of the factors of production which limits the development of productive forces (although the production of precious goods and artistic developments may know considerable development). Often, progress in productive forces entails an enlargement of uneconomic, unproductive activities. This is the case with the Siane of New Guinea, who by substituting steel axes for stone ones diminished by 40 per cent men's labour hours spent on subsistence activities. The time 'gained', initially, was devoted to furthering those activities which traditionally were considered the most highly valued: war, ceremonial occasions, travelling.[33] This did not upset the traditional social structure, but it was a change of tradition which in turn modified relationships between groups and led to further changes.

If modern anthropology has confirmed the argument that the relationship between the development of productive forces and the development of social inequalities is not mechanical, it has on the whole shown that social competition in class societies provides the major incentive to surplus production and, in the long term, leads indirectly to progress in productive forces. In Melanesian segmentary societies the individual must create for himself his own personal authority. For this he must accumulate a 'store of power' (Malinowsky), that is to say, he must amass pigs, 'shell currency', food and create a network of obligations and a 'following', by distributing goods with calculated generosity. To demonstrate his power he must devote himself to patronising enterprises which extend beyond the narrow framework of each local community and domestic economy. On the level of society he appears as an indispensable means for creating supralocal forms of organisation. At the same time, his renown becomes the community's renown and the community identifies with him in as much as he identifies with it. However, to keep himself 'in power', the 'big-man' must constantly maintain his pressure over members of his faction, asking more from them and delaying more and more the moment of their reward. Begun in reciprocity, his control ends in exaction. Undermined from within and challenged from outside, his power collapses leading to the 'big-man's' fall in favour of some rival.[34]

This outline, which I have taken from Marshall Sahlins, describes the mechanism which shapes social inequality and power within societies which are relatively egalitarian and more or less segmentary in type.[35] It reveals an important fact. In practice, inequality is not created, is not justified ideologically, except through services rendered to a community. It always presupposes, and in fact develops, a form of economic dis-equilibrium between individuals and groups, a disequilibrium which is transformed into an advantageous *social* relationship both for the community and the individual who claims to play a 'central' role. Therefore, up to a certain point, economic and social inequality represents an advantage as far as the development of social life is concerned and, in practice, results in the community *identifying* its interests ideologically and factually with the interests of certain individuals. Inequality, at this stage, can appear as a normal condition of development, if not the norm of such development.

In essence, this observation corresponds to the basic thesis Marx put forward in *Formen*, and Engels in *Anti-Dühring*, whereby 'it is always the exercise of social functions which is at the basis of political supremacy'; and this brings us back to the question of the development of inequality in primitive societies, the appearance of social classes and the State. Marx's convergence here with modern anthropology goes to prove the *immediacy* of the main *essentials* of Marx's analyses when he bases his arguments on the origins of the State and 'the Asiatic mode of production'.

There is still a long way to go before we reach the State. Nor does the stage we have just described necessarily, or directly, lead us there. Another stage sees the substitution of provisional forms of authority built largely on individual superiority, for *hereditary* forms of authority based on superiority, by a constant minority, of 'birth'.

How and why does this substitution occur? We do not know the complete answer, nor indeed anything definitive about this problem which Engels left to one side, declaring that 'heredity of functions...comes about almost as a matter of course in a world where everything happens in a natural way.'[36]

We shall confine ourselves to a few suggestions. Societies in which heredity functions and statuses exist are not all of the same pattern. Morton Fried[37] distinguishes two important categories, 'ranking societies' and 'stratified societies', according to whether there is real political control by men or a control more or less elaborated from the means of production. Every gradation of this scale is possible. To illustrate it, we have chosen three Pacific societies: one Melanesian, the Trobriands, the other two Polynesian, Tikopia and Hawaii.

Malinowsky's description of Trobriand society still remains a *chef-d'oeuvre* of modern anthropology, although some of the author's interpretations are contested today. One of the most debated points[38] is the nature of the powers exercised by the chief of Omarakana, a village dominating the Kiriwina district, the richest in the isle, and Malinowsky called this personage the 'paramount chief', the 'supreme chief' of Trobriand, thus suggesting the existence of a form of centralised government.

However, Malinowsky's evidence seems to imply another interpretation. The basic political unit of society is the village. Even the most powerful chiefs mainly exercise their authority over their village and only secondarily over their district. The village community as a whole cultivates the gardens, goes to war, performs religious ceremonies, undertakes commercial expeditions. Its political and economic autonomy is important. It is directed by the eldest member of the dominant subclan. The chief of the village may or may not be a man of rank. When he combines these two titles, his position is very much stronger. He then exercises a certain authority over a district, that is to say a group of villages which adjoins his own, for purposes of war and the great religious ceremonies. All men of rank belong to a hierarchy, the head of which is the Omarakana chief. He is the most powerful ritual expert, controlling rain and sun. Men of rank wear distinctive adornments, but are mainly differentiated from commoners by the existence of special taboos, the number of which increases as the hierarchy is ascended. People of high rank, and chiefs, possess no judicial or executive authority over people of inferior rank from villages unconnected with their own. When a chief asks for help from members of his village, his district or strangers, he must compensate them. The necessary resources are furnished him through polygamy, the chief's privilege, and the gift (*urigubu*) which each brother-in-law must give to his sister's husband. A ranking chief marries a sister of each village chief in his district, and they in turn owe their brother-in-law a significant part of their harvest and valuables. The ranking chief is thus seen as a 'glorified' and glorious brother-in-law to the whole community. His exceptional wealth is used to promote grand ceremonies and, generally, to integrate a number of villages with the 'district economy'. The chief is therefore the instrument of a much greater economy than that of the village and *a fortiori* the domestic units of production.

The chief has no public force at his disposal to regulate conflicts; these remain the concern of lineages. The chief avails himself of a single weapon, sorcery, and the best sorcerers are at his disposal. Trobriand society therefore does not recognise any central government. What then is the meaning of the hierarchy which reigns there, linking all political and territorial units on the isle, i.e., the local lineages?

Uberoï suggests that the rank of local lineage may be considered as the combined result of three factors: a. an economic advantage, signifying that a village has fertile gardens or is particularly well placed for fishing; b. the degree to which this village plays the role of integrating centre with its neighbouring economic powers; c. its position in the net-work of overseas alliances, its role in the famous inter-island exchange cycle, called the Kula. Uberoï concludes:

I think it is these three factors which combine to determine the relative status of the different villages and of the local lineages dominant therein. When two Trobrianders meet who are not related by kinship or marriage, and one bends his knee to the other, this behaviour is to be understood as a symbolic recognition of the relative standing of their respective villages. Thus Omarakana is the most fertile district on the island actively participating in the Kula Ring sea-going expeditions and controlling the largest network of matrimonial alliances and ceremonies while at the opposite end of the pole we find the Bwoytalu an endogamous group who have the worst gardens, and no sea-going canoes.[39]

In Trobriand society we have an example of a hereditary hierarchy which binds different lineages and local village communities *without* functioning as a unique, integrating *political* structure. The chief's power lies in supporting economic and religious relations which extend the framework of particular village communities, without however integrating them into a single economic or ceremonial network covering the whole island. Chiefs are those who possess the most potent magical powers and they must use these on behalf of their community. Their privileges are thus the obverse of their duties and the reward for exceptional services rendered to the community at every level, imaginary or real. Trobriand is also the most celebrated example of the importance and mode of exchange in primitive segmentary societies. Apart from the exchange of necklaces and bracelets, the great maritime expeditions mean that indispensable raw materials may be procured: stone for axes, rattan, clay, etc. The Kula exchange constitutes a vast *political* association linking segmentary societies and which had to maintain the regular performance of vital trade *without help from a central government* which might have guaranteed peace between the different trading groups.

If, by comparison with the 'big-man', the Trobriand chief commands by birth exceptional rights over the results of trading and labour within the community, he nevertheless has no special control over the factors of production which remain in the hands of local lineages. This step we find in Tikopia.

Having published in 1936 an analysis of the social structure in Tikopia, mainly concerning kinship relations, R. Firth[40] subsequently wrote *Primitive Polynesian Economy*, 1939 in which he says:

> I analysed the economic structure of the society because so many social relationships were made most manifest in their economic content. Indeed, the social structure, in particular the political structure, was clearly dependent on specific economic relationships arising out of the system of control of resources. With these relationships in turn were linked the religious activities and institutions of the society.[41]

The Tikopian economy, like the Trobriander, is not a subsistence economy,[42] but one where the production and exchange of 'precious' goods plays a considerable role. The chief occupies a dominant place in the economy. He has ultimate control of the land, the long boats and the most precious goods of his clan. He is the 'titular owner' of these and this privilege is based on the fact that he has supreme control of fertility, of land and sea, and that he is the privileged intermediary between the clan, his ancestors and the gods. In the production process, he takes the *initiative* in agricultural and fishing activities, ensuring the *direction* of cooperative exercises: communal fishing, sago cultivation etc. He controls the correct utilisation of most of the basic natural resources. He makes sure of their conservation by imposing taboos which protect them from immediate consumption. He engages specialists and pays them to construct sea-going long boats and great fishing nets. He receives and distributes a large quantity of goods, encouraging their accumulation by organising big ceremonies which integrate the society into something bigger than the clan. He has the right to material assistance from members of his clan but cannot exercise any material sanction against those who refuse this assistance. He settles differences and, in some cases, resorts to force, helped by members of his lineage against serious offenders, murderers, etc.

The chief therefore enjoys a twofold inequality. Socially and spiritually the inequalities are natural and irreducible, while in the economic sphere they are chiefly by degree. Within his domestic unit, the chief and his family participate directly in production. In communal undertakings, he plays a guiding role but is spared the hardest tasks. He is not responsible for any losses, his harvests are gathered by members of his clan. He may not cook his own food. On the whole economic relations are personal relationships between individuals. The profit motive exists but is subordinated to the social role of the accumulation or use of wealth. Economic transactions, as all social relations, obey a 'code of reciprocity'.

As in Trobriand, there is no central government, although the chiefly hierarchy is more restricted and in the matter of rites there is one supreme chief who conducts them. The structure is shaped like a pyramid which is more clearcut than Trobriand. The base is formed by the commoners, many of whom descend from chiefs but have no royal status as such (genealogical distance in relation to eldest son), or have lost it. Apart from controlling the redistribution of goods, the main difference lies in a direct control over the tools of production and a directive role in the productive activities on a communal scale. The chief, however, is not expected to participate in the materially productive tasks, even if he manages them.

In Hawaii,[43] on the contrary, the chief no longer works at all. The social hierarchy has three levels: the chiefs' families, headed by a supreme chief of the island; the level of administrators, generally distant relatives of the chief, or men of high rank in their locality; lastly, the commoners who form the mass of the population and are mostly distant relatives of the chiefs and their councillors. A considerable number of taboos surround the person of supreme chief. A commoner may not touch any object used by the chief: his shadow may not fall on the house or clothes of the chief. Special adornments and perhaps a special language distinguish the latter from other men. Marriage with commoners is scrupulously avoided. The chief descends directly from the godhead and has special ritual functions, including the consecration of temples. Official ceremonies celebrate the birth, marriage and death of members of the aristocracy. The supreme chief controls the use of land, sea and any water destined for irrigation purposes. The immediate producer keeps watch over the use of his plot of land. He may be dispossessed if he refuses to contribute to collective works or manages his land in an unproductive way. Redistributions are, in fact, redistributions of control in local groups between a chief's entourage, after his accession to power or following a war. This entourage constitutes a kind of 'primitive bureaucracy', supervising production in domestic units placed under its control.

The necessary resources for great communal enterprises, public works and ceremonies are collected from the mass of the population and end up in the hands of high ranking chiefs, who then redistribute them. Taboos are imposed on the use of natural resources in order to permit their conservation and accumulation. The supreme chief has the means of coercion at his disposal and punishes those who infringe his rights, the punishment varying with the status of the accused. The chief's will, in short, is the supreme law. Assassination, rebellion, emigration limit the tyranny of his, or his servants', powers and make for an alternation in the periods of decentralisation and centralisation in Hawaii's political history. An analogous structure exists in Tonga, Samoa and Tahiti where, however, irrigation is of little importance. The difference in comparison with Trobriand and Tikopia is considerable in spite of many common elements. The land and the factors of production are no longer the property of direct producers alone. The latter must produce a surplus used partially for enterprises of collective interest which exceed the possibilities of local communities. The mobilised surplus, for certain ceremonial occasions, assumes considerable proportions. Figures such as 40 000 pigs and 20 000 calabashes of taro have been quoted. On the basis of the appropriation of excess products in local communities and the unequal control of production factors, a class division has been built up. A central government exists. It has, as one of the essential characteristics of the State, the right to levy tribute on commoners, but this State remains embryonic in so far as a veritable public force does not appear to exist and the territorial organisation of the population is but little developed. Revolts occur, not in order to abolish the system but to restore it to bearable limits.

To find a fully developed State structure, we must leave the Polynesian area and look at the traditional African States or the States and empires of pre-Columbian America. Without going into details, the population of these societies is divided administratively[44] and central authority is effected through territorial subordinates who are either appointed or hereditary.[45] The State has a public force at its command and the power of levying taxes on labour and goods is considered one of its essential attributes. Local groups, organised according to kinship relations, have, in part, lost control of the land. The State decides on land occupancy and usage. In the economic and political spheres, the State organises activities on a level unattainable by local groups, but these always assure protection and cooperation among members. Autonomy in local groups is more or less reduced by new obligations to authorities outside kinship groups and local communities. A network of new relations is developed mainly outside kinship relations and this now constitutes the framework for new forms of social promotion and status. The State is responsible for peace within the defence or attack from outside.

The State promotes work of general interest, controls foreign trade and, in general, the circulation of precious goods.

The State is incarnated in the person of a sovereign belonging to one of the lineages able to justify their supremacy by a mythical charter, legends and the capacity to contact supernatural beings,[46] who look after the wellbeing of the nation. In Africa a specialised priesthood sometimes existed. In pre-Columbian States this was pretty widespread. The incarnation of the State in the person of a sovereign has been described by Radcliffe-Brown in terms which extend beyond the African framework.

> In Africa it is often hardly possible to separate, even in thought, political office from ritual or religious office. Thus, in some African societies it may be said that the king is the executive head, the legislator, the supreme judge, the commander-in-chief of the army, the chief priest or supreme ritual head, and even perhaps the principal capitalist of the whole community. But it is erroneous to think of him as combining in himself a number of separate and distinct offices. There is a single office, that of king, and its various duties and activities, and its rights, prerogatives and privileges, make up a single unified whole.[47]

Perhaps this fusion of multiple functions and powers in the person of a single man only appear, to Western eyes, as a sign of 'despotic' power which knows no other law than that of a sovereign's arbitrary will.

A State, therefore, on the whole, when embodied in a sovereign of noble descent, dominates peasant peoples[48] organised in communities within which kinship relations still play an essential role. The population owes the State part of its labour and production. Surplus is destined partly for consumption by the ruling class (a consumption which takes markedly sumptuary forms) and partly for enterprises of collective interest, real or imaginary.[49] Slavery exists, but plays only a secondary role in production.[50]

These few examples are sufficient to reveal the diversity and complexity inherent in the development of inequality within primitive societies. These latter, we repeat, are as diverse as any class society. A variety of economies: the Bushmen economy, the hunter–gatherers living in bands in the Kalahari desert; the Kwakiutl, where competition for goods and counter-goods in order to acquire titles assumed the dramatic and well-known form of 'Potlatch'; the Trobriands, capable of organising maritime exchanges with islands 100 to 150 miles away; the great Polynesian kingdoms; the former Ghana, Mali and Mexican empires. To call them all examples of 'primitive communism' is to disregard essential differences by giving them the same label. The common ownership of land, as Marx repeatedly stressed, may take, like private ownership, the most varied forms. We would not give credit to a historian who drowns all differences between Graeco-Roman and capitalist forms of private ownership merging societies of distinctly separate classes into the general rubric 'Societies where private ownership exists'.

Moreover, our examples permit us to locate and formulate in 'operative' terms, some of the problems which anthropology and history must study more thoroughly if humanity's past is to cease being a mystery. Here are some of them:

1 How does it come about that there are heredity functions and statuses in certain primitive societies? It is worth remembering, that primitive society, right from its simplest form, carried different statuses for men and women (based on the sexual division of labour), to which may be added differences between elder and younger sons.

2 Under what conditions is an economy of redistribution developed, which changes and partially replaces the mechanisms of reciprocity, which traditionally ensured the exchange of goods and services within or between groups.[51]

3 How are social relations of a new type built outside the sphere of kinship relations? For example, age divisions, voluntary religious, political and economic associations. These new relations may combine harmoniously[52] with kinship organisations or react against them. They may also be found in State societies.

4 How is it that, in addition to inequality in the redistribution of the social product, there is an inequality in the control of the factors of production?

These questions have already been tackled in an incomplete way and we don't need to go over them all again. Let us point out, however, that they often verify Marx's central thesis, that social inequality protects the collective interests of primitive communities and is an essential factor in their progress. All our examples, in one way or another, encourage us to take up some of Marx's fundamental theses and, in particular, those of 'the Asiatic mode of production'.

Up to what point can this last concept be brought back from oblivion and 'revived' by modern science?

The formula is ambiguous because it is a concept which has long been used by many non-Marxist authors[53] who discovered it in the works of K. Wittfogel and caricatured and impoverished it. According to K. Wittfogel 'the Asiatic mode of production' originated in 'hydraulic' societies. When it appears in non-hydraulic societies, it must have been borrowed from or imposed by a hydraulic society. Marx's and Engels' proposition is quite different. Great productive works, hydraulic or other, as well as non-productive works are only *one* of the possible bases for the appearance of State power dominating primitive communities and, mostly, they follow and do not precede this appearance. Religious functions are another basis, as also in a general way 'the necessity to safeguard common interests and to combat antagonistic ones'. 'The State, to which primitive groups of communities belonging to the same tribe come with the sole aim of safeguarding their communal interests and defending themselves from outside enemies, acquires as a result the function of maintaining by force the conditions for existence and the domination of the ruling over subject classes.'[54]

The very essence of the 'Asiatic mode of production' is the existence of *primitive communities*, where there is communal possession of land and where it is still partly organised on the basis of kinship relations, along with a *State power* which expresses the real or imaginary *unity* of these communities, *controlling* the use of essential economic resources and *appropriating directly* a portion of the labour and production from those communities it dominates.

Therefore, in its essence, the 'Asiatic mode of production' is *one form of transition* from classless to class societies. Considered as such, its structure combines and unifies relations of production and the social organisation characteristic of classless societies, together with the relations of production and the new domination forming a class society.

The 'Asiatic mode of production' therefore expresses in *one specific* form, the contradictions involved in the passage from classless societies to class societies and this specificity consists in the fact that the exploitation of classes is effected through communal forms of ownership and the possession of land.

It is not therefore the existence of great works directed by a central power which will cause a society to belong to the 'Asiatic mode of production',[55] but the existence of communities which collectively possess the essential means of production, ultimate control remaining in the hands of the State.

We can understand that, using this definition, the concept of an 'Asiatic mode of production' seems to have a much greater application, in both time and space, than either Marx or Engels could foresee;[56] as a result, the adjective 'Asiatic' is no longer apt. It would seem applicable to some traditional African kingdoms, where, on the whole, great productive works did not exist, but where intertribal, indeed, international, trade was developed for precious goods: gold, ivory, skins, slaves, controlled by tribal aristocracies. This could also have been the case in the Thai States of the Indo-China peninsula which controlled trade routes between China and India.[57]

Should we return to Marx and revive a concept elaborated in 1858?

Not if the concept is to be revived just as Marx constructed it. Yes, if we can remove the *dead parts* and *change* it into a new concept, using the knowledge and learning of our own time.

What are these dead parts?

First of all, the notion of 'oriental despotism'. This concept does not belong to political science but to ideology. It evokes a much more oppressive power, embodied in the arbitrary wishes of an absolute sovereign. It is facile and useless to contrast this, as Voltaire and the Jesuits did in the 18th century, with the Chinese emperors' concern for good government. It is enough to quote the judgments of two contemporary authors when they speak of the totalitarian power of the Incas; they reveal the vague and subjective nature of this concept. According to R. Karsten, 'The totalitarian rule of the Incas was not an unbearable tyranny. The most wonderful side of the Inca civilisation, in addition to its political system was its social legislation (in general).' According to Baudin, the *socialist* empire of the Incas was 'a *menagerie* of happy men' built on 'the individual's self-effacement'.[58] These judgments teach us little about the Incas and a lot about their authors, but we cannot hide the fact that, paradoxically, Marx and Engels would have been much closer to Baudin than to Karsten.

However, this paradox is only apparent because it directly expresses another dead part of Marx and Engels' propositions – the idea, modified, however, in 1881 – that 'the Asiatic mode of production' signifies a thousand years of stagnation and misery, an unrealised journey toward civilisation and, dare we say it, more or less a failure. Of course, in 1881, the rural community, the basis of 'oriental despotism', appeared in a new light, dynamic, rejuvenated; but the weight and influence of previous arguments outbalanced this new aspect which was not developed. Modern archaeology[59] has shown sufficiently often that from Greece was derived the West and not 'civilisation', the West being a particular form of civilisation which finally became dominant. If we are considering the dynamics of productive forces, then the appearance of the State and class societies, which Marx and Engels classified under the 'Asiatic mode of production', testify, on the contrary, to a gigantic progress in productive forces. If the Egypt of the pharaohs, Mesopotamia and the pre-Columbian empires belonged to 'the Asiatic mode of production', then this mode of production corresponds to the era when man wrenched himself free from the economy of soil husbandry, invented new forms of production, improved agriculture, cattle breeding, architecture, invented arithmetic, writing, trade, currency, law, new religions, etc. Thus, in the initial stages, the 'Asiatic mode of production' signified not stagnation but the greatest progress in productive forces, all based on previous communal forms of production.

However, Marx's argument seems to retain a certain validity for more backward eras which were to see societies of the 'Asiatic' type sinking into a thousand-year stagnation. There is no point in denying the inequality and slow development of many non-Western, class societies. But we should remember that some, like China at the beginning of the 16th century, were more advanced than western society. The break and separation were caused by the development of capitalism itself.[60] However, this is not the theory which is being questioned. Some of Marx's arguments suggest the idea that the

'Asiatic' mode of production must *necessarily* entail a thousand-year stagnation. Now, the 'Asiatic mode of production', like any mode of production, may evolve in *several* ways; this evolution depends on its *internal* structure and *historic setting*. The internal structure of the 'Asiatic mode of production' combines both communal and class structures. The 'Asiatic mode of production' has, therefore, only been able to evolve, change and sometimes disappear in so far as the communal relations of production have been destroyed and replaced by *different* forms of private ownership. When such a process does not develop, the 'Asiatic mode of production' petrifies and consequently sinks into relative stagnation. An example of the first was China, or Japan, very different in ways and eras. Perhaps this means that with the development of individual ownership, seignorial or peasant, certain forms of the 'Asiatic mode of production' give birth to forms more or less *analogous* to the European, feudal relationships[61] though the role of State may be such that the 'feudalities' retain some of the characteristics peculiar to the 'Asiatic mode of production'. But the second way, evolution 'slowed down', happened in many cases wherever the State found it easy to exact income in the form of forced labour and on products from communities and therefore slow down changes in techniques and the development of trade. Here and here only, Marx's argument is partially confirmed. It may have happened in other ways too, for example, after the collapse of the palatine economies in archaic Greece.

And so, our problem is *not* whether we 'return to Marx', since this would be going back to a state we have already *gone beyond* in scientific terms. For a Marxist, the problem is in finding a theoretical concept which takes into account the methods of his time (scientific or otherwise) and in applying the analyses inherited from Marx as often as possible. Only on such terms will historical materialism, as a general world conception, not stultify into a petrified corpse of dogmatic prescriptions.

And so, disencumbered of its dead parts, faced with *all* the available knowledge of our times and enriched by a new theoretical analysis of kinship structures, religious and economic structures in both class and primitive state societies, the concept of the 'Asiatic mode of production' – or some equivalent, but better-named concept – can and must be used by modern science.

But, we need not only a new concept but a new way of looking at problems. The question of the origins of classes should be looked at from two aspects, one in which classless societies are dominated by kinship relations (anthropology) and the other in which we see the first forms of class societies (archaeology, history). If we take history into account we also make analyses of particular societies and epochs; we put forward and elaborate the theory of social relations, their evolution, the theory of kinship relations, religion, forms of power, etc. The science of History mobilises and unifies all human sciences. In this way we may discover the *hidden* logic of social structures and behaviour patterns, which at first sight, if applied to ancient or non-Western societies, seem strange, even absurd. Such a method challenges both the positivism of many Marxist historians and the narrow evolutionism of the 19th century.

Any discussion of the 'Asiatic mode of production', therefore, goes beyond it toward the constitution of a comparative theory of social structures and the construction of a multilineal scheme of the evolution of societies.[62] And in this process, Marxism can and should play an essential role. It can only do so by going more deeply into the analysis of its own principles. Now, the basic principle of Marxism is the theory that social life has its ultimate basis in the mode of production of material life.

Can we support this argument when we see that kinship relations in primitive society play the *dominant role*? How can we understand both the *dominant* role of kinship within primitive society and the *determining* role, in the final analysis, of economics; and more generally how do we understand the dominant role of a structure in a particular type of society?

Marx had already evoked the question after *Capital*, when he wrote to one of his critics:

> In his estimation my view [is] that each special mode of production and the social relations corresponding to it, in short, that the economic structure of society, is the real basis on which the juridical and political superstructure is raised...so that the mode of production determines the character of the social, political and intellectual life in general...All this is true for our own times, in which material interests preponderate, but not for the Middle ages in which Catholicism reigned supreme, nor for Athens and Rome, where politics reigned supreme. In the first place it strikes one as an odd thing for anyone to suppose that these well-worn phrases about the middle ages and the ancient world are unknown to anyone else. This much, however is clear, that the middle ages could not live on Catholicism, nor the ancient world on politics. On the contrary, it is the mode in which they gained a livelihood that explains why here politics, and there Catholicism, played the chief part...On the other hand Don Quixote long ago paid the penalty for wrongly imagining that knight errantry was compatible with all economical forms of society.[63]

The initial error is to consider economics and kinship in primitive society as two independent structures similar to infrastructure and superstructure. In fact the economist will easily distinguish the productive forces (hunting, farming, breeding, etc.), but he will not be able to 'isolate' the 'autonomous' relations of production. Or at least, he will perceive them in the functioning of kinship relations themselves. These determine the individual's rights regarding land and its products, his obligation to receive, give or cooperate. Kinship relations also determine the authority some people have over others in political and religious matters. Finally, they constitute, as Lévi-Strauss shows, 'l'armature sociologique' of the 'savage mind', one of the schemes in which the mythic representations of the culture-nature man-animal-plant relationship are organised.[64]

In *this* kind of society, therefore, kinship relations *function* as relations of production, political relations, and as current ideologies. Here, kinship is therefore *both* infrastructure and superstructure.

This plurifunctionality of kinship in primitive societies illuminates, in our opinion, two facets on which there has been unanimity since the 19th century: the *complexity* of kinship relations and their dominant role. Kinship functions *directly*, internally, just as economic, political and ideological relations function symbolically expressing the content of social life, man's relationship with man and nature.[65]

The economy–kinship correspondence does not appear as an external but as an internal relationship, but not so as to confuse the economic relations between kin with their political, sexual relations, etc. *Unity* of functions does not imply a *confusion* of functions. At the same time, this plurality of kinship functions is made necessary by the general structure of productive forces, their low level of development which imposes the sexual division of labour and the cooperation of both sexes in order to subsist and reproduce their way of life.[66] We must analyse along these lines the complex reasons for the appearance of unilineal, bilineal, etc., kinship relations.

If we wish to explain the evolution of primitive societies, we have to explain the appearance of new *incompatible functions* alongside the maintenance of former social *structures*. The question of passing from class societies to the State may, therefore, be partially reduced to a knowledge of the circumstances wherein kinship relations *cease to play the dominant role* unifying all the functions of social life.

We might suppose that the appearance of new forms of production modifies place of residence, demography, the relative importance of the sexes, demanding new relations of production, new forms of authority. Beyond a certain *limit*, kinship relations no longer correspond to new social conditions. They evolve up to the point where, outside of kinship, new social relationships are built, which in the long term will play the dominant role once held by kinship relations. These last will slip into a different, secondary role, and the new social relations, charged with new functions, will come to occupy the vacant *central* place. New political relations, centralised tribal power, appear in certain societies seeming to extend *kinship*: to derive from it yet oppose it. It is not, however, kinship which mysteriously changes into political relations. It is the political function of former kinship relations which are developed on the basis of new problems.

The scientific study of the evolution of social structures (kinship, politics, religion, economics, etc.), is therefore only the study of function and form;

the importance accorded the position of each of these structures with regard to types of economic and social formation and their transformation. Now this relationship of each social structure with every other constitutes the very structure of society. It is the basis for the *causality* peculiar to each of these social structures together with their reciprocal *correspondence*. But the correspondence exists only within certain *limits* and it is these limits which reveal the historical and objective content of each structure.[67]

For a theory which explains the differential evaluation of societies, we need to find a scientific theory of kinship, politics and ideology. We must also be ready to recognise that under certain circumstances, kinship is economics, and that religion may function directly as in relations of production. This hypothesis enables us to abolish the myth of a 'state' of mankind in which men live without economics, without kinship relations; where men merely aim to subsist without *time* for inventing *de luxe* products such as religion, kinship etc. Once mankind exists, *functions exist* with a particular content and form; History is nothing more than the history of their *transformations*. In this sense Marx was right to dismiss questions of origin and to declare that man's problem was not in his original unity with his conditions of production, but his separation from them.

Where kinship relations are not just a 'superstructure', when they are specialised and do not merely exist as social relationships ensuring the reproduction of the human species while retaining an economic aspect, though not directly intervening in production, there must be very special historical conditions.[68]

The same applies to religion when it is no longer just an ideology, a personal affair, a non-scientific concept of the world. We should resist projecting onto society as a whole, modern categories which correspond to specific social relations. It goes without saying that only by analyses such as these can we elucidate the difficulties encountered in the economic and political development of societies where kinship relations, religion (Islam, Hindu, Buddhist) forms of power (royalty, tribal chiefs, etc.), have quite a different content from Western capitalist and socialist societies. The failure of certain development schemes in Asia, Africa, Latin-America should remind us of this. And these failures are not due to the 'irrationality' of 'native' behaviour.

In an era when, for the first time there is the possibility of human progress without the development of new exploiting classes or the retention of former ones, Marxism, cleansed of all dogmatism, has as much responsibility for scientific revolutions as social ones.

PART III

Money and its fetishes

5

'Salt money' and the circulation of commodities among the Baruya of New Guinea†

PRECIOUS GOODS AND MONEY IN PRIMITIVE SOCIETIES: A FEW PRELIMINARY REMARKS

At the beginning of this century Boas[1] and Malinowski,[2] uncovering and analysing the potlatch of the Kwakiutl Indians and the *kula* of the Melanesians in the Trobriand Islands, began to destroy the traditional image of primitive man worn down by the forces of nature and trying hard to stay alive. He was seen to be busy, apart from his subsistence activities, accumulating precious objects, feather head-dresses, pearls, pigs' and dolphins' teeth, copper plaques and transforming them, by clever strategy of gifts and various kinds of presentations, into 'stores of wealth' (Malinowski), into a means of acquiring the most valued roles or status in his society. Within the complex network of kinship relations, relations of production and power in primitive societies, the gift was revealed to be the dominant form of exchange and competition between individuals or groups. It was found necessary to elaborate the theory of the gift.

Mauss, the first (1924)[3] to apply himself to the task was followed by Firth,[4] Einzig,[5] Polanyi,[6] Dalton,[7] Sahlins,[8] etc. In carrying it out an ideological difficulty immediately became apparent, which has not yet been entirely overcome. At first sight all the ethnographic material suggested that to understand it we would have to revive notions of political economics and see in primitive forms of competition and exchange 'archaic' forms of commercial competition and consider the gift as a kind of 'compound interest loan' and precious objects as types of currencies. Primitive transactions seen in the light of market-economy categories, seem to differ only in degree and not in kind from modern capitalist economies.[9] A close look however showed that primitive transactions do not easily fit into such readymade categories. It had to be admitted that the Trobriand islanders, far from confusing *kula* with normal trade distinguished it from barter, since they had another term for this (*Gimwali*).

It also had to be admitted that potlatch was unlike a loan since it is the lender who forces his rival to accept the gift, while with the loan it is the debtor who asks to borrow.[10] Above all the fact could not be ignored that precious objects, primitive 'currencies', were only rarely exchanged and hardly ever for land or labour;[11] also that their accumulation and circulation among individuals and groups did not lead to a general development of productive forces as is the case with the accumulation of capital in capitalist trading societies.[12]

Precious objects in primitive societies were not capital and rarely functioned within these societies as a form of currency, i.e., as a means of commercial exchange;[13] they were objects to show off, to give away or redistribute in order to create a social relationship (marriage, admission to a secret society, intertribal political alliances); they were objects for healing breaks in social relations (ancestral offerings, compensation for murders or other offences); for creating or symbolising a superior social position (potlatch deluxe objects accumulated and redistributed by important people, chiefs or kings). They served as a means *of social exchange*, of multiple and complex value in a distinct and separate sphere of circulation, within limits determined by the very structure of the social relations of production and power.

Nevertheless, we generally forget that all these precious objects, whether fabricated or obtained at the price of great labour or large payments, were *rare* products, which when bartered, possessed an *exchange value*.[14] In Malaïta, for example, currency armbands of white pearl came from the Kwaio who exported them to their neighbours. From the barrier reefs, one person could not collect, polish or pierce more than two armbands of pearls (at the most) per month. Dolphin teeth came from the Lau, fashioned by fishermen of remarkable skill who lived on small islands where agriculture was impracticable, and who exchanged these teeth for pigs and vegetable foods. The Yap millstones came from far distant islands and veritable sea expeditions were undertaken to extract them, hew them and bring them back.[15] Throughout the interior of Africa, Asia and New Guinea cowries circulated which came from distant shores, generally from India, and were obtained through the exchange of local, rare products.[16] Therefore when *entering or leaving* these societies, precious objects provisionally took the form of bartered commodities at fixed, or barely fluctuating prices. *Within* each society they usually ceased to circulate as commodities, and became objects to *give or distribute* in the social process of social life, kinship relations, relations of production and power, etc.

Therefore, if our analysis is correct, we must perforce conclude that *very often* the precious objects we encounter in primitive societies have a *dual nature*: they are both goods and non-goods, 'money' and gifts, according to whether they are bartered between groups or circulate within the group.

They function primarily as commodities if they have to be imported or produced for export. Subsequently they function as prestige objects, as objects of social exchange when circulated within a group through the mechanism of gifts and other forms of distribution. The same object, therefore *changes* its function; of the two functions, the second is the *dominant* one because it takes *root* and *meaning* within the requirements of *dominant structures* in primitive social organisation, kinship and power.[17]

In addition, it should be noted that a precious object does not simply function as a commodity when imported or exported between groups, but each time it is bartered between members of a group, when not given or distributed. It then circulates within this group as a commodity, even though it might circulate mostly as a non-commodity – as an object to give or an object of social exchange.

Finally, it should be made clear that when a precious object circulates as a commodity, this does not necessarily mean that it becomes 'money'. An additional condition is required for this: the possibility of exchanging it for *several* goods of various kinds. For example in Malaïta, a necklace of red pearls may be exchanged in return for pigs or tools of carved stone, or in return for food, raw or cooked, etc., and in this case it functions as money.

To sum up, more often than not, precious objects circulating between and within primitive societies were both objects of commercial exchange and objects of social exchange, goods for bartering and goods to exhibit or use as gifts, commodities which sometimes turned into money or symbols, visible signs of the history of individuals or groups receiving their innermost meaning from the social structures. They were, therefore, multifunctional objects whose functions did not merge even when superimposed or combined, objects which circulated always within strict limits, determined by the very structures of these primitive societies where labour and, more especially, land were never transformed into commodities obtainable by the exchange of other goods.

If this is correct, we can now understand why the analyses or statements made by economists or anthropologists about primitive currency are contradictory, or appear to be.[18]

There may be two basic reasons for these contradictions. When taken on the level of the facts themselves, the object described by the anthropologist has been perceived either functioning primarily as bartered merchandise[19] or functioning primarily as an object of adornment or as a gift; secondly, in the anthropologist's very way of thinking, the theoretical distinctions between commodities, money and objects of social exchange have not been clear and have made for confusion in the perception and analysis of the facts themselves.[20] Now, on the basis of these distinctions a very thorough rereading of the vast documentation which has accumulated on 'primitive money' becomes necessary and, indeed, possible.

We can also understand why most primitive peoples, right from first contacts, have shown that they understood the reasoning behind both gifts and bartering in the simple circulation of goods and why some of their precious objects have been called archaic forms of our money, even though it was rare for their money to be manipulated as capital invested for profit or accumulation.[21]

Finally, we can understand why, under certain circumstances, from Antiquity to the present day, these precious objects became ever more divested of their dominant characteristic as gift objects and came increasingly to be regarded as commercial objects,[22] retaining for a long time the 'traditional', or as is sometimes said, 'ethical'[23] aspect.

With these preliminary remarks we can now present the material collected in New Guinea on the fabrication and circulation of salt money among the Baruya.[24]

BARUYA SOCIETY

The Baruya[25] number about 1500 people spread over a dozen or so villages or hamlets in the subdistrict of Wonenara, which in June 1960, was the last region in the Eastern Highlands of New Guinea to come under Australian administration. Their language, material culture and social organisation all belong to an original ensemble of tribes now known under the name of 'Kukakuka', an offensive term used by some of their neighbours and made general since its adoption by the Australian government. Linguistically, the Kukakuka are not related to the Highland tribes or to the Melanesian languages of the coastal tribes of Papua or New Guinea.[26] Their number is estimated at about 50 000, the majority living in the northern part of a vast, extremely rough and hilly territory, stretching from the Vailala river in the West to the River Bulolo in the east and the River Watut in the North on the outskirts of Kerema on the Papuan coast. In Papua, some groups, under little administrative control, lead a 'nomadic' existence in a forestal region which is extremely difficult of access and protected from contacts because of its great distance from the patrol-posts of Menyamya, Kantiba and Kerema.

The Kukakuka are warlike tribes, mostly cannibal, whose raids sow terror amongst the neighbouring tribes and they live in a state of perpetual war.[27] Victims of the discovery of gold deposits on their eastern frontier in the Wau region, at the beginning of the century, they now make it difficult for gold-seekers to enter the country and put up a lively resistance to the Australian government's efforts to control and pacify them.[28]

The Baruya claim descent from the refugees of the Yoyué tribe living in the Menyamya region, who had to flee their original territory after a conflict which put them in opposition to other segments of their tribe, who on that occasion had become allies of their former enemies. The exodus took place, according to our calculations, about two centuries ago. The refugees settled in the Marawaka region, some three days' march to the north-west of Menyamya and gradually, through wars and matrimonial alliances, took possession of part of the territory of the local tribes, the Andjé and Usarumpia. At the beginning of the twentieth century they penetrated the neighbouring valley of Wonenara driving back the former inhabitants. Together with the Baruya, they constitute the frontier groups of Kukakuka to the west. Beyond them are the Awa, Taiora and Fore tribes, profoundly different in language and culture though similar in other ways to the tribes of the Eastern Highlands studied by Read, Watson, Langness and Salisbury.

The social organisation of the Baruya is that of an acephalous tribe composed of thirteen patrilineal clans, eight of which descend from the first refugees and seven from segments of the lineage of enemy or neighbouring tribes, with whom the Baruya once exchanged women and who chose to reside with their allies. Lineages are the basic social unity. Each village consists of from three to five lineage segments belonging to different clans. Individuals enjoy considerable freedom to choose their place of residence, even though patrilocal residence is preferred. A hierarchical division of the male population into four age-classes makes for a further break in the ensemble of clans and lineage descents, bringing together all the villages and unifying the society in ideological (the initiations' cycle) and military spheres.

Agriculture is the principal economic activity, along with pig-breeding and production of vegetable salt in considerable quantities. The villages are situated between 1600 and 2000 metres up in the high valleys of the Kratke Range, a mountainous chain which reaches 3720 metres in height. Vegetation is *rain-forest* type with large expanses of grassy savannah (*kunai*) resulting from slash-and-burn farming. Rain is abundant with seasonal variations quite marked. Hunting and gathering plays a minimum role with regard to food supplies but has great ceremonial significance. Until about 1940, the polished stone adze, the digging stick, the bamboo knife and bone chisel, constituted the main elements of the Baruya equipment. Before the arrival of the Whites, the steel axe and machete penetrated the region through intertribal commercial routes and rapidly took over from the neolithic equipment.

The staple food is sweet potatoes, cultivated in a relatively intensive way with periods of short fallow, mainly in the deforested zone. Cassava is much less important than the sweet potato as a food, but it is of prime importance in the ceremonial and social spheres. It is cultivated in the minor forest soils which are left fallow for twelve to twenty years. Drainage techniques, irrigation with bamboo pipelines and the bark of the screw-pine, lightly-banked terraces against the sloping levels to prevent surface soil erosion on the steepest inclines, are all evidence of a more complex type of farming than simple burning and superficial scratching out of the soil.

The lineage is the collective owner of the soil. Hunting and farming territories are shared by all the clans and lineages. Right of ownership is clearly fixed, but the use of the soil is extremely flexible. Ownership is founded, for each tribe as such, on rights of conquest and, for each lineage, on the work done by ancestors in clearing the forest. Work is based on a sexual division of labour and is done both collectively and individually.

SALT PRODUCTION

Technology

The diet of New Guinea natives is based chiefly on the consumption of tubers and, apart from a few communities with abundant resources of meat or fish, this entails a high sodium deficiency. Salt must be got by some means or other. On the coast, salt is obtained from sea water and is often exchanged with hinterland tribes. The state of the terrain, the distance and the constant war between tribes prevent sea-salt from reaching tribes living far inland. The latter, or at least some of them, produce their own salt either from salt mines or by extracting it from plants gathered or cultivated in the bush.[29]

The Kukakuka tribes all manufactured salt, but nowhere did it reach the amplitude and degree of specialisation as among the Baruya. They made their salt from the ashes of the *Coix gigantea* Koenig ex Rob, a plant[30] which originated in south-east Asia; as seedlings it is planted in areas naturally or artifically irrigated (by means of canals or ditches).[31] The cultivated areas vary from 2 to 30 acres divided into small plots, boundaries being marked off by different varieties of flowers or shrubs.

This salt plant is cut each year during the dry period and then springs up again. It is left to dry for a week or two; it is then mounted on a stake compiled of special kinds of wood and burnt for a day or two. The heap of ashes is protected under a thatched roof and remains there for several months. A filter is then constructed, composed of a row of gourds, blocked at the bottom by a wad of *Triumfetta nigricans*, which retains all impurities. The gourds are filled with the ashes (600 to 800 grams) and fresh water is slowly poured over them. The water, in passing, becomes saturated with the mineral elements and flows into a gutter made of leaves which discharges the water into long bamboo canes, which are subsequently transported to the place where the salt is manufactured. From time to time the water flowing from the gourd is tasted and when there is no longer any salty flavour, the gourd is emptied and refilled with new ashes.

The salt-making equipment is the property of a specialist. It includes an oven, composed of a tunnel 3.50 metres in length, 30 cm high and 30 cm wide. The walls are made from fire-proof, flat stones, cemented with the hardened deposit of the salt plant ashes. At the top of the oven a series of 12 to 15 moulds have been hollowed out, each 80 cm long and 12 cm wide in the middle. Each mould contains a bucket of impervious banana leaves and the top is kept open under pressure of a framework of light bamboo-cane. The salty water is poured into the buckets when the oven reaches a suitable temperature. This is maintained at a constant heat during the five days and nights which it takes for the evaporation and crystallisation of the salt solution.

The specialist supervises the oven temperature to ensure that the solution in the buckets does not boil (the temperature is kept between 55 and 65° C). With a special spatula, he stirs the water surface to prevent any skin formation. He removes any impurities which form or fall into the buckets. Finally and what is more important, he is the master of salt magic. At the end of five to six days evaporation is complete and the crystallised salt appears as very hard bars, 60 to 72 cm long and 10 to 13 cm wide. The bars are then carefully lifted out and the sides scraped to present a perfectly regular shape. A group of men wrap them in dried banana leaves and long narrow strips of wettened bark, carefully tied with overcast stitch, which harden as they dry out. The packing affords adequate protection against humidity and makes for easy transport without danger of breakage. The bars are stocked in the huts on a support above the hearth.

15 bars on average represent 25 to 30 kg of salt. The oblong shape of the oven means that the bars at the two side ends are shorter than those in the centre. The Baruya classify the bars into three categories according to size, giving them different names and allocating them different rates of exchange. Out of 15 bars, four or five are small, four or five medium-sized, six are large.

The social division of labour

The process of salt production, therefore, is divided into two phases separated by quite a long period. The first consists in gathering, incinerating the salt plants and building a cover to protect the ashes from bad weather. The second consists, strictly speaking, in the manufacture of the salt, namely, the filtering, the evaporation and the packaging. Both men and women participate in the work of the first phase and according to the importance of the task, the work is performed individually or collectively. On the other hand, the manufacture of salt is essentially man's work, surrounded by independent rituals and sexual prohibitions which ward off any risk of female pollution. It also brings in a specialist for the delicate operations of evaporation and crystallisation. These specialists are few in number, two to five for each village out of a population averaging 30 adult males. Their recognition as such is due to their magical powers and technical know-how. If their descendants also manifest a disposition and the ability for it, they transmit their secrets to them.

In Table 1 we have drawn up the basic data showing the duration of each operation and the kinds of work, individual or collective, male and/or female which each require. We then calculated, from the duration of the operations, the amount of social work necessary for the production of fifteen bars of salt. For this we abstracted the difference between male and female labour, which we felt justified in doing since, in the tasks of cutting, collecting, transport, stacking of the salt-plant stalks (in all of which they participated), the women showed practically the same efficiency as the men. A more delicate problem is that of the conversion into days of straightforward work, the supervision work of the specialist (discontinuous supervision over a period of five days and five nights). We have reduced this specialist work to three days of simple continuous work.

Table 1 reveals that work of any complexity is essentially male, which is also the case in the construction of houses, the digging of canals for irrigation, the installation of pipelines, the manufacture of weapons, etc. It can also be seen that collective work prevails slightly over individual work and that the number of individuals working collectively is quite few, varying from two to six. Taken as a whole the manufacture of salt requires the participation of eight to ten men and eight to ten women, in other words, twenty-one people.

What was the effect of the introduction of steel equipment to replace the traditional methods of production based on neolithic equipment? Without going into details, let it be noted that the technological changes have only diminished the time spent on cutting the canes and the wood for burning. Before 1940, the salt plants were cut with long knives of tapered bamboo cane and the wood for burning with the stone adze. It can be estimated that 50 per cent more time was needed to cut the plant, i.e., three days instead of two. The whole process must have required approximately twenty-seven days instead of twenty-one, which corresponds to 30 per cent supplementary labour.

In comparison, agricultural work, tree-felling, clearing the undergrowth, the construction of fences round gardens to protect them from domestic or wild pigs, the digging of drainage and irrigation ditches, have undergone much more significant changes. In the social sphere, the increase in productivity of individual work has diminished the social significance of collective labour by making cooperation in work less necessary. Cooperation is based on the mutual aid certain individuals owe to the salt owner through kinship ties, or which they provide as friends or neighbours on the understanding that he will do the same for them on another occasion.

Table 1

	Process of production								
	Production of raw material						Salt manufacture		
	(1)	(2)	(3)	(4)	(5)	(6)	(7)	(8)	(9)
Nature and order of operations	Cutting and laying-out the canes	Cutting and transporting the wood for burning on the pile and in the oven	Making the pile	Collecting and stacking up the dry canes	Supervising incineration	Making a shelter for the ashes	Filling the bamboos with fresh water for filtering and transporting to workshop	Supervising evaporation	Packaging the bars
Transformation of product	*Coix gigantea* Koenig				Ashes		Solution	Crystallised salt	
Forms of work	Collective – women (2)	Individual – Male		Collective – male and female (10 people)	Individual – male		Individual – male		Collective – male
Time taken for each operation	2 days	2 days	1/2 day	1/2 day	1 night	1 day	2 days	5 days and nights	1½ hours per bar
Quantity of social labour	2×2 = 4 days	2 days	1/2 day	1/2×10 = 5 days	1/2 day	1 day	2 days	3 days	22 hours = 3 days
	Total quantity of social labour to produce 15 bars of salt = 21 days						Quantity of social labour per bar = 1¼ days		

Table 2

Distribution of the quantity of social labour = 21 days	
(*a*) According to the sexual division of labour	
Male 13 (61%)	Female 8 (39%)
(*b*) According to type of work	
Individual 9 (42%)	Collective 12 (58%)
Specialised 3 (14%)	Non-specialised† 19 (86%)
If we take operations (3, 5, 7, 8, 9) of Table 1 as more complex forms of work than operations (1, 2, 4, 6) we get:	
Simple 9 (42%)	Complex 12 (58%)

† By non-specialised work we mean work which may be undertaken by any worker within the limits of the sexual division of labour.

Salt manufacture terminates with a collective meal (*tsàmouné*), generally offered by the beneficiary of this mutual aid. Sweet potatoes and cassava are served in abundance and eaten with bits of salt collected from the moulds or scraped from the bars during the process of smoothing the edges before packing them. Juicy sugar-canes complete this 'deluxe' meal, and the guests, whether they have helped or not in the salt manufacture, will linger on for a long time talking and discussing, their discourse only barely interrupted to masticate betel or to inhale enormous puffs of green tobacco from their long bamboo pipes.

SALT TRADE AND DISTRIBUTION

Salt circulation among the Baruya assumes two forms: redistribution and commercial exchange.[32]

Redistribution

Salt lands. All lands adapted to salt culture (flat and well-irrigated zones) were appropriated by different lineages during the conquest of the Marawaka and, later, Wonenara valleys. The desire to seize salt lands is one of the acknowledged reasons for certain wars with the Andjé and the Usarumpia, neighbours of the Baruya. In theory, all lineages have salt lands; in practice this does not work for a large number of their segments. The reason for this is the history of the group itself, its expansion toward the north-west at the beginning of the twentieth century and the invasion of the Wonenara valley. The first occupants of this valley divided and reclaimed lands suitable for salt production and because of the distance, ceased working on those they possessed at Marawaka. These continued to be worked by members of their lineage who had not emigrated, by allies or simply by friends.

Then, about 1940, following the Marawaka valley invasion by enemy groups from the east and south-east, a small band of refugees went to join the Wonenara valley inhabitants. A large number of them no longer wished to return to Marawaka after the enemies had been forced to cede their conquered territory. They settled in the Yanyi and Wiaveu villages, but unlike the colonists who had arrived at the beginning of the century, they came too late to find new salt lands in the vicinity, and they lived too far away from the old ones to make working on them feasible.

In the Wonenara valley therefore there is an unequal distribution of salt lands between the different segments of lineages which is advantageous to the first colonists. However, inequality in the owning of salt lands does not lead to any inequality in the redistribution of the salt itself and this can be explained in two ways: firstly, the proprietors frequently allow their in-laws, their maternal relatives or friends the right to use their lands (i.e., to cut and burn the canes). Sometimes even, they authorise permanent use of a plot by a relation or friend. Secondly, those who cut the salt (whether owner or user) are obliged to redistribute a part of their product.

Redistribution of the product. Salt is redistributed by the owner among his in-laws (brothers- and sons-in laws), his cross-cousins, mainly those on the maternal side, sometimes a few friends (particularly his co-initiates). Out of fifteen, five or six bars will be redistributed. The remainder are destined for family needs and for himself, and sometimes, if they are still living, for his father and mother. The bars are kept above the hearth and will be produced on various ceremonial occasions (approximately half a bar per year), or used as a form of exchange.

Salt exchange

Exchange for services. Out of those that remain, the salt owner must again deduct one or two bars for the salt specialist. Occasionally he will give one or two bars to a sorcerer, if he has cured a member of his family or himself. Finally and even more infrequently, if he himself is not able to go to neighbouring tribes to trade his salt and should he have need of some important article (a steel axe), he will entrust a friend to go and barter in his place giving him one salt bar for his trouble.

Exchange for goods. (1) Bartering within the group. In certain cases, bartering is practised among the Baruya. When a man has a son, or younger brother, who has to go through the initiation rites which will make him a man,

Table 3

	Objects and their use		Rate of exchange	Trading partners
Means of production	Split stones	large	1–2 LB*	Tchavalié, Kokwayé,
	Adzes	medium		Yopénié, Yoyué,
		small	1 MB*	Youndouyé
			⅓, ¼, ⅕, ⅙ of a bar according to length of stone	
	Steel axes		From 1–4 LB, on average 2 or 3	Nangravanié, Tchaégananié, Nondanié, Watchakè, Yoyué
	Machetes		1 LB	Yoyué
Weapons	Round pierced stone for stonecrushing		1 MB	Yoyué
	Bow			
	Barbed arrows (20–30)		½ LB	Youndouyé
Luxury goods	*Ceremonial attire*			
	(1) Necklace of pigs' teeth		½ LB	Youndouyé, Wantékia, Yopénié
	(2) Shells			
	(*a*) gamshell (polished mother-of-pearl)		3 LB or 1 cowrie bracelet 3–4 metres long	Tchavalié, Kokwayé Yopénié, Yoyué
	(*b*) cowries		1 SB*	Youndouyé, Nangravanié,
	narinna (young girls)			Tchaégananié, Yoyué, Nondanié
	small cowries		6–7 necklaces = 1 LB	Youndouyé, Yoyué, Tchavalié
	tambu		1 set = 1 LB	Tchavalié, Kokwayé, Yopénié, Yoyué
	(*c*) ampwakameunié		1 cowrie bracelet 3–4 metres long	Kokwayé
	(*d*) ndjammeunié		1 set = 1 LB	Kokwayé
	(3) Feathers			
	(*a*) aralla		1 set = ¼ LB	Demboulié, Wantékia,
	(*b*) niutniuvé		1 set = ½ LB	Tsimbari

	(c) kalavé	1 wing = ½ LB	Youndouyé, Tsimbari, Andjé, Usarumpia, Boulakia, Tchavalié, Kokwayé, Yopénie, Wantékia
	(d) bané	1 wing = ½ LB	Wantékia, Tsimbari, Boulakia, Watchaké
	(e) worié	10 feathers = ½ LB	Youndouyé, Wantékia, Tsimbari, Andjé, Usarumpia, Boulakia
	(f) willa	10 feathers = ½ LB	Yopénié
	(4) Pearls		
	pearl seeds	1 article = 1 LB	Kokwayé, Yoyué
	European	1 article = 1 LB	Andjé
	Magical charms		
	nuts (niaka) bark of	Bits of salt	Yoyué, Tchavalié
	cinnamon tree	Bits of salt	Tsimbari, Wantékia, Boulakia
	Pigs		
	male	2–3 LB	} Yoyué
	female	4–6 LB	
	Dogs		
	male	1 MB	} Tchavalié, Yoyué, Yopénié
	female	1 LB+1 MB	
Current consumption goods	Bark cloths	1 LB = 5 large cloaks 5 loin cloths with Wantékia, Boulakia 1 LB = 6 large cloaks with Youndouyé	Wantékia, Demboulié, Tchavalié, Kokwayé, Yopénié, Boulakia
	Salt from other groups	1 large bark cloak	Kokwayé, Tchavalié
	Small knives	⅙ LB	Watchakès, Yoyué
Services	Salt specialist	2 LB	} Baruya
	Friend 'commercial traveller'	1 LB	
	Sorcerer	1–2 LB	

* LB = large bar, MB = medium bar, SB = small bar.

he must provide him with a cross-belt of pigs' teeth, an emblem of his new status. If he himself does not own a cross-belt, he will offer pieces of salt to the pig killers in exchange for the jaw bones. Often, he also gets a piece of the meat. He makes the cross-belt himself. In fact, the Baruya prefer to get hold of small necklaces of pigs' teeth from their neighbours and mount these on the cross-belt. In other instances, extremely rare, a man may offer salt to a friend in exchange for the stone in a ceremonial mace.

In reality, exchanges inside the group are of little importance, since the circulation of goods is primarily regulated by the play of reciprocal loans between relations or between neighbours and friends.

(2) Exchanges with foreigners. Salt was the object of very active exchanges between the Baruya and neighbouring tribes, some of whom lived over a four days' march away. Except for the Youndouyé, whose language and customs are different and with whom the Baruya maintained a constant state of trade and peace, all the Baruya neighbours were alternatively their allies or their enemies.

The exchanges related to a range of products which we have classed in four categories.

(*a*) Production resources: split stones for the fabrication of adzes (small picks) and, since 1945, steel axes, machetes,

(*b*) Weapons: bows, arrows, stone bludgeons,

(*c*) Luxury goods: ceremonial adornments made from feathers, shells, pearls, magic charms, pigs,

(*d*) Current goods for consumption: bark wrappers, lime for chewing betel.

Salt is also exchanged for dogs, which may be classed in the category 'weapons', because they are principally used for chasing marsupials, who figure obligatorily in the most important ritual acts. Rates of exchange vary according to the products exchanged. A large piece of split stone is worth one or two salt bars, a male pig from two to three, a female from three to six, a steel axe from three to six, a feather headdress only one. Rates differ according to tribes, but once a rate is established with a particular tribe, it tends to remain the same (See Table 3).

The trading routes were opened by daring individuals whose names pass down to posterity. They ran the risks (being killed or eaten) involved in making first contacts with a neighbouring tribe, managed to establish friendly relations with certain members of the group and to effect a form of trade-and-protection pact with them. Normally this pact carries over from generation to generation and a man inherits the trading partners of his father. Each partner undertakes to house, feed and protect his guest and, if unable to provide it himself, will do his best to find the merchandise the other desires from within his own group. Transactions between his partner and possible purchasers are carried out inside, or at the door of, his house. This space, both geographical and social, restricted to the confines surrounding the dwelling of a segment of the lineage, and where the stranger is assured in advance of being able to meet possible purchasers with complete safety, functions therefore like a 'miniature market', each time a seller is present. This type of market (space and transaction) which is somewhat 'sporadic', is distinct from the periodical or permanent type of market habitually described by anthropologists and economists (See Table 4).

Table 4

Distance (in days on foot)	Names of trading partners	Distance (in km)
½	Youwarrounatché (N.), Youndouyé (N.W.) Andjé (S.), Usarumpia (S.W.)	10–15
1	Tchavalié (E.), Wantékia (W.), Nangravanié (N.)	15–20
2	Nondanié (N.), Watchakès (N.E.), Boulakia (S.W.), Yopénié (S.E.)	20–35
3	Kokwayé (S.), Yoyué (S.)	35–50
3+	Wéiaganatché (E.), etc.	50+

However, even when normalised and peaceful, exchanges continue to be dangerous. If the visitor has shown himself to be too hasty during the bargaining, he risks becoming the victim of acts of witchcraft directed against him by the discontented purchaser or by another witch whom the purchaser has engaged to avenge him. Often, for this reason, the visitor carefully covers his stomach and chest with special bluish-coloured clay, which diverts poisons or sickness against him.

Thus, trade signifies peace, even if it is more often an armed peace. From this aspect, therefore, the network of exchanges at any given period expresses the political relations between tribes and simultaneously reveals the complementarity of their economies. Therefore, apart from a description of mechanisms, microeconomic exchanges which link small groups of partners in pairs, it is essential to make an analysis of the overall mechanism of Baruya exchanges; this makes them appear to be a decisive link in a vast intertribal and interregional system of exchanges (See Table 5).

Before the introduction of steel tools, the Baruya did not have at their disposal stone-beds or quarries where the stone was of the required hardness or quality to fabricate their tools of production or their maces. They, therefore, had to import them and to do this they had to possess or produce an

Table 5

Friends	Friends and/or enemies	Neutral
Youndouyé* Yoyué†	(1) All immediate neighbours: Usarumpia, Andjé, Wantékia, Youwarrounatché, Goutlutché, Tchavalié (2) Distant groups: Watchakès, Yopénié, Kokwayé	Nangravanié Nondanié Boulakia Tsimbari Wéiaganatché

* Legend has it that between the ancestors of this group and the Baruya there was a trade and peace contract.

† They descend from Baruya ancestors.

exportable resource. There is little need to emphasise that, seen in this light, intertribal exchange was not based on the economic decisions of any individual, but was a practical necessity both anonymous and collective. The stones came from the north-west and south-west of the Okapa region (tribes of the interior) and the south-east along the route leading to the Yoyué in the Menyamya region.

Moreover, the Baruya live at a high altitude, 2000 metres up, and it is too cold to grow the tree varieties used in making their bark cloaks (*ficus*). In addition, and for the same reason, their forests are lacking in the kinds of birds whose iridescent feathers serve as ceremonial adornments (different varieties of birds-of-paradise: *Paradisaea raggianna, Paradisaea Rudolfi, Paradisaea minor*, etc., or the cassowary, *Casuarius unappendiculatus*).[33] On the other hand, trees and birds are plentiful in the lower valleys, to the west and south-west, leading towards the marshlands of the Papuan Gulf or, in the north-east, over the slopes descending to the River Markham.

Thus, to procure for themselves the means of production indispensable to their agriculture, to protect themselves from the cold, and to ensure that, in the functioning of their social life, there are present the material resources of its symbolic expression, the Baruya had to find, in their environment, a precious resource to exploit and exchange. This resource was found in the very morphology of their habitat, in the vast flat areas of the valley beds and the alluvial banks descending in tiers to the River Wonenara. The Baruya, it seems, immediately recognised which sections they had to draw off for irrigable surfaces and decided to exploit (and conquer) them systematically. One person confided to us that the Baruya clans of the Yoyué tribe, after taking refuge with the Marawaka, were visited by representatives of brother tribes who had stayed in the Menyamya district after the war against Tépadéra. The visitors had come to look for the refugees in order to resettle them on their territory. When they saw the Marawaka salt lands, they counselled the Baruya against returning and strongly encouraged them to remain where they were and produce salt. And that is what happened. Not only did the Baruya *plant* huge areas with salt, creating a kind of primitive commercial agriculture, but they *improved on* the production techniques known to most Kukakuka groups and invented the ovens with moulds capable of producing twelve to fifteen bars at a time and which constituted permanent workshops under the control of specialists. Thus, faced with the objective necessity of trading in order to live, the Baruya responded by showing intelligent utilisation of their environment and with technological and social invention. In so far as this invention revolved around trade, one can say that they 'enhanced' the value of their material resources.

Since the salt trade is destined to satisfy the needs of a population which today numbers about 1500 people, we may roughly calculate the volume of these exchanges. Suppose each member of the society requires one bark cloak per year and if we assume the average rate of exchange to be 1 bar for 6 cloaks, the group must annually produce 250 bars of salt to protect themselves from the cold. If we take 12 bars of salt as the average oven batch then at least 21 people would have to make salt in order to distribute 250 bars and knowing the average rate of yield for a hectare of salt planted, it is possible to calculate the area which must be cultivated to afford protection from the cold.

On the other hand, there must be 1500 cloaks available for Baruya in neighbouring tribes. As, according to our calculations, a tree aged six to ten years provides the raw material for 3 cloaks, these tribes must use up 500 of their trees each year to satisfy the Baruya demands (therefore they would plant them some years in advance). We shall see later how much work this exchange of 'salt–bark cloaks' represents for the groups concerned. But, to be complete, a total analysis of a system of exchange must be historical.

About 1920, different varieties of cowries and glass beads appeared among the populations in the north and south, to such an extent that they came under the control of the Australian government who used these articles instead of money. Steel axes and machetes arrived in 1940.

From all the information we received, it would seem that from 1920 to 1960, in order to procure pearls, shells, steel tools, the Baruya, who were not yet under White control, planted, produced and exchanged more salt than ever before. During this time, they went still farther afield to trade and came in contact with groups (five or six) who up till then were unknown to them and spoke different languages. Therefore, with *no outside pressure*, the Baruya had changed their production technique by sustituting the steel axe for the stone adze; they had enlarged the scope of their luxury objects (pearls, shells) and, at the same time, they had had to intensify their salt production and increase their commercial contacts. The present period is witnessing a rapid disintegration of their system of exchange, even though the Baruya salt, consumed principally during ceremonies, is not directly in competition with European salt, which can be bought in the Lutheran Mission shop. Construction works at the Wonenara landing-strip and *patrol-post* were paid in cowries, axes, machetes. Work on the plantations brought in ready cash which immediately found its way to a shop opened by a Kainantu commercial company and, later (1967) to the Lutheran Mission shop. Exchanging salt for bark cloaks remains the last solid remnant of the system, but already the Baruya partners are demanding to be paid in shillings. Finally, the ceremonial adornments and magic charms, which formed a small part in the business of exchange, are less and less required, since the government stopped wars, and the missions have morally discredited initiation rites.

By 1967, it was already too late to discover the traces of stone-axe exchange or to resuscitate the spectre of neolithic economy. Tomorrow the Baruya salt will be a useless accessory stowed away for ever in the museum of primitive cultures.

SOME THEORETICAL ANALYSES

Taking our ethnographical analysis as a basis, we may attempt the reply to three inevitable questions. (1) Is Baruya salt a primitive form of 'money'? (2) What is the basis for the exchange value of this money? (3) If there is both money and exchange, is there also profit?

Is Baruya salt a primitive form of 'money'?

When salt production first started, there was, as we have seen, an objective necessity for the Baruya to export in order to import the necessary means of production for their agriculture; the means to protect themselves from the cold (which constitutes a serious problem at an altitude between 1500 and 2300 metres); the means to satisfy their need for symbolic expression in social relations (ceremonial adornments) and to ensure their control over supernatural forces (magic charms). By reason of its variety of basic functions (subsistence, ideology), the exchange does not constitute a marginal activity, an occasional supplement of the functioning of Baruya society, but a strategic element of its structure. To go further, we might say that this society cannot subsist without exchange. We have arrived, therefore, at the antipodes of primitive, so-called 'subsistence' economies.[34] In the historical and archaeological sense, Baruya society constitutes an important example in that it throws light on the economies of neolithic societies, many of whom had to import raw material to make their tools and equipment. Theoretically speaking, its example brings to light all the difficulties in the concept of surplus in the way that economists of classic Marxist or Keynesian schools often deal with it. It was not after being sure of their subsistence that the Baruya turned to exchange and selling off their surplus. In fact, salt for them was a product primarily destined for exchange, and therefore a commodity.

This merchandise has an exchange value primarily because it has a use value: it is consumable.[35] Certainly, what salt is consumed by the Baruya themselves is minimal; it is not because salt is physically scarce, but because it is exclusively an object of ritual consumption. Therefore, salt is a commodity whose use value is that of a highly-prized ritual object by its ideological and social significance as much as by its biological usefulness, its gastronomic flavour and the difficulties in production. Salt is therefore a 'price' commodity, a luxury, which one usually does without, but which must make its appearance every time daily life gives way to ceremonial activity. Moreover, though salt is not physically scarce among the Baruya, it is among all groups who do not manufacture it and who also reserve it for ceremonial occasions and requirements.

Salt is a price commodity, but is it 'money'?

In order for a commodity to function as 'money', it must be able to be exchanged for a *whole lot* of other goods, it must function as a *general* equivalent for the lot. Let us go back to Table 3 and look at the example showing the circulation of a cross-belt made from pigs' teeth. It cannot be exchanged for a stone axe or a pig, dead or alive. It could be exchanged for feathers, but the possibilities for its conversion to another product stop there. Its circulation therefore involves a simple swop and if it is a commodity, it is not money. Stone axes and pigs could, virtually, be converted into any other commodity, but this is not the case, perhaps because they are too scarce.[36] On the other hand, only salt may run the whole gamut of possible conversions. Therefore it functions as money.

Because bird-of-paradise feathers, stone axes and even the services of a witch may be converted into salt, they become comparable to a certain extent. Salt in the form of bars, big and small, capable of being divided into pieces, offers a convenient unit of measurement for initiating business relationships. Its extremely careful packaging means it may be easily transported and will last for years. Salt has, therefore, a general equivalence, and is an inevitable intermediary for the acquisition of all goods which are socially available or necessary. A general equivalence does not imply a universal equivalence, since common consumption goods, sweet potatoes, cassava, etc., land and labour are not commodities and stand outside the sphere of 'salt money' exchange. This general equivalence does not only apply to the Baruya, but also their neighbours, the Youndouyé, for example, who come first to exchange their bark cloaks for Baruya salt before trading the latter for stone axes with the Awa and Tairora.

Baruya salt is therefore a primitive form of money and, since it is 'primitive', this money offers us an exceptional opportunity to probe the mysteries of the theory of value.

Baruya 'salt money' and the basis for its exchange value: labour or scarcity?

If you ask a Baruya his reasons for exchanging 1 salt bar for 5 or 6 bark cloaks, instead of 1, 2 or 18, you generally get a reply in the form of two answers, neither of which excludes the other. First he will emphasise that he doesn't trade for himself alone, but also for his wife or wives, his children, his brother's children, etc. In this way he is referring to the importance of collective needs. On other occasions, on the contrary, he refers explicitly to the long and arduous work entailed in the production of salt. According to our observations, in a bargaining situation, the former type of argument is generally employed first, aimed at appealing to his partner's sense of compassion: 'My children have nothing to wear..., etc'., and, later, when the other remains impassive, he will bring work into the picture. A Baruya once told us: 'When we bargain, work is invoked only in the last resort. Work belongs to the past, it has almost been forgotten. We only bring it up when the other man goes too far.'

The balance of exchanges is therefore primarily regulated by the volume of social needs. In any one exchange, bargaining determines a position of equilibrium between supply and demand. If it is thought that the visitor has laid down an insufficient number of cloaks before a bar of salt, or that the cloaks are of poor quality, then the salt will not be offered to him. The latter will then add one or two more cloaks and the salt bar will be handed over. If one or the other asks too much, the transaction will be cut short. Nevertheless, bargaining or haggling is rare and generally each partner knows what he *must* give in order to receive. The two act as if there were a 'normal' rate, a 'correct price' for the goods exchanged and this rate is known by the tribe and all its members. However, it is worth noting that rates are not the same for all tribes. The Wantékia, for a bar of salt, give five large cloaks and five bark loin-cloths (all of which corresponds to 7 cloaks), that is to say a rate slightly higher than the Youndouyé give (5 or 6). In this connection innumerable problems present themselves which we can only touch on. For the Baruya, though their trade with other tribes was of vital importance, it was at the same time constantly threatened and interrupted by fluctuation in their political relations, alternately peaceful and warlike. For this reason they did not solely trade with groups who offered them the 'best prices'. Moreover, those tribes who offered the best prices frequently had little to exchange, except the Yoyué with whom the Baruya would constantly speak of their common origin, their blood ties (which rule out pettiness). Finally, another reason why some groups would trade their products for low rates with the Baruya was their infrequent contact with them, their ignorance of the rates which other groups had settled with the Baruya and their lack of knowledge concerning the terms of salt production. For example, when the Baruya made contact with the Watchakès for the purpose of obtaining stone axes, they offered them one bar of salt for one axe and this rate was accepted until, one day, a Baruya, who had not taken advice from those who had been before and who was terrified by the cannibal Watchakès, threw three bars of salt on the ground and fled with the axe proferred him. He had applied the rate which the Baruya used for the Yoyué. After this the Watchakès refused to exchange for less than three bars of salt and the guilty one was copiously reviled for his cowardice and stupidity.

This is a very important example, because it shows exactly under what circumstances a 'normal' rate is established. It is fixed when regular and important exchanges exist between neighbouring, yet foreign, groups, who do not know the circumstances of production or the efforts required by their partners to procure the merchandise. It is not perhaps by chance, that the Baruya describe those groups with whom they trade the most – the Youndouyé, Tchavalié, the Kokwayé – as being 'hard, miserly'.

However, once fixed, what do the objectivised social conditions for forming a normal rate of exchange consist of? Is it the relationship between two equivalent quantities of work output, as certain economists recalling Marx, even Ricardo, never cease to hope?

In order to explore this problem, we shall take a trading example of the present day which is both the most regular and the most important – salt traded for bark cloaks between the Baruya and a tribe with whom they are tied by a pact of 'eternal friendship', the Kénasé (whom the Baruya call Youndouyé and the Australian administration, Asana). According to our calculations, making a bark cloak requires five hours of intensive labour which can be broken down into three distinct operations (See Table 6).

Every man and woman knows how to make the bark cloaks. There is no specialisation in the work beyond the simple sexual division of labour. The most delicate work (thinning the bark without making holes in it), and the hardest (the stone-beater weighs between 800 and 1000 grams) is done by the women. A woman can beat out a loin cloth or a cloak in one day, but this represents eight hours of intensive and continuous labour.

Table 6

Nature and order of operations	The process of production (1) Cutting and removing the bark from the tree	(2) Scraping the bark inside and out with a bamboo knife	(3) Beating the bark with a stone to make it supple
Form of Labour	Individual male	Individual male	Individual female
Hours of work	½	1½	3

If we analyse, in terms of labour, the exchange of 1 average bar of Baruya salt, which equals 6 Youndouyé bark cloaks, we get:

1½ days ⟷ 4 days of work (5 hours × 6)

The *normal* rate of exchange is therefore an *unequal* rate since the Baruya receive almost three times more than they give. The normal exchange is not an equivalent exchange.

Leaving aside the substitution of steel knives for bamboo, which has practically no effect on productivity, the production process of bark cloaks has remained entirely traditional. If we take two days as being the amount of time required for producing a Baruya bar of salt, before the introduction of steel tools, the exchange still remains unequal:

2 days ⟷ 4 days

The Baruya must know this, because they say that they 'gain', and their salt, agreed unanimously by their trading partners, is considered dear. From this, the last question we must ask if we are to throw light on the fundamentals of salt value is as follows:

Why is it that the Baruya and Youndouyé, knowing each other as they do and having lived always at peace with one another, consider this unequal rate as normal? (Unequal to our mind and in terms of the exchange of social labour.)

We suggest the following answer, which tallies with what we have been told: salt is dear because it is a 'luxury' product and its production requires a knowledge of technique and magic which other neighbouring tribes do not possess. What the Baruya ask for and what their partners normally agree to pay for, is the *monopoly of a double rarity* – product and know-how. By the same logic the Baruya were paying a lot for certain things like stone axes, *gamshells*, which were precious to them. The exchange was established on a level which expresses both the need and the labour involved (or the effort to procure a resource), but labour seems to play a secondary role; this could only be defined as a kind of minimum below which the rate of exchange must not descend, while the need, the rarity of the product, could be defined at the maximum limit attainable.[37]

'Primitive', therefore, does not mean 'simple'. Primitive reality not only contains the seeds of some future, therefore complex, conditions, but may also present 'developed' forms of social practice, the *analogy* for which may be found in other moments of historical evolution. This conclusion will be reinforced once we have analysed two other cases of Baruya salt exchange.

In the Menyamya district, the Baruya obtain certain nuts (*niaka*), which, used with cinnamon sticks, possess the magical power of attracting 'crowds' of possums on roads used by hunters. These nuts are also sucked, during ceremonies, by young married men who have just had their first child, in order to purify their mouths and bodies against the dangerous pollutions which result from sexual relations with their wives. These nuts are exchanged in the Menyamya district for pieces of salt. Probably they come from south of Menyamya, from Papua, where they are collected by local tribes. Here, we have an example of a thing which has 'social utility', which is a commodity, and therefore has a relatively high price corresponding to the amount of work involved in collecting nuts and transporting them in small quantities.

We shall conclude with another 'complex' example. If a man wishes to buy a young sow from the Yoyué, he will need at least four large (Tchameunié) bars of salt. Very often, he lacks the required number and will borrow a couple or so from a brother or brother-in-law. Later, when the sow has given birth, he gives in return one piglet for each bar of salt borrowed. If this is translated into salt money, he will have borrowed one bar of salt and returned the equivalent of two or three bars of salt, if the young pig is male, and four or five if female. This corresponds to an 'interest rate' of 100 to 400 per cent. However, this is a rare case and it is more important to note that no one, to our knowledge, *accumulates* salt *in order to lend it*. This example brings us to our last question: Is the Baruya salt exchange governed by profit seeking?

Exchange. Money and profit

The constituents for an answer are already there; they merely have to be put together. We have seen that in the Wonenara valley there exists, in favour of the first colonists, an unequal distribution of salt lands among the different lineage segments. This situation does not mean unequal distribution of the salt itself, since the owners allow their families, relations or friends the right to use temporarily or permanently their salt lands, and more especially since every person who cuts salt is obliged to redistribute part of his takings. A widow, an old man, an orphan will receive salt and necessary goods, bark cloaks, knives, etc. The 'interest rate' example, when salt bars are borrowed in order to buy a pig, reveals a fact which betrays the essence of the exchange process: no one accumulates salt for the purpose of lending out or making profit. There is certainly a material advantage and moral prestige to be had from lending, but no profit is sought to the detriment of the debtor. The underlying principle and aim of exchange lies in the satisfaction of social needs, consumption and not profit-seeking. Political authority and social prestige in a clan, lineage or an individual resides less in land wealth or salt than in ritual or war-like functions, the number of wives or children. Baruya society recognises a certain hierarchy of clans and individuals, but nothing resembling the 'big-man' of the Western Highlands societies, where a vast network of men and merchandise are manipulated and, of course, there is nothing which evokes the noble Trobriand lineages or the Polynesian aristocracies.[38]

Is it the same in the relations between the Baruya and their commercial partners, and does the profit which they draw from certain unequal exchanges signify exploitation of one group by another?

The answer seems negative to us for two reasons. The inequality, as we have seen, lies in the unequal exchange of work.[39] Now, with the Baruya, as with most primitive societies, *labour is not a scarce resource*. Productive activities occupy, at least for men, only a part of the time available (we estimate a third of their time is devoted to productive activities). What counts in group exchanges is the reciprocal satisfaction of their needs and not a well-kept balance of their labour expenditure. For this reason, the inequality of exchange expresses the comparative social utility of exchanged products, their *unequal importance in the scale of social needs and the diverse monopolist positions of exchange groups*. What counts is that there is *enough* to satisfy their needs and, recalling the words of one of them: 'If we receive enough, then work belongs to the past, it is forgotten.'

There is therefore *inequality without the exploitation* of man by man. Baruya salt exchange belongs to the sphere of the *simple* circulation of commodities. It constitutes *a case of simple market economy, welded to a non-market economy*, based on the individual and collective works of direct producers redistributing their products by way of kinship channels and neighbourly intercourse.

CONCLUSION

Our analysis of Baruya 'salt money' illustrates the previous theoretical comments. Salt, to the Baruya, is:

(1) A precious object, of a particular kind, because it enters, along with pigs, into the category of things 'good to eat, yet scarce and essential', i.e., meat and salt.

(2) A precious object, because it is consumed exclusively during vital moments of social life: birth, initiation, marriage, i.e., within the framework of ceremonies and rites 'celebrating' them. Salt is, therefore, invested with all the significance attached to the most solemn and decisive moments in the life of individuals and of the group.

(3) A precious product because its manufacture cannot be effected without the art of specialists who must possess both technical and magical know-how in order to bring about its crystallisation. In short, it is to the salt maker's magical powers that salt-field owners must turn if they wish to get that 'white and heavy' salt which other tribes covet and are ready to 'pay' a good price for.

(4) A precious product, because, thanks to it, the Baruya can procure all *that they lack*, and which to them is necessary for subsisting (stone axes), protection from the cold (bark cloaks), adornment and finery (feathers, pearls), compensation for murder, initiation of their daughters and warriors (magic nuts), arming themselves, etc. Salt is therefore precious, because it allows the Baruya to overcome the limits of their resources, limits imposed by their ecology and economy.

Salt is, thus, both a commodity produced for others and an object given 'among themselves'. In so far as it is the only commodity which is exchanged for all others, it plays the role of money. Conversely, all goods substituted for it *become by this exchange* commodities and leave neighbouring tribes, *in this form*, passing to the Baruya where they again lose their quality of commodities in order to become objects for display or for giving in the same way as salt itself; among the Baruya, salt is never an object for barter, it is an object for giving or distributing, an object of social exchange.

We can understand now why, in some Baruya huts, suspended above the fire-place there are bars of salt a generation old, blackened from soot and shrivelled. '*Not for anything in the world*' would their owner exchange or eat this salt because for him, it is a symbol of past friendship, of a pact sealed with his enemies, a dumb language which at every moment reminds him of a past which must never fade away. The bars are now no longer any good to eat, to barter or to give away. They are only 'good for thinking'.

6

Market economy and fetishism, magic and science according to Marx's *Capital*†

Selecting and analysing ideas about fetishism and magic in Marx's *Capital* at first seems merely an excuse to linger over some of Marx's brilliant formulae – considering the form rather than the content of his theory. But as these terms crop up at every crucial point in the development of his theory we may assume that they express at least one, if not several, fundamental Marxist principles. The essential texts are found in the first section where he speaks of the basic nature of 'commodities' and in the last section which is devoted to capitalist forms of income and their source. By then, although the work remained unfinished, Marx had completed his theoretical project, which was to study the 'internal organisation' of the capitalist mode of production, its 'hidden essence' as distinct from its visible movement and the concurrent 'illusions'.

What is meant by the 'fetishism of commodities' and why should profit, interest, wages and land rent assume the same character?

How are we to begin a scientific analysis of the capitalist mode of production and to what end? Through the analysis of commodities, replies Marx, and not from choice but from practical necessity: 'The wealth of those societies in which the capitalist mode of production prevails, presents itself as 'an immense accumulation of commodities', its unit being a single commodity. Our investigation must therefore begin with the analysis of a commodity.' (C, I, 35).[1]

What is a commodity? Firstly, it is any external object which has the property of satisfying any kind of human need. It or its properties constitute its use value, its social usefulness. An object which is of no use to anyone but its producer cannot be exchanged nor can it become a commodity. Its exchange value becomes apparent only when it is exchanged for a pipe or two silk handkerchiefs or their equivalent in money.

Its value, therefore, seems to be something which does not change even though the object itself may be exchanged in differing proportions for other objects. For objects to be exchanged in differing proportions they must have something in common of which they represent one more or one less. This common something cannot have anything to do with use value, since the latter is distinct and radically different. We are left with one possible explanation, the fact of it being the product of human labour. 'A use-value or useful article, therefore, has value only because human labour has been embodied or materialised in it.' and this value is precisely that 'something common', which is revealed in relation to the exchange of goods.

Before pursuing this further, let us briefly outline Marx's method at the beginning of *Capital*, a method which so many authors have unfortunately considered to be a 'dialectic' deduction of 'categories', drawn up on somewhat Hegelian lines. Marx did not choose this starting point. It was imposed by the very nature of *social relations* in the social period he was proposing to analyse. This starting point does not involve a 'notion', but the *forms* under which various objects playing the role of commodities appear. The analysis of these forms obliged Marx to look for the practical conditions underlying the possibilities for exchanging goods. For this to exist, all goods must have something in common and it is the nature and origin of this common something which had to be discovered. It is not in their quite different and incommensurable use values that this element resides, it is therefore in one property only that they have this common something, the fact that they are all the products of labour. From this it follows that the nature of the value, its 'substance' is discovered: it is human labour, coagulated, materialised, crystallised. Marx, therefore, did not proceed with an ideal, logical 'deduction' about the concept of value, beginning with the concept of commodities. To stress the importance of this point, it is enough to remember how he insisted, shortly before his death, on the original character of this method, as seen in his celebrated notes to A. Wagner's *Treatise on political economy*: 'I do not start from "notions", neither from the "notion of value", and consequently I have not "divided" it in any way. That from which I start is the simplest representation of the *social form*, in actual society, the product of work, that is, commodities.'[2] 'My *analytic* method does *not start from man*, but from the *given socio-economic period* which has nothing in common with the method based on notions of German thinkers ("with some remarks, one can struggle in wonder, with some, construct a system").'[3]

But let us carry on with an analysis of value. Its essence is materialised labour, we might imagine that the value of commodities is going to vary with the sloth or skill of the producer, i.e., the concrete, individual forms which the work takes for production.

In fact, the time determining the value of commodities is that labour time 'socially' necessary for its production and not that time spent concretely, individually by such and such a producer: 'The labour-time socially necessary is that required to produce an article under the normal conditions of production and with the average degree of skill and intensity prevalent at the time ...The labour-time changes with every variation in the productiveness of labour.' (C, I, 39–40). It is therefore the *average* amount of work spent on the production of a commodity which determines its value. From this it may be understood that the concrete labour of any one producer produces value only in so far as it is composed of work expended by all the other producers engaged in the same production, coinciding with the labour time socially necessary for its production and, thus, becoming an inseparable element from the labour force of society as a whole. [The total labour-power of society, which] 'is embodied in the sum total of the values...counts here as *one homogenous* mass of human labour-power, composed though it be of innumerable individual units.' (C, I, 39). Commodities in which equal quantities of labour are embodied, or which can be produced in the same time 'have the same value'. (C, I, 39).

Human labour has therefore a twofold character, concrete and abstract, according to whether it is related to the use value of commodities or to the worth of these commodities. For Marx, this discovery was so important theoretically, that he wrote: 'I was *the first* to point out and to examine critically this two-fold nature of the labour contained in commodities...this point is the *pivot* on which a clear comprehension of Political Economy turns.' (C, I, 41; Godelier's italics.)

If we take Marx's estimation of his work seriously, as we should, then we must conclude, that in his opinion, the discovery of the dual nature of human labour provides the missing link in the theory of value as propounded by the classical economists, a link enabling a proper questioning and resolution of certain fundamental theoretical problems. Whereas, since W. Petty and A. Smith, human labour was recognised as being the origin and substance of the value of commodities, it was not known (except in a few instances[4]) that labour forms the value of commodities only by becoming abstract human labour, socially necessary labour. Marx was therefore aware of having made a leap forward in the theory of value which meant he could 'do what bourgeois economy has never attempted: (to) trace the genesis of money-form.' (C, I, 47). Now – and here we arrive at the very crux of our research – this genesis is going to reveal simultaneously the enigmatic, fetishist nature of all commodities and therefore of all money. What does it mean to trace the genesis of 'money-form'?

It is to develop 'the expression of value implied in the value-relation of commodities, from its simplest, almost imperceptible outline, to the dazzling money-form. By doing this we shall, at the same time, solve the riddle presented by money.' (C, I, 48).

And so, by 'tracing the genesis' of money, Marx analysed the way in which the value of a commodity appeared, the form in which its content (*abstract* human labour) and its magnitude (*socially* necessary labour) are *revealed*.

Now, the value of a commodity can never be revealed if this commodity is considered in isolation, separate from all others. In this case it is only the use value of the commodity which is manifested, its property as a useful object. In order to reveal its value it has to be exchanged for other commodities. Once it enters into an exchange relationship with other commodities, its own value finds in this *relationship* a *form* which expresses it. This relationship, this form, constitutes the 'exchange value'. The 'exchange value' of a commodity is 'the phenomenal form proper'[5] to its value, 'a representation, characterised by the value contained in this commodity' (i.e., the social expenditure of work crystallised in it), but this 'exchange value' is not the 'value' of the commodity.

The distinction between 'value' and 'exchange value' is often ignored by people commenting on Marx, and yet it is fundamental: 'In my opinion, the "value" of a commodity is neither its use-value nor its exchange value.'[6]

The 'exchange value' of a commodity is the value relationship established in exchanging the commodity for other commodities. This relationship does not create the 'value' of the commodity because the value is born with the production process of the commodity and not in the process of its circulation between producers. Circulation does not create the value. The value *exists* before the commodity is circulated. Once commodities circulate, or are exchanged, they enter into value relationships which may or may not correspond to their value. They may be sold, for example, for a price exceeding their value.[7]

Let us now analyse the exchange relationship between two commodities, since this relationship constitutes the 'form' of the appearance of the value and the starting point for tracing the genesis of money. Let us take a simple example: commodity A (cloth) is exchanged for commodity B (coats) in the proportion $xA = yB$, 20 metres of cloth = 1 coat. The value of A is expressed therefore in a fixed quantity of B. It is expressed 'relative to' B and B is opposite it as an 'equivalent'. Therefore the value of A is expressed in two ways – one relative, the other as an equivalent. If the equation is reversed, A becomes the equivalent form of B. Thus, in this 'expression relationship', both play a separate role, though correlative and exclusive of the other's (a commodity cannot be its own equivalent). So, in this relationship only the value of *one* is expressed. The second commodity, playing the role of equivalent, merely furnishes the first with the 'material for expressing'[8] its value without expressing its own value. It plays a 'passive' role.[9]

How can this *relationship* between two commodities *contain* 'the whole *Mystery* of the form of value', and therefore the *fetishist* nature of the commodity and money? In order to understand this a closer analysis of the opposite poles in this expression relationship is required, the relative form and the equivalent form. The coat equivalent of the cloth expresses the value of the cloth by the use value of the coat. Now, to weave cloth and to cut coats are two *distinct*, concrete forms of work. As soon as the coat becomes the equivalent of the cloth, the work involved in B is confirmed as *identical* to the work involved in A. Therefore the two concrete forms of work are brought together as equal, abstract human labour.

Since the value of A may be expressed in object B having a *different* use, the 'relative form' of the value of A demonstrates the fact that the value is not a property of *things* exchanged, but a *social reality*, the necessary social labour for production.

On the other hand, since commodity A alone, in the simple relationship $xA = yB$, expressed its value and, for this expression, needs B, it would seem that commodity B *naturally* possesses the capacity to express the value of any commodity. Thus, any commodity, once it plays the role of equivalent, seems to possess *in itself* the capacity to measure the value of other commodities. The 'equivalent form' of a commodity does not reveal the essential value (which is a social reality, human labour); it turns the value into a characteristic of things, thus creating the fetishist nature of commodities, transforming them into mysteries.

Hence the enigmatic character of the equivalent form which escapes the notice of the bourgeois political economist, until this form completely developed, confronts him in the shape of money...He has not the least suspicion that the most simple expression of value such as 20 yards of linen = 1 coat, already propounds the riddle of the equivalent form for our solution. (C, I, 57–8). (See also p. 48: 'The whole mystery of the form of value lies hidden in this elementary form. Its analysis, therefore, is our real difficulty.')

In brief, the 'form' of the value of commodities is derived from the very nature of the commodity. This is why, essentially, any commodity has a *twofold* reality; the use value and the value *it needs* in the relationship of *two* commodities (one being use value and the other exchange value) in order to *make its essence apparent.* But the very essence of the value disappears in its mode of appearance. The value, social human labour and therefore abstract, social reality and non material, can only be expressed in a form, the 'equivalent form', which conceals it by making it appear a natural characteristic of things.

Now, this 'form' of value only appeared at a particular period in the historical development of society, when market production made its appearance, and it developed along with it. Whereas initially in primitive societies market exchange was pretty casual and the form of value was merely the simple relationship of one commodity with another, $xA = yB$, taken a stage further as and when the number of commodities increased; the form of value then was able to be developed, the value of A being expressed in a large number of equivalents: $xA = yB$, $xA = zC$, $xA = vD$, etc. This happens with cattle, for example; in some societies they may be exchanged for other commodities, though the latter may not be exchanged for anything else.

At a more advanced stage in market production, it became possible and necessary for any commodities produced to express their reciprocal values by the *same* equivalent. *One* commodity alone became the *general* equivalent for the value of all others. Since then, social labour and the market found a unit of form and expression which was lacking before.

The particular commodity, with whose bodily form the equivalent form is thus socially identified, now becomes the money-commodity, or serves as money. It becomes the special social function of that commodity, and consequently its social monopoly, to play within the world of commodities the part of the universal equivalent. (C, I, 69).

Historically speaking, it has been precious metals which have gradually acquired the monopoly for this position, becoming money. Thus the term for the relative value of commodities in money became the 'price' of these commodities.

With the appearance of money, the 'false appearance', which the equivalent form gives to the 'value' of commodities, finally became consolidated.

What appears to happen is, not that gold becomes money in consequence of all other commodities expressing their values in it, but, on the contrary, that all other commodities universally express their values in gold, because it is money. *The intermediate steps of the process vanish in the result and leave no trace behind.* Commodities find their own value completely represented, without any initiative on their part, in another commodity existing in company with them. These objects, gold and silver, just as they come out of the bowels of the earth, are forthwith the direct incarnation of all human labour. Hence the magic of money. (C, I, 92).

And so, the ideal genesis of money is complete, a genesis which completely explodes its mystery. What did this 'genesis' consist of? Again, a few epistemological observations seem necessary. Marx did not start from a concept, but from a practical fact, the exchange relationship of commodities, i.e., the *social form* by which is expressed the value of *any* commodity. In starting his analysis, he chose the *simplest* form of this relationship, the relationship of two commodities only and he distinguished and defined the different functions these two fulfilled in the relationship. In order to analyse these functions, he used the theoretical results obtained from his previous research, on the one hand, the definition of the nature of value (acquired from the classical theorists) and, on the other hand, his own discovery of the twofold nature of labour. Then he followed the development of the form of value from the simple relationship of two commodities up to the complex relationship of all commodities with each other.

A transformation in the exchange relationship of commodities appeared once the exchange of commodities became generalised and assumed a complex form. The 'equivalent' form assumed the form of money. This transformation corresponded to internal necessities in the development of market production. For the exchange of commodities to become generalised, the equivalent form of the value of commodities had to take on a *general* form, that is to say a *unique* form for the totality of all commodities.

The transformation in the exchange relationship of commodities, corresponding to a stage of generalised exchange of commodities, resulted therefore in the *specialisation of a single category* of commodities as a function of the general equivalent in the value of other commodities. The specialisation of one element in this structure corresponds to the greatest complexity in the structure of market exchange.

At the end of this analysis we find, therefore, that the concepts of money and price are scientifically defined and constructed.

This abstract analysis dealing with changes in 'forms' of value, immediately reveals the *historical* nature of the concepts, the economic categories of money, price, etc. These changes appear to be internal conditions (i.e., both cause and effect) in the development of market production itself within certain societies, beginning with a particular period in history and corresponding to successive stages of its development – from occasional bartering in primitive communities up to the appearance of gold and silver coins in Eastern and European antiquity. The order for the appearance and definition of concepts, in this instance, corresponds to the order in which gradually more complex market relations appeared in the history of certain societies. Thus, Marx's analytical methods demonstrate both the *realities* analysed by thought and the *concepts* constructed by thought to explain them. Marx's method does not allow theory any *speculative alienation*; he does not give us ideal realities without a history, nor does he give us idealities reflecting a reality which itself has no history. We shall return to this point.

The general result of Marx's analysis is to reveal the absurd, ridiculous nature of those spontaneous representations made by people living in market societies. His analysis destroys the false appearances, the pseudo 'evidence' (as well as the elaborate representations made by those 'vulgar' economists who take it upon themselves to 'systematise' spontaneous representations): 'A commodity appears at first sight a very trivial thing, and easily understood. Its analysis shows that it is in reality a very queer thing, abounding in metaphysical subtleties and theological niceties.' (C, 1, 71).

The complexity and mystery do not arise from the use value of commodities nor from the fact that they are products of labour. In any given society, the 'usefulness' of commodities is evident in itself and men, in any society, are interested in the time required for the production of those objects they use.

The complexity and mystery arise only as a result of the mode of appearance of the value of commodities, of the social 'form' they assume as soon as the commodities enter into a relationship of mutual exchange.

The existence of the things *qua* commodities, and the value-relation between the products of labour which stamps them as commodities, have absolutely no connexion with their physical properties and with the material relations arising therefrom. There it is a definite social relation between men, that assumes in their eyes, the *fantastic form of a relation between things.* In order, therefore, to find an analogy we must have recourse to the mist-enveloped regions of the religious world. In that world the productions of the human brain appear as *independent beings endowed with life, and entering into relation both with one another and the human race.* So it is in the world of commodities with the products of men's hands. This I call Fetishism which attaches itself to the products of labour, so soon as they are produced as commodities, and which is therefore inseparable from the production of commodities. (C, I, 72; Godelier's Italics).

In essence, therefore, the fetishism of the market world consists in the form of appearance of value which has the property of concealing the real nature of value while *showing* precisely the opposite. It is not man who deceives himself, it is reality deceiving him, by inevitably appearing in a concealed form and presenting itself upside-down in the spontaneous awareness of people living in the market world. This mode of appearing upside-down thus constitutes the necessary starting point made spontaneously by people when dealing with economic relations. These representations and the ideological developments consolidating them, created as much by the 'vulgar' economists as other categories of ideologues, constitute in people's awareness *a more or less coherent domain of spontaneous phantasms and illusory beliefs referring to the social reality in which they happen to live.* Now we can understand why such illusory representations and notions cannot become the starting point for a scientific analysis of social reality.

The fetishist nature of commodities is not, therefore, the effect of alienation of the consciousness, but the effect in and for the consciousness of the dissimulation of social relations in and behind their appearances. The fetishism of the commodity is not the unique, subjective result of one person's experience, but the general and objective result of collective experience, the product of society. Since its foundation exists outside consciousness, in the objective reality of social relations historically determined, this fetishism can only disappear with the disappearance of these social relations. The scientific discovery:

that the products of labour, so far as they are values, are but material expressions of the human labour spent in their production, marks indeed an epoch in the history of the development of the human race, but, by no means dissipates the mist through which the social character of labour appears to us to be an objective character of the products themselves. The fact, that in the particular form of production with which we are dealing, viz., the production of commodities, the specific social character of private labour carried on independently, consists in the equality of every kind of that labour, by virtue of its being human labour, which character, therefore, assumes in the product the form of value – this fact appears to the producers, notwithstanding the discovery above referred to, to be just as real and final as the fact, that, after the discovery by science of the component gases of air, the atmosphere itself remained unaltered. (C, I, 74).

A scientific knowledge of the structure of market relations does not do away with the spontaneous consciousness people have for these relations (even for scientists). It certainly modifies the role and the effects of this consciousness on their behaviour, but it does not suppress it. In order to abolish it, a social revolution is required linked to the very development of productive forces, a development and revolution which would make possible and necessary the very functioning of the capitalist mode of production, the most historically developed form of market production, the ultimately complete form of this production, since man's labour in it has also become a commodity.

All forms of society, in so far as they reach the stage of commodity-production and money circulation, take part in this perversion. But under the capitalist mode of production and in the case of capital, which forms its dominant category, its determining production relation, this enchanted and perverted world develops still more. (C, III, 806).

What are these developments? Here we shall merely suggest them in a roughly schematic way, as otherwise we would have to analyse minutely and completely the whole of *Capital*.

Capital is primarily money (i.e., the general equivalent for the value of commodities). But all money is not capital. For money to function as capital it must bring in profit. In the simple circulation of commodities, a commodity M_1 is sold for money and this money is used to acquire another commodity M_2. In finalising the process, M_1-A-M_2, money has definitely been *spent* and has functioned as a simple means of circulating commodities M_1 and M_2. In the circulation of money as capital, an amount of money A_1 is '*advanced*' in order to buy a commodity which is subsequently sold. In finalising this process an amount of money A_2 will be found in the hands of the owner of A_1, so that A_2 equals the sum A_1 previously advanced plus something more, a plus value or surplus value: $A_2 = A_1 + \Delta A$. Thus, in this process, the value initially advanced is not only maintained but enhanced, money is transformed into capital. In the simple circulation of commodities, the owner of commodities M_1 sells merely to obtain commodities M_2, because he needs them and does not produce them. The simple circulation of commodities serves only as a means to an end external to it, the appropriation of useful things for the satisfaction of needs. The circulation of money as capital, on the contrary, appears to possess an end in itself by continually changing money into commodities and commodities into money:

Value is here the active factor in a process in which, while constantly assuming the form in turn of money and commodities, it at the same time changes in magnitude, differentiates itself by throwing off surplus-value from itself; the original value, in other words, expands spontaneously. For the movement in the course of which it adds surplus-value, is *its own movement*, its expansion, therefore, is automatic expansion. Because it is value it has acquired the *occult* quality of being able to add value to itself. It brings forth living offspring or, at the least, lays golden eggs. (C, I, 153–4).

Here we find the same vocabulary which was used to describe the fetishist nature of commodities. This characteristic which till then had found its most complex form in money, now completes its development since, as soon as it functions as capital, money seems to possess in itself, not only the property of being the value, but also of enhancing value, of generating itself.

In the relation of capital to profit, i.e., of capital to surplus-value... *the capital appears as a relation to itself* [a]: a relation in which it, as the original sum of value, is distinguished from a new value which is generated. *One is conscious* that capital generates this new value by its movement in the processes of production and circulation. But the way in which this occurs is cloaked in *mystery* and *appears to originate from hidden qualities inherent* [b] in capital itself. (C, III, 48: *a.* Marx's italics; *b.* Godelier's italics).

In order to explain the genesis and functioning of the capitalist mode of production, the basic scientific problem lies in explaining the origin and nature of surplus value.

For money to turn into capital, and therefore to be enhanced, we must be able to buy on the market a commodity which, when used, has the property of creating value. This commodity exists, it is labour power. But for labour power to be shown on the market as a commodity for sale, there have to be very special, unique historical conditions. The producers have to be separated from the means of production and deprived of the money to buy them. They must be simultaneously obliged to sell their labour power to the money owners, and the owners of the means of production, and yet be *free* in themselves (otherwise they would be selling themselves with their labour and would be slaves and not wage-earners). Since the 15th century in different European countries[10] these conditions were gradually appearing in the stage known as the primitive accumulation of capital, which saw both the dissolution of the feudal economic structure and the birth of the component elements of the capitalist system. The basis for this whole evolution was expropriation from the agricultural workers.[11] Money thus only became productive capital[12] from the moment when a new social relationship, a relationship of two social classes, capitalists and workers, was established in the production process of commodities. Capital, as the famous formula has it, is not what it seems, 'a thing, but a *social relation* which is established between people by the intermediary of things'. Once more the social and historical nature of economic categories, here capital, surplus value, wages, is shown and demonstrated by Marx's analysis of them in their 'genesis'.

> Nature does not produce on the one side owners of money or commodities, and on the other men possessing nothing but their own labour-power. This relation has no natural basis, neither is its social basis one that is common to all historical periods. It is clearly the result of a past historical development, the product of many economical revolutions, of the extinction of a whole series of older forms of social production. (C, I, 169).

Since, in essence, capital is the social relation between capitalist and worker, how does surplus value come into this relationship? What the capitalist buys from the worker for a wage is the use of his labour power. Labour power is therefore a commodity, the value of which is measurable, as with any commodity, in the labour time socially necessary for its production, i.e., the production of the material means required for its training and maintenance. When a man works, that is to say when he uses his labour power in the service of the capitalist, he creates not only the equivalent of the value which his wage represents, but something more than the value, which is not paid to him. This unpaid work, this plus value, constitutes the origin and substance of surplus value. The capitalist–worker relationship is therefore immediately revealed as an exploitation relationship of man by man, an exploitation which is concealed by the wage: 'This phenomenal [wage] form, which makes the actual relation invisible, and, indeed, shows the direct opposite of that relation, forms the basis of all the juridical notions of both labourer and capitalist, of all the mystifications of the capitalistic mode of production.' (C, I, 540).

In fact, for both capitalist and worker, in practice everything takes place as if the wage paid for all the labour provided by the worker (including in the wage – bonus, overtime, etc.). Wages, therefore make unpaid labour seem like paid labour and, correlatively, make profit seem inevitably the product of capital. Profit is only a form of surplus value, 'a form in which its origin and the secret of its existence are obscured and extinguished.' (C, III, 47)[13]. Each social class therefore seems to draw its rightful revenue from the production and circulation of goods. The economic categories of wages, profit, interest on capital, revenue, therefore express the visible relations of day to day business and as such have a *pragmatic utility*, but no scientific value. While the circulation of goods *does not create* the value, but *realises* it, and while the surplus value created by this circulation in the production process *is divided* among different types of capitalists (industrialists, financiers, landowners) and takes different forms of profit, contract, interest, ground rent, in appearance everything takes place *as if* capital, labour and land were autonomous sources of value, combined and added to make the value of merchandise. The appearance of economic relations hides and contradicts their essence.

The final pattern of economic relations as seen on the surface, in their real existence and consequently in the conceptions by which the bearers and agents of these relations seek to understand them, is very much different from, and indeed quite the reverse of, their *inner but concealed essential pattern* and the *conception corresponding* to it. (C, III, 205; Godelier's Italics).

It is an *enchanted, perverted,* topsy-turvy world in which Monsieur le Capital and Madame la Terre do their ghost-walking as social characters and at the same time directly as mere things. It is the great merit of classical economy to have destroyed this false appearance and illusion, this mutual independence and ossification of the various social elements of earth, *this personification of things and conversion of production relations into entities,* this *religion* of *every day life*... Nevertheless even the best spokesmen of classical economy remain more or less in the grip of the world of illusion which their criticism had dissolved... On the other hand, it is just as natural for the actual agents of production to feel completely at home in these estranged and irrational forms of capital-interest, land-rent, labour-wages, since these are precisely the forms of illusion in which they move about and find their daily occupation. (C, III, 809–10).

This text on capital ties up our analysis concerning the idea of fetishism *chez* Marx, and completes our demonstration of the necessary link relating the analysis of commodities at the beginning of Marx's work, to the analysis of profit, interest and revenue at its end. Between these two extremes lies the intermediary and fundamental link, the analysis of the 'capital form' of money and the discovery of the real substance of wages and surplus value, i.e., the real substance of capitalist relations of production.[14]

A product of history, characteristic of the mode of appearance of social relations in societies where market production has developed, a collective illusion in the minds of members of these societies, which, having no basis, can only disappear with the disappearance of the social relations which gave birth to this illusion, the fetishism of commodities (and all the social forms which have developed as a result of it – money, capital, interest, wages, etc.) constitutes the breeding-ground for a world of mythical representations, where irrational beliefs in the magic power of things are nourished, where people are induced to resort to magic in order to reconcile themselves with the occult powers responsible for these things. At the end of Marx's analytical dissection, the daily life of people in capitalist societies with their ways and notions about conducting economic affairs, spontaneous or systematised by vulgar economists, this world, so rational in appearance, seeming to testify at every moment to the 'rationality' of capitalist society and its economic system, is shown to be an absurd world of myths and irrational illusions dominated by revered fetishes. In Marx's remarkable expression this ideological and practical world is revealed to be the *religion of everyday life* for people living in bourgeois society. We may well ask whether these myths, these beliefs, these spontaneously magico-religious patterns of behaviour, differ from those found in 'primitive' societies. Do they not fulfil the same functions which deceptively serve to 'explain' and 'justify' kinship relations, incest prohibition, the origin of plants, animals, techniques, the sexual division of labour there? Perhaps after all '*la pensée sauvage*' is merely thought at a spontaneous level, the primitive level, in which the visible movement of social relations is immediately reflected. From this we may understand that scientific thinking is merely the same way of thinking,[15] instructed by history, tamed to a certain degree by man; scientific thinking proceeds to the substance of things by turning away from their appearances in order to come back to them and explain them as arising from the internal link and relationship of things, their inner sequence.[16] By this reverse motion the false appearance of things, the illusion of unscientific spontaneous consciousness in the world, all dissolve. We might compare this approach with Freud's when, underlying the various manifestations of mistakes, slips of the tongue, forgetfulness, dreams, mental illness he discovered the existence of an active and structured reality – the unconscious.

In short, the final fetish to exorcise, the last myth to destroy is the dogmatic illusion that scientific knowledge depends on the brilliance of a few great thinkers, Aristotle, Marx or Freud. We need only remember Marx's tribute to Aristotle in *Capital*. Aristotle concluded his analysis of the value relationship between commodities in the *Ethics*[17] (taking the example 5 beds = 1 house = so much money...): 'Without exchange there could be no association, without equality there could be no exchange, without commensurability there could be no equality. Strictly speaking no doubt things so widely different can never become commensurable.'

The affirmation of their equality to him seemed contrary to the nature of things, to their specific substance. What Aristotle was unable to discover was that things so concretely different as a house and bed could be equal in substance in so far as they could be similar quantities of the same reality, the socially necessary labour for their production, the equal expenditure of equal and abstract human labour. And Marx added:

There was, however, an important fact which prevented Aristotle from seeing that to attribute value to commodities is merely a mode of expressing all labour as equal human labour, and consequently as labour of equal quality. Greek society was founded upon slavery, and had, therefore, for its natural basis, the inequality of men and of their labour powers. The secret of the expression of value...cannot be deciphered...in a society in which the great mass of the produce of labour takes the form of commodities in which consequently the dominant relation between man and man is that of owners of commodities. The brilliancy of Aristotle's genius is shown by this alone, that he discovered, in the expression of the value of commodities, a relation of equality. The peculiar conditions of the society in which he lived alone prevented him from discovering what 'in truth' was at the bottom of this equality. (C, I, 60).

We may now understand why scientific analysis follows 'a course directly opposite to that of their actual historical development' (C, I, 75). The latter starts from simple forms (barter or swopping, for example) and leads to complex ones (capitalist market production). Knowledge and learning, on the other hand, may only start from the complex forms if they are to discover the content and sense of the simple ones. 'The anatomy of man is a key to the anatomy of the ape',[18] the higher explains the lower, on condition that 'the differences are not obliterated'.

Our task therefore is to unearth the real history underlying the great discoveries of brilliant people like Aristotle, Marx or Freud, so that the dogmatic and fetishist nature of these discoveries are left behind and lead us on beyond them, a little further into the invisible and the unapparent.

PART IV

The 'phantasmatic' nature of social relations

Feuerbach starts out from the fact of religious self-alienation, the duplication of the world into a religious, imaginary world and a real one. His work consists in the dissolution of the religious world into its secular basis. He overlooks the fact that after this work is completed the chief thing still remains to be done.

Marx, Four Theses on Feuerbach,
On Religion, op. cit., p. 70.

7
Fetishism, religion and Marx's general theories concerning ideology

THE MARXIST CONCEPT OF THE FETISHISM OF COMMODITIES

The essence of the fetishism of commodities

This concept is not a casual by-product of Marx's thought. In the pages of *Capital* where it crops up it is not a 'theoretical block', Marx succumbing once again to the fascination of old philosophical notions of alienation and reification as evinced in the 1844 Manuscripts. This would deny the rigour of his new method which, paradoxically is to be found in the first section of *Capital*'s first book, the most difficult and most thoroughly worked out.

We must first stress Marx's basic distinction, often ignored by Marxists, between 'value' and 'exchange value' – 'In my opinion, the "value" of a commodity is neither its use-value nor its exchange value.'[1]

The 'exchange value' of a commodity is the value relationship established practically during its exchange for another. This relationship does not *create* the 'value' of the commodity, because the value derives from the process of production and not from the process of exchange or circulation. The value is more or less 'realised' in accordance with the price for which it is exchanged, but the exchange itself does not create this value.

When commodity A is exchanged for a certain quantity of commodity B, A's value is expressed in a certain quantity of B, and B plays the role of an 'equivalent' for A. In the exchange relationship A and B, it *seems* that commodity B is *naturally* qualified to express commodity A's value. Once a commodity plays the role of value equivalent to any other commodity it immediately appears as though it possesses *in itself* the ability to measure the value of other commodities. The 'equivalent form' of a commodity therefore *masks* the value's essence which is that of being a social reality and an expenditure of social, therefore abstract, labour; it makes this value a feature of things, thus creating the enigmatic and fetishist nature of commodities. With the development of market relations, the equivalent form of the value of commodities is determined for a particular category of commodity which then plays the role of general equivalent for the value of other commodities, i.e., the role of money, money itself becoming capital each time it is invested for profit.

We can now see how even the simple relationship between two commodities involves all the mysteries of market production, since it represents the whole mystery of value, money, capital. We can also see how this mystery reaches its completed form with the appearance of the capitalist mode of market production.

It is an enchanted, perverted, topsy-turvy world in which Monsieur le Capital and Madame la Terre do their ghost-walking as social characters and at the same time directly as mere things. It is the great merit of classical economy to have destroyed this false appearance and illusion, this mutual independence and ossification of the various social elements of wealth, this *personification* of things and conversion of production relations into entities (C, III, 809)[2] (Godelier's italics).

Therefore, fetishism in the market world consists basically in the fact that the apparent form of value has the property of concealing the real essence of this value and *shows* the exact *opposite*. Consequently, it is not man who deceives *himself* over reality, it is reality which is deceiving *him*, by inevitably appearing in a form which conceals and presents itself the wrong way up to the spontaneous consciousness of people living in the commercial world. This topsy-turvy appearance thus constitutes the *necessary starting point* for representations made spontaneously by people in their economic relations. These representations and the ideological developments which consolidate them, generated as much by vulgar economists as other species of ideologists, constitute in people's awareness a *more or less coherent domain of spontaneous fantasies and illustory beliefs pertaining to the social reality* in which they live. Now we can understand why these representations and spontaneous notions cannot form the starting point for a scientific analysis of this social reality.

The fetishist nature of commodities is not, therefore, the result of alienating the consciousness, but the effect in and for the consciousness of the dissimulation of reality in social relations from and behind their appearance. As soon as a product of labour circulates as a commodity, its commodity form conceals the origin and content of its value, i.e., the human labour required for its production and, irrespective of social relations, what it was that organised this production (slave, feudal, capitalist, socialist modes of production). In the capitalist mode of production, as labour power becomes itself a commodity, its value assuming the form of wages, not only are the origin and content of the value concealed, but also the origin and content of the surplus value, i.e., the very nature of capitalist relations of production in so far as they represent an exploitation of the workers by capital.

Now we may understand that the fetishism of commodities, having no foundation in the consciousness, only outside it, in the objective reality of social relations historically determined, cannot disappear from the consciousness except with the disappearance of these social relations; and secondly, that the scientific knowledge of the value content and capitalist relations of production does not abolish for the scientist (or, more simply, for the Marxist) the *spontaneous illusory* awareness he has for these realities.

Since the basis for illusory, spontaneous economic representations does not lie in the consciousness, but outside it, in the reality of social relations, we can understand why Marx stressed the fact that 'the mysticism which obscures the products of labour in the present day' did not exist with other modes of production before the appearance of the capitalist mode of production, and will not exist again after the disappearance of this mode of production. ('It is only at a definite historical epoch in a society's development that the product of labour becomes a commodity.' (C, I, 61). To illustrate this point Marx gives three historical and two imaginary examples.

Three historical cases and two imaginary examples of the absence of fetishism in commodities

(*a*) Modes of production based on the 'direct association' of producers, on forms of 'communal labour'. Marx here means two kinds of economic and social organisation: first, primitive societies where the direct association of producers exists in its 'natural primitive form'; and secondly, peasant forms of family production whereby each family produces enough to satisfy their particular needs. What each family produces 'appears as the different products of its labour and *not as commodities* reciprocally exchanged'.

Correlatively:

> The different kinds of labour, such as tillage, cattle-tending, spinning, weaving and making clothes which result in the various products, are in themselves, and such as they are, direct social functions, because functions of the family which just as much as a society based on the production of commodities, possesses a spontaneously developed system of division of labour. The distribution of the work within the family and the regulation of labour time of the several members, depend as well upon differences of age and sex as upon natural conditions varying with the seasons.

And he concludes:

> The labour power of each individual, by its very nature, operates in this case merely as a definite portion of the whole labour-power of the family, and therefore, the measure of the expenditure of individual labour-power by its duration, appears here by its very nature as a social character of their labour (C, I, 78).

This text is important for several reasons. Marx brings primitive peoples and peasants together; or at least from among the forms of peasant production, he links those not oriented to commercial exchange but based on the direct association of producers who maintain kinship relations. Moreover, Marx establishes a kind of kinship, even affiliation, between primitive communities, (ancient peasant communities which arose as a result of different forms of the dissolution of joint property), and the modern European peasant communities where various forms of private ownership exist (derived from Rome, or the Germans, and modified by the feudal and, later, capitalist modes of production). Thanks to this affiliation Marx was to associate social anthropology with rural sociology within the general framework of historical development.

More important still, Marx, far from making the family and kinship relations in primitive or peasant societies an element of the superstructure, as certain Marxists still persist in doing, saw them clearly as relations of production, elements of the infrastructure. Modern anthropology confirms this analysis for many primitive societies.

We should extend this and make an inventory (from primitive and peasant societies) of different associations of producers which go beyond the family framework and kinship relations, being based on age or religion, etc. We shall have to cope with the problem of the different forms of cooperation among producers imposed by the ruling class or the State (forced labour). Marx does this when dealing with his second category concerning the modes of production in old Asia and the ancient world in general.

(*b*) Within these modes of production, 'The conversion of products into commodities...holds a subordinate place, which, however, increases in importance as primitive communities approach nearer and nearer to their dissolution. Trading nations properly so-called, exist in the ancient world only in its interstices, like the gods of Epicurus...or like Jews in the pores of Polish society.' (C, I, 79).

Thus, in these societies, the fetishism of commodities exists, as does market exchange, but it is not the dominant feature of the economic ideology because market production plays but a secondary, limited role. The societies Marx mentions are ancient forms of class societies, from Asia and Europe where class relations developed as former communal relations of production disintegrated. Strictly speaking Marx meant those societies dependent on the Asiatic or slave mode of production. 'Those ancient social organisms of production are, as compared with bourgeois society, extremely simple and transparent.' (C, I, 79).

Summarising, Marx gives two reasons for the simplicity and transparency of primitive modes of production, 'Asiatic' or 'slave': 'They are founded either on the immature development of man individually, who has not yet severed the umbilical cord that unites him with his fellowmen in a primitive tribal community, or upon direct relations of subjection.' (C, I, 79).

Nevertheless, Marx, while declaring that in these old modes of production the phantasmagoria of the fetishism of commodities did not exist, or only to a very limited extent, insists that 'all social life' is hidden behind 'a mystical cloud which conceals the view'. Here we are confronted by a new form of fetish, illusory representations that have made a hoax of reality and we must seek for the basis of this reality.

(*c*) The third example analysed by Marx is the feudal mode of production; thus we have another stage of historical development: The Middle Ages in Europe.

Here instead of the independent man, we find everyone dependent, serfs and lords, vassals and suzerains, laymen and clergy. Personal dependence here characterizes the social relations of production just as much as it does the other spheres of life organized on the basis of that production. But for the very reason that personal dependence forms the ground-work of society, there is no necessity for labour and its products to assume a fantastic form different from their reality. They take the shape in the transactions of society of services in kind and payments in kind. Here the particular and natural form of labour, and not, as in a society based on production of commodities, its general abstract form is the immediate social form of labour. Compulsory labour is just as properly measured by time, as commodity-producing labour...No matter, then, what we may think of the parts played by the different classes of people themselves in this society, the social relations between individuals in the performance of their labour appear at all events as their own mutual personal relations, and are not distinguished under the shape of social relations between the products of labour. (C, 1, 77).

From the point of view of a comparative theory of history, this is a valuable quotation. To the extent that numerous class and caste societies in the ancient Asiatic and European world were based on relations of exploitation, not those of the slave-owning Graeco-Roman type, but on the submission of village or tribal communities to a central power, on labour tribute, on payment in kind, on services, on ground rent or forced labour which local communities gave to the State or 'Despot', these relations assumed the appearance of relationships 'between individuals', characteristic of the feudal mode of production. This is the reason for so many historians believing they had discovered feudal relations in ancient Egypt, Creto-Mycenaean society, among the Mongols, in the African States of the Middle Ages, swelling the number of 'exotic feudal systems', about which Marc Bloch has spoken so ironically.

(*d*) A return to the Asiatic mode of production and State forms of 'oriental despotism'.

In fact, the relationship is not between individuals but between communities and the State personified, incarnated in the person of a chief, a despot. In order to analyse this relationship we must turn back to the text of *Formen* taken from the *Grundrisse der Politischen Ökonomie*, in which Marx stressed that the despotic ruler of the first, oriental class societies *personified the unity* of all local communities; he represented a community superior to the local ones, their general interest being contrary to the particular interests of individuals and also, more importantly, to individual communities: 'Ultimately this higher community (exists and) appears as a *person*...This surplus labour is rendered both as tribute and as common labour for the glory of the unity, in part that of the despot, in part that of the imagined tribal entity of the god.'[3]

Whatever way relations of exploitation *are personified* in class societies of the 'Asiatic type', in the actual person of a sovereign or in the imaginary personage of a god (therefore indirectly as priests or anyone serving this god), the important thing is that these class relations constitute the development of a new process (begun even within primitive societies) heralding the appearance of hereditary chiefs (and aristocracies). Once the *common interests* of all members of a community are incarnated in the person of one of its members (or a section, the family, the clan), this person will represent on a *higher* level, the community of which he is a member. He is therefore both in the *centre* of it and *above* it. Responsible for the common interests, he controls the surplus labour destined to satisify these interests; having more responsibilities than other members in the community, he has more rights and this inequality of status forms a *hierarchy* in the ensemble of community membership, often involving kinship relations which members uphold or relinquish with the chief and his family.

We are now faced with non-commercial social relations within which relations of dependence and exploitation take fantastic forms, obscured behind a mystical cloud. Before analysing the basis for these we should quote two standard cases which Marx has analysed where social labour is unable to assume the fetishist nature of market relations of production.

(*e*) The case of Robinson Crusoe. For reasons of pedagogy and also to caricature Smith and especially Ricardo, Marx analyses the form which the products of Robinson Crusoe's labour would take after his shipwreck on the island. He stresses that:

> Moderate though he [Robinson] be yet some few wants he has to satisfy and must therefore do a little useful work of various sorts...In spite of the variety of his work, he knows that his labour, whatever its form, is but the activity of one and the same Robinson and consequently, that it consists of nothing but different modes of human labour. Necessity itself compels him to apportion his time accurately between his different kinds of work. Whether one kind occupies a greater space in his general activity than another depends on the difficulties, greater or less as the case may be, to be overcome in attaining the useful effect aimed at. (C, I, 76–7).

In this way Marx analyses a borderline case, Robinson Crusoe on his island, and although he is not analysing a social relationship, man's relationship with man, he recalls the following banal truism: that every isolated individual, in order to satisfy his different needs, has to divide his time differently, taking into account his requirements and the means at his disposal. Thus, the unique force of this individual will be divided into different and complementary activities analogous to the unique force of a society where labour resources are divided between different productive sectors and complementary activities.

Marx's conclusions concerning this ideal case are the very same as those he draws from the study of older social organisms, primitive tribes, slaves of the ancient world, oriental despotism, etc.:

> All the relations between Robinson and the objects that form this wealth of his own creation, are here so simple and clear as to be intelligible without exertion even to Mr. Sedley Taylor. And yet those relations contain all that is essential to the determination of value. (C, I, 77).

(*f*) With this ideal example of a single individual, independent but isolated from society, Marx compares another case, ideal for his time, that of the labour of free, yet associated, individuals, i.e., of communist society originating from the abolition of all capitalist and market relations of production and all other forms of precapitalist relations of production:

> Let us now picture to ourselves, by way of change, a community of free individuals, carrying on their work with the means of production in common, in which the labour-power of all the different individuals is consciously applied as the combined labour-power of the community. All the characteristics of Robinson's labour are here repeated, but with this difference, that they are social instead of individual. Everything produced by him was exclusively the result of his own personal labour and therefore simply an object of use for himself. The total product of our community is a social product. One portion serves as fresh means of production and remains social. But another portion is consumed...A distribution of this portion among them is consequently necessary...The social relations of the individual producers, with regard both to their labour and to its products, are in this case, perfectly simple and intelligible and that with regard not only to production but also to distribution. (C, I, 78–9).

The common element in these real or imaginary examples as analysed by Marx is that relations of production are, or should be, simpler in structure and more transparent to the consciousness (both spontaneous and scientific) than market relations of production and above all capitalist market relations of production. And these non-capitalist relations of production above all offer no basis for masking social relations as relationships between things. At the same time Marx speaks of the 'masks' worn by men in feudal society and, more generally, of the 'mystical clouds' which obscure social life in pre-capitalist societies.

We must therefore analyse the problem of the nature and bases inherent in these illusory representations of reality in precapitalist societies. Marx's answer is clear. The basis for these mystical representations is:

They can arise and exist only when the development of the productive power of labour has not risen beyond a low stage, and when, therefore, the social relations within the sphere of material life, between man and man and between man and Nature are correspondingly narrow. This narrowness is reflected in the ancient worship of Nature, and in the other elements of the popular religions [i.e., pre-Christian whether tribal or state religions]. The religious reflex of the real world can in any case only then finally vanish, when the practical relations of every-day life offer to man none but perfectly intelligibile and reasonable relations with regard to his fellowmen and to Nature. The life process of society which is based on the process of material production, does not strip off its mystical vest until it is treated as production by freely associated men, and is consciously regulated by them in accordance with a settled plan. This, however, demands for society a certain material ground-work or set of conditions of existence which in their turn are the spontaneous product of a long and painful process of development. (C, I, 79–80).

FETISHISM, RELIGION AND A GENERAL THEORY OF IDEOLOGY

Marx's insistence on using religious metaphors to characterise ideological forms assumed by social relations in precapitalist societies, or by the mechanism of the fetishism of commodities in capitalist societies, seems to indicate that for him, religious forms of ideology play a dominant role in history. What is Marx's theory for the basis of religion and the ideological forms close to it? 'The *low* stage of development of the productive power of labour . . . the *narrowness* of relations between man and man and between man and Nature, *is ideally reflected* in the old religions.' (C, I, 79; Godelier's Italics.)

Here we have a negative reason, privative in a way, since it consists in the limited degree of primitive man's practical domination over nature, in the absence of a complex division of labour, in ignorance of the profound mechanisms of nature and history. And Engels, twenty-three years later, writing to Conrad Schmidt, gave the same explanation:

These various false conceptions of nature, of man's own being, of spirits, magic forces, etc., have for the most part only a negative economic element as their basis; the low economic development of the prehistoric period is supplemented and also partially conditioned and even caused by the false conceptions of nature. And even though economic necessity was the main driving force of the progressive knowledge of nature and has become ever more so, it would surely be pedantic to try and find economic causes for all this primitive nonsense.[4]

Thus what Marx and Engels provide is a mechanical explanation, a summary economic determinism for the appearance of religious forms of ideology. We must therefore seek for a general explanation and determine exactly what *positive effect* this negative causality has in social life and in the social consciousness of primitive men. This *effect on the consciousness*, consists in the fact that nature *presents itself*, in practice, to primitive man – who in a limited way, effectively influences the order and course of things – as a mysterious reality, superior to man, as a *superior power to man* and society. From this we arrive at the theoretical question: how can primitive man represent in his consciousness this nature which *exists* in practice and *is present in his consciousness as a sphere of mysterious and superior powers*?

Marx's and Engels' reply is clear and, as we shall see closely corresponds to findings in modern anthropology concerning religion: primitive man, in considering nature, thinks by ANALOGY. The primitive mind pictures nature spontaneously as being analogous to the world of man. What are these analogies? They *represent* the invisible forces and realities of nature as 'subjects', i.e., as beings endowed with consciousness, will-power who communicate among themselves and with man. Nature, beyond its visible appearances, is a double for the consciousness, containing in addition, imaginary other worlds inhabited by sublime beings personified by invisible forces, the mysterious and superior powers of nature. The dreams and vague ideals created by human thought present themselves as a coherent and organised world of illusory representations, a world which dominates man's actions and awareness. 'In the mist-enveloped regions of the religious world the productions of the human brain *appear* as *independent* beings endowed with life and *entering into relation* both with one another and the human race.' (C, I, 72; Godelier's Italics.)

Thus for Marx, primitive thinking (*à l'état sauvage*, as Lévi-Strauss would say) has pictured nature by investing the invisible realities which populate it with the *attributes* of man, consciousness, will and even corporeal being. Thus, spontaneously, unconsciously, human thought builds a *double, imaginary ideal of the human world*, of a society peopled with fantastic personages who represent, in an illusory way, the invisible realities of nature, the superior powers who regulate the order and course of things.

All religion, however, is nothing but the phantastic reflection in men's minds of those external forces which control their daily life, a reflection in which the terrestrial forces assume the form of supernatural forces. In the beginning of history it was the forces of Nature which were at first so reflected, and in the course of farther evolution they underwent the most manifold and varied personifications among the various peoples. Comparative mythology has traced back this first process, at least in the case of the Indo-European nations, to its origin in the Indian Vedas.[5]

If these texts of Marx and Engels are analysed closely, we find that, for them, the basis of the fantastic character of religious representations is twofold:

a. primitive thinking spontaneously represents the non-human, material and unintentional reality of nature as a world of people, therefore building illusory representations of the world;

b. primitive thinking spontaneously gives an independent, objective existence to vague ideals, idealities, which have no real existence, except in the thought itself, therefore representing itself in an illusory way, by a false awareness of itself; it alienates itself by its own representations, since it perceives them as outside of itself.

Thus, spontaneously, unconsciously and by the same process, primitive thinking:

– treats the world of things (and objective relations) as a world of people, and

– treats the subjective world of mythical, religious idealities, as an objective reality, independent of man and his thinking.

We see why Marx, in *Capital*, insisted on the 'analogy' of religious forms of ideology with the spontaneous representations of the origin and nature of the value of commodities. If we take as an example of the fetishism of commodities, its most developed, most complete form, i.e., the way in which money used as capital appears to the spontaneous consciousness, we see that: 'The value here is like an automatic substance *endowed with its own life*. . . In short, the value seems to have acquired the occult quality of being able to add value to itself. . . But the way in which this occurs is cloaked in mystery and APPEARS TO ORIGINATE FROM HIDDEN qualities inherent in capital itself.' (C, I, 154; Godelier's italics and capitals). 'It is the great merit of classical economy to have destroyed this false appearance and illusion, this mutual independence and ossification of the various social elements of wealth, THIS PERSONIFICATION OF THINGS AND CONVERSION OF PRODUCTION RELATIONS INTO ENTITIES, this RELIGION of everyday life.' (C, III, 809–10; Godelier's capitals).

By constructing mythical and religious ideals in order to represent the hidden reasons and invisible forces of nature, and by spontaneously investing them with an existence *analogous* to that of man, yet *independent* of him, primitive thinking makes the relationship of things with each other assume the 'fantastic form' of a social relationship analogous to that of men with men. At the same time, invisible forces, by being personified, become the imaginary characters of myth and religion, and Nature is divided into two worlds, 'the sensible and the suprasensible', the sun is both an astral being and a god, etc.

The basic consequences of this analogous and illusory representation of nature are twofold: firstly, religion presents itself (as science was to later) as a means and a way of knowing reality and explaining it, i.e., accounting for the cause and effect which constitute the order of things; secondly, religion, because it represents these causes in a human shape, i.e., as beings endowed with consciousness and with powers *superior*, yet analogous, to those of men, immediately presents itself as a means of action for influencing these ideal characters, analogous to man – characters, therefore, able to hear, to listen and understand appeals and reply to them favourably. For this reason, any religious representation of the world is inseparable from some form of (imaginary) practice, such as prayer, sacrifice, magic, ritual. It is because the world of the invisible is peopled with imaginary realities endowed with awareness, volition and more especially, a superior efficiency to that of man, yet analogous to man's when exercising an influence over people or things, that man can conceive of the notion that he may influence in a practical way the consciousness or volition of these imaginary characters who rule the world. It is the content itself of religious representations in the world which establishes religious practice and this makes religion not only a system of representations but a practice which is considered objectively and truly effectual. As against a certain school of anthropology, which arbitrarily claims a difference in essence between magic and religion, it should be restated that religion exists spontaneously in a theoretical form (representation–explanation of the world) and in a practical form (magic and ritual influence over the real), therefore as a means of explaining (in an illusory way, of course) and transforming (in an imaginary way, of course) the world – influencing the order of the universe.

Therefore, in origin and content, religion is the spontaneous and illusory representation of the world, yet this representation is such that, by its very content, from within, it establishes and demands a corresponding practice and observance.

We should extend this analysis and show that religion is not only an influence on the world, but also an 'influence on oneself'. For example, any ritual or magic practice is accompanied by some kind of restriction or prohibition supported by the one who officiates and/or the public. Any religious influence on the world, on the secret forces which direct the world, involves and initiates man's influence over himself in order to communicate with these forces, reach them, be heard by them and obey them. The magic power is satisfied by imposing restrictions (food, sexual, etc.); the reverse of power is obligation. Taboos, prohibitions, constraints do not mean any restriction of power, rather an accumulation of it.

Starting from this analysis we could put in their place and explain all Marx's and Engels' theories on the history of religions, because religious ideology, like any ideology, the unconscious product of man's relations with nature and himself, evolves with the development of these relations. According to Marx and Engels, the general meaning of evolution would be just that. In primitive society, there is little sign of inequality initially; only the inequality of male and female and between generations. As society gradually becomes hierarchised, as social POWERS begin to form and class, caste and State societies make their appearance; as society progressively becomes 'obscured', LOSES DIRECT CONTROL over itself – a control which it possesses at the level of primitive forms of social organisation – then ideology seizes hold of the social powers and confers on them supernatural attributes, which from time immemorial have been invested in the forces of nature.

But it is not long before, side by side with the forces of Nature, social forces begin to be active; forces which present themselves to man as equally extraneous and at first equally inexplicable, dominating them with the same apparent necessity as the forces of Nature themselves. The phantastic personifications, which at first only reflected the mysterious forces of Nature, at this point acquire social attributes, become representatives of the forces of history.[6]

Afterwards, a new stage in religious thought was reached, resulting in the deification of social relations, personified by those who ruled over society: the deification of kings, priests, etc. And Marx and Engels cite other religious mutations (historically speaking those corresponding to the long transitional period from classless primitive societies to the first forms of class societies): the transformation from polytheism to monotheism in Christianity and Islam for example.[7] But it is not our business to analyse Marx's concept about the history of religions; we are concerned to explain the basic content in the hypotheses of the nature and foundation of ideological consciousness in general.

One of Marx's major points in these theses is his emphasis on the fact that religious ideology is the *dominant* form of primitive people's spontaneous ideology and that this continues in most subsequent stages of historical development, including the capitalist stage.

For example, in the well known *Formen*, Marx wrote that for primitive peoples 'the natural common body' (which he indifferently refers to as the spontaneously evolved tribal community, herd) 'appears not as the consequence but as the precondition of the joint [temporary] appropriation and use of the soil' and that existence in and belonging to a community are 'the first precondition of the appropriation of the objective conditions of life, and of the activity which reproduces and gives material expression to, or objectifies (*vergegenständlichen*) it (activity as herdsmen, hunters, agriculturists, etc.)'. He adds that these preconditions 'are not the *product* of labour but appear as its natural or divine preconditions.'[8] Marx clearly demonstrates that it is not only the higher powers of nature which are reflected illusorily in the spontaneous religious consciousness of primitive peoples, but their social conditions for existence, i.e., necessarily belonging to a community whose conditions of appearance remain unknown (here we have what anthropology calls myths on the origin of societies, tribes, clans, etc.).

With the appearance of classes and primitive forms of State (the oriental 'despot' type), and on the basis of the 'Asiatic' mode of production, practical access, for the individual, to the conditions of production (for example, the land) did not just depend on his belonging to a local or even tribal community, but to a superior community, the State, personified, either in a real way by a sovereign, or in an imaginary way, 'the imaginary tribal being which is God'. Apart from belonging to his community of origin, access to the material conditions of existence 'is mediated through his existence as a member of the state, through the existence of the state – hence through a *precondition* which is regarded as divine, etc.'[9] In these texts dating from 1857, Marx gives us an example of 'illusory' religious representation and not the unknown powers of nature any more, but the unknown conditions for the appearance of various 'spontaneous' primitive societies, the appearance of 'sacralisation' and 'divinisation' of these new social powers, once social relations of domination and dependence in class and State relations appeared.[10]

Briefly, Marx and Engels are saying that for primitive mankind, nature and society *spontaneously* assume 'fantastic, mystical' forms, in a word SACRED forms. The fundamental role of religious ideology in the development of forms of political awareness and strife is thus theoretically clear. This is why Marx and Engels dwelt so much on the political role of religious heresies and on the religious forms of political strife. In precapitalist societies 'in order to speak about the existing social conditions it was necessary to omit the sacred element'.[11]

We should add 'to replace it with another', i.e., with another sacred content, that of a subversive religion, 'heresy'.

This is why, for Marx: 'The difference between the present upheaval and all earlier ones lies in the very fact that man has found out the secret of this historical upheaval and hence, instead of once again exalting this practical, "external", process to the rapturous form of a new religion, divests himself of all religion.'[12]

Before concluding, let us go over the basic points of our analysis so that we may extend it further. If we define ideology as the sphere of illusory representations of the real, and we consider religion to have been in the course of mankind's development, the dominant form of ideology within classless societies and first forms of class societies, then our findings permit us to make a step toward a general theory of ideology and more immediately to grasp Lévi-Strauss's meaning in *La Pensée sauvage* and *Mythologiques*.

We should start from the fact that, on the basis of the low development of productive forces characterising primitive societies, man's control of nature is very limited and the structures of social life are relatively simple. Under these conditions, nature can only *appear* in the consciousness as a domain of powers superior to man who must simultaneously represent, explain and attempt to control them. The foundation for this appearance of nature in the consciousness is thus outside the consciousness. It is objective, not subjective. It is based on and expresses a particular type of man's social relations with man and nature.

How can thought spontaneously represent these invisible realities which are also superior to man? By ANALOGY. Analogy is the general principle organising the representation of the world in and through primitive thinking. This means that thought represents the non-human world (nature) and the hidden causes of the human world (history) analogously with man's relations to them. The hidden causes, the invisible forces which regulate the world are represented as superhuman characters, i.e., beings endowed with consciousness and will, power and authority, therefore *analogous* to man, yet *different*, in that *they do what man cannot do*; they are superior to man. These characters form an ideal society, maintaining relations among themselves and with human society. The invisible world is considered as a completely analogous society to that of human society; or at least analogous within the *network of intentional social relations existing between men*, thus analogous with a human society *reduced* to the network of relations which pass through the consciousness of its *subjects*.

From this point of view we can understand two facts as analysed in modern anthropology.

a. Because primitive thinking is done by analogy, the whole logic of myths, as Lévi-Strauss has shown, is a logic of metaphor and metonymy, i.e., it is based on two major forms of analogy.

Moreover, because the causes which are invented to explain the order of the world are represented by superhuman 'characters', mythology unfolds like a great recital, as in a theatre where all kinds of literary genres are employed such as plays, epics, comedies, poetry . . . Because it is constructed by analogy, the mythico-religious world represents the world in the theatrical sense of 'putting on a performance', and this corresponds to Marx's concept in *Darstellung*. Marx used this concept to indicate the spontaneous illusory representations of economic and social relations as they are perceived by the economic agents who support these social relations.

b. Because primitive thinking is by analogy, religion and magic are logically and practically inseparable; they constitute the fundamental and complementary forms for an explanation (illusory) and the transformation (imaginary) of the world.

But the relationship 'primitive society – mythical thinking' is even closer. Here we should mention as being of extreme theoretical importance, the *Mythologiques* of Lévi-Strauss. He shows that kinship relations form the backbone of the mythical world, the *sociological scheme* of organisation. All myths, in which the origin of fire, water, food, cooking, man, animals, stars, death, etc., are 'explained' are myths describing the adventures of superhuman characters also related to one another, such as parents and children, brother and sister, wife givers and takers, husband and wife, elder and younger sons; and they all undergo the conflicts of these kinship relations.

In most primitive societies, kinship relations *objectively* constitute the *dominant* structure of social relations, the basic scheme for the organisation of society. There is therefore a close correspondence relationship between the objectively dominant role of kinship relations in social life and their role as the sociological backbone in the ideal world of myths.

The role, as the sociological scheme of mythical worlds, cannot be *deduced from nature nor from formal principles of thought.* It can only be drawn from the very content of social relations in primitive societies. Therefore it has its foundation in the society at a particular stage of its historical development.

In short, and this could perhaps form the premiss for a Marxist theory of mythico-religious consciousness, two components may be isolated from this consciousness, two possible conditions for its genesis and content.

(1) An *effect* IN *the consciousness* of a particular type of social relations and a certain type of relations with nature which have as a basis a low level of development in productive forces.

What does the effect in the consciousness from this negative cause consist of? Primarily because to man the sphere of natural and societal forces uncontrolled by him, seems to him like a sphere of *superior powers.* This is an objective fact and the basis for this representation exists therefore outside consciousness in objective reality.

But this effect in the consciousness does not itself create the phantasm, the illusory representation. An additional condition is required to transform the representation of forces and invisible causes into a phantasm, the intervention of another mechanism based in man himself.

(2) We shall call this other mechanism an '*Effect* OF *the consciousness* ON *itself*'.

By this, we mean that man spontaneously represents the world – the causality of invisible levels of nature and society, by analogy with his own experience – to a conscious being, endowed with a will who acts on himself and others intentionally.

Human thought spontaneously, that is to say both consciously and unconsciously, gives sense and form to the effects in the consciousness of man's relations with man and nature; it refers to categories of conscious human experience and in particular, it uses those kinship relations which happen to play the dominant role in social life; these relations serve as an example of the organising sociological scheme for the imaginary world of myths (EFFECT IN the consciousness of the social structure).

At the intersection of the network of effects *in* the consciousness of man's relations with man and nature, and the effects *of* the consciousness on its content, the mythico-religious consciousness of the world (ideological representation) is constructed by analogy, consciously or unconsciously, with the visible and intentional relations of men in society. This unconscious basis explains why primitive people themselves cannot provide any information on the *real* process for the genesis of myths. This can only be discovered and reconstituted by scientific analysis.

At this point we are faced with the fundamental question involving the differences and relations between mythical, philosophical and scientific thinking. We shall deal with the analysis later, but we can already outline the problematique suggested by our analysis.

Basically, these three forms of thinking answer the same need, the same purpose; this is to explain the world, to discover the causes and connections relating to phenomena. Causality, in the sphere of mythical thinking, is represented by the action of imaginary characters; these are enlarged images of man himself and they act within a society which is reduced to the intentional and reciprocal relationships between individuals and organised along lines which reproduce the real schemes of social life. Now, in the case of philosophical and particularly scientific thinking – because philosophy while being a substitute for, is but a continuation of mythical thinking – it seems that gradually mankind erased the 'intentional' representations in order to find anonymous and unintentional causalities.

Advances in philosophy and science have been made by *gradually obliterating this network of intentions which man spontaneously had attributed* to the image of his own world; progress has scratched at the surface of things, destroying bit by bit, fragment after fragment those imaginary representations which invest things with the coherence or incoherence of a system of intentions, in order to replace them by the representation of unintentional relations between men and things. The difference between causality, as mythical thinking images it, and causality as a philosophic category or a scientific concept, is that thanks to these idealities of a new kind, the unintentional relations existing in nature and society have been better grasped and represented.

And this is why Aristotle excluded from philosophy the old mythical forms of world representation, saying in his *Metaphysica* (B. 4): 'Why should we examine seriously the spurious wisdom of myths?'

Hegel, two thousand years later, also excluded it when he stated: 'the myth, in general, is not an adequate means for expressing thought' (*Lessons in the history of philosophy*).

Though it lies outside the scope of this article, we, in fact, should show what it is, in speculative philosophy, that constitutes illusory representations of the real, of a different kind than those encountered in mythical thinking, but equally dependent on an ideological consciousness of reality.

If such is the unconscious and inevitable foundation for religious forms of ideology, we can understand why Marx criticised 18th century materialist theories which saw in religion merely the work of imposters, the result of plotting priests.[13] We can also understand why religion linked from within, and by, unconscious mechanisms, to determined social relations, cannot be suppressed by any decree issued in the name of scientific or political awareness. Similarly, if the fetishism of commodities is to disappear, all forms of market production must also disappear, just as 'This religious reflex of the real world can only finally vanish when the practical relations of everyday life offer to man none but perfectly intelligible and reasonable relations with regard to his fellowmen and to Nature.' (C, I, 79). This doesn't mean that the unconscious, the unknown or obtuse will not go on living in social life or in the life of each individual, but in practice it means that man will not be amenable to social powers which alienate him, nor will he any longer see in the unknown elements of nature a mystery or a threat.

8

The non-correspondence between form and content in social relations†

NEW THOUGHTS ABOUT THE INCAS

It was on the non-slave-based forms of dependence that the majority of primal class societies developed together with the states characterising ancient and recent history in pre-Columbian America, pre-colonial Africa, etc. The Inca Empire grew up in less than two centuries and this lightning growth was exceeded only by the Aztecs who, when entering the valley of Mexico in the 12th century, were hunter and warrior tribes with no knowledge of farming or weaving. Before their conquest by the Incas and their integration into the Tahuantinsuyu, the Empire of the Four Quarters, the mode of production for many Andean tribes was based principally on the production of tubers within the Ayllu, a local village community inhabited by a kinship group of the lineage type. Land ownership was communal and land was redistributed periodically between extended families, who were not allowed to convert their right of usufruct into a right of transfer; so, there was no form of private property as distinct from communal ownership. There was also a form of communal labour, based on mutual help among the villagers (the *minga*) in the performance of various productive tasks. The village chief (the *curaca*) was the first beneficiary of this village mutual aid, and communal lands were especially cultivated for maintaining the tombs of local divinities as well as the local chiefs.

When they fell under the Inca domination, these communities, or at least the social groups organized into communities of this type, underwent a profound change. All land, rivers, mountains, herds of lamas, game were declared state property. A section of these lands was definitively expropriated and became state or Church property. The remainder was returned to them through the 'kindness' of the Incas, on condition they worked the lands now appropriated by State or Church in the form of forced labour. Relations of production were therefore thrown into confusion; on those lands retained for subsistence, the communities lost their former right of communal ownership, controlling rights of possession and use only. On these lands, production and customary forms of soil and usage still assumed the same communal form as before the Inca conquest, nevertheless a new mode of production was established on a régime of forced labour.

Forced labour was not an individual matter; the whole village participated in it and the Inca state provided the food and drink, in the same way as, in the traditional Ayllu, the beneficiary of communal mutual aid had provided for those who helped him. The State provided the tools and seed and insisted that the people go to work in holiday clothes, with music and song. In this way the former forms of economic reciprocity together with the ideology and ritual linked with them, were now used for the functioning of economic relations of exploitation and servitude, characteristic of a new form of production of the type known as the 'Asiatic mode of production'. In order to organise its own economic basis on a stable level and to ensure growth, the Inca State checked all lands, peoples, animals and produce. For this, it needed to create an administrative organisation which would cover the population and control it directly or indirectly; it also needed to popularise the cult of the Inca, son of the Sun, and the cult of the Sun father, and to maintain an army to suppress revolts, etc. This body of institutions corresponded to the new mode of production; and it is known that this very mode of production was by 1532 fully developed, the State having been forced to transfer entire populations in order to set up military colonies and thus control local populations who were too unruly. They had therefore totally or partially broken with the traditional ties linking these tribes with the soil. In other respects, a new development occurred, a traditional form of personal dependence called *yanacona*, by which individuals taken away from their community of origin, the Yana, were attached to the person of an aristocratic master and remained in the service of his lineage for life. The descendants of these Yana generally inherited this position. This form of exploitation certainly existed before the Inca conquest, but assumed greater social significance with the development of a kind of individual ownership (not, however, private) of lands and herds given by the Inca State to certain strata of the nobility.

We will go further with our analysis of the Inca social and economic formation, because, apart from the fact that it offers us a remarkable example of non-western class society, it leads us to some theoretical observations which may open up new paths in the field of anthropology. The surprising thing about the economic basis of the Inca social formation is that, while the dominant mode of production actively maintained part of the former communal relations and was supported and moulded by them, it also used them for its own mode of production and reproduction, while destroying and suppressing another part of these traditional relations. For example, in the words of the chronicler, Gobo: 'Only on the day of their marriage do men become liable to tax and take part in public work.' This meant as John Murra shows in his remarkable thesis, *The Economic organization of the Inca State*, that the passage rite of marriage within a local community became a means of access to a new status and, as a symbol of this status, into a subject liable to take part in the forced labour required by the Inca State, therefore a member of a community very much larger and basically different from the Ayllu or local tribe.

By compelling the peasants to come in their holiday clothes to work on the lands of the State and the Sun, by providing them with food and drink, the Incas were employing the former mode of production based on reciprocal obligations between members of local communities, where both the form and the obligation were known and understood by all; in this way they shaped new relations of production, founded on oppression and domination, since the producers had now lost part control of their labour and its product. Moreover, the Incas, while retaining the cult of local gods, added the cult of the Sun god and his son, the Great Inca, in honour of whom the peasant would offer his labour, as was already demanded by his own traditional and local divinities. The old kinship relations and the former village and tribal political relations *without a change in either form or structure, had now changed their function*, since they were required for furthering a new mode of production.

It is this mechanism which John Murra has shown and dissects when he writes: 'When the Crown elaborated a system of forced labour, the communities' reciprocal obligations, known and understood by all, served as their model.' The practical problem confronting the Incas after their conquest, was twofold: to allow the subjugated people to continue to produce their means of subsistence in accordance with traditional practice; and to oblige them to produce for the State in forms of production which they would understand and which, up to a certain extent, would be justified in their eyes. In order to resolve this problem, exceptional efforts of political and social invention were required, both collectively and individual – as tradition has credited the almost legendary emperors, Pachacuti, Manco Capal and, particularly, Vilracocha – but, at the same time, it should be said, that the means for solving these problems partially existed already within the previous mode of production.

Among these means, there were: Firstly, the fact that production was based on different forms of simple cooperation; secondly the fact that the land was owned by the community as a whole and that the individual possessed only rights of usufruct to the plots, which were redistributed more or less periodically; thirdly, the fact that – equally in the sphere of the material process of production as in the individual's relation to the basic means of production – the land, the community *existed and appeared* as a reality *superior* to the individual and as the practical condition for his survival; fourthly, the fact that the function of representing the community, of controlling the process of its reproduction as such, (i.e., as a unit superior to the individual in so far as it was the unit of common interest), was the responsibility of a particular family and, in this family, of the individual who could best fulfil this function. This person was the *curaca*, the 'chief' of the local or tribal community, being also chief of war. By this function, the *curaca*, and his family, personified the community more than any other person; he in some way incarnated the society in so far as he was a reality superior to others and he personified his superior unit. The function of representing and defending the common interest of all members of the community put the member who played this role out of the common run of men. A kind of internal aristocracy existed, in the proper sense of the word: *aristos* in Greek meaning the 'best', i.e., one who best represents the community; fifthly, in organising the process of production, their labour force, taken from members of the local community, the Ayllu, was utilised to reproduce their own existence and those members of the community in need, widows, the old, infirm, etc.; it was also utilised in the form of supplementary work destined to reproduce the community *as such*. This supplementary work was spent in cultivating the *curaca's* lands. The *curaca* had the right, as all members of the community, to lands in sufficient quantity to support his family and to work on them with mutual help from the community. But additional lands were allotted to him and he was provided with supplementary labour to cover the 'costs' of his duties as representative of, and person responsible for, the community such as it was. Depending on the situation and in accordance with the scope of his functions (village chief or tribal chief), the chief either still participated directly in the process of production or, having ceased to be a direct producer, took part in the process of production merely by controlling the use of land, guiding the process of production and organising the ritual and ceremonial activities at each phase of the agricultural process.

Alongside the supplementary labour on behalf of the community's representative, we should also mention the labour involved in waging wars, i.e., defending or conquering lands and the irrigation canals; in short, protecting or enlarging the population's production resources. In order to cope with population increases, and thus allow the community to reproduce itself on the same basis, extra labour was expended in the form of local irrigation works, enlarging already cultivated lands with terracing, destined to increase the community's production resources. Finally, supplementary land and labour were devoted to the cult of ancestors and local divinities (gods of the land, rain, etc.), and to the upkeep of tombs and altars. Some lands were reserved for maize production for the beer drunk at ceremonial libations. Llamas were bred for ritual sacrifice, woven materials were produced for burning, etc. Dedicating resources (land, animals, maize, woven stuffs) and labour (farming, artisan, etc.), for the cult of ancestors and gods answered a twofold necessity: on the one hand to show recognition for the dead, invisible but still surviving, and to the gods, thanks to whom the community existed and was still alive, thus honouring and glorifying their ancestors and the supernatural powers and thereby fulfilling the community's obligations towards them. On the other hand, in so far as ancestors and supernatural beings seemed to be powers capable of controlling soil fertility, rain, death, illness, victory in war, hence permitting or impeding the reproduction of the community and controlling all situations outside man's direct responsibility, it was necessary to try and stop, or divert the actions of, evil powers by arousing, attracting or multiplying the actions of benevolent powers. They therefore had to develop a method of indirectly controlling these powers which were themselves directly controlling the natural and supernatural conditions of the reproduction of the community; this method would require these powers to intervene, or abstain from intervening, in the life of the community and its process of reproduction. To this end, they sacrificed, they offered material wealth and labour to the invisible powers, within the framework of symbolic practices aimed at influencing (in a make-believe way) the conditions of reproduction in social life.

These five elements belonging to the old mode of production did not disappear after the Inca conquest. The former mode of production continued to ensure both the subsistence of local communities and these *five elements provided the operational bases and shape of the new mode of production.* The victorious community appropriated all lands and natural resources from the conquered communities. All that the victors needed to do was to apply traditional tribal law: so long as the individual is a member of the community, he is entitled to his rights, if he does not belong he is deprived of all rights. The superior community, personified in the Inca chief, who represented both it and the State, hence became the collective landlord, and all conquered territory became 'crown' property. This meant that the collective form of land appropriation was, as it had been before, the social form of relations of production attached to the land; it meant that the State took the place of the local community as landlord and thus constituted, for the individual, a new community superior to his traditional one and upon which he depended for survival. Therefore, for the individual, both before and after the conquest, his conditions for existence were assured by belonging to a community superior to his own.

The State, now the pre-eminent owner of all lands in the kingdom, directly appropriated some of these lands by transforming them into crown or church lands, leaving 'out of kindness', the use (not the ownership) of the remaining territory to the communities, thus graciously permitting them the means of subsistence in return for working those lands which had become State and

Church property. Henceforth, the State, the new superior community, by replacing the traditional community as collective landowner and by taking on the former function which guaranteed families and individuals their means of existence, automatically assumed the right to demand supplementary labour from the conquered community, since such labour had been expended traditionally to permit the reproduction of the community as it was. The superior community therefore merely added an additional surplus labour which assumed the same forms as the traditional one. The State provided the peasants who worked on the expropriated territory with food, drink and seed, thus identifying with the traditional local powers and giving forced labour the shape of traditional relations of village and tribal reciprocity. The victorious community – direct owner of part of the material resources in numerous local communities and simultaneously owner of a vast amount of the producers' surplus labour – was, in fact, founded on a new type of economic base, which, in appearance had the form – if enlarged to gigantic proportions – of the former mode of production.

At the same time, the functioning of these new relations of production necessitated the development of institutions and a new social stratum, a State bureaucracy responsible for controlling and supervising the reproduction of the new mode of production. For example, in each province, a governor was appointed whose title signified 'one who sees all', and he saw to it that the State and Church lands were worked and that the forced labour tasks were carried out without any delays. The new mode of production therefore gave to politico-religious functions a new dominant role in production organisation and in the reproduction mechanism of the new mode of production. Whereas, before, the old mode of village production had determined the dominant role of kinship relations within the traditional community, the new mode of production both destroyed the dominant role of kinship relations in the new social organisation, leaving it with a secondary role, that of continuing to organise the subsistence of local communities, and also transferred the dominant role to the new politico-religious relations, which completely overwhelmed the former village and tribal framework.

We can now grasp the ideological consequences which arose as a result of the fact that the former relations of production (village mutual aid, surplus labour, etc.), gave their form to the new relations of production (forced labour). The fundamental consequence was that the new relations could only come about in a form, an appearance, which masked the economic agents, in spontaneous ideological representations, making the new, real content, the exploitation of man by man, in these new relations of production disappear. Owing to the fact that the former relations of production both continued to survive and gave form to the new relations of production, the old ideological forms could both serve as material and as a scheme of representation for the new social relations and could only do so in accordance with their proper content which represented the obligations of community members *vis-à-vis* their community of origin, obligations *vis-à-vis* a superior reality, hence benevolent yet compelling. The old ideology was therefore able to *represent* the new relations, but could only do so by making them *appear as something else*, something analogous to the former mode of production and which simply extended it. Two effects came about as a result of this, inevitably characterising the whole ideology of domination: the *concealment*, the disappearance on the representation level of the oppressive nature of the new mode of production, and the *justification* for this oppression in the eyes of both dominant and dominated classes. It provided all social groupings with *good reasons* for continuing to direct or be directed; in short, it constituted an adequate ideological form for the functioning of the new mode of production and its economic, political and religious proceedings. Thus, it constituted an ideology which corresponded to the conditions of reproduction in the new economic and social formation. Let us point out, and this influences ideological theory, that it was because it *was not a direct* reflection, an immediate transposition of new relations of production, that the former ideology answered the reproduction needs of these relations *best*. It was because the former ideology represented the new relations in a form which did not allow their real content to be seen, that it corresponded best to their content. We can already imagine the difficulties which partisans of a theory which regards ideology as the direct and simple reflection of the economic infrastructure of a society, will encounter. Other theoretical observations of general significance may be made from this brief outline of the Inca mode of production. They concern the role of war and violence in the formation of this mode of production and the role of large labour operations. We have already tackled the problem of war remembering that the very form of tribal collective ownership usually implies that any individual or group foreign to the tribal community is deprived of any ownership rights. In wars this right is only exercised by violence (whether this be really so or whether there is submission without fighting) and the defeated enemy is deprived of any right to his own soil. However, war in itself is not enough to create a new mode of production. Over a certain period it may support a victorious tribe's domination and allow the wealth of vanquished tribes to be pillaged while the traditional mode of production remains the same, but it is not enough to create a mode of exploitation which continually reproduces itself, and therefore one which could subsist in times of peace and develop. War is an important element in numerous modes of production (except in the case of hunter–gatherers where its importance seems much less). With war, territory and production resources are protected or else new ones are added. Violence, initially necessary for expropriating from foreign communities, cannot subsequently furnish the means whereby the vanquished are regularly forced to produce supplementary labour for the conquerors. This does not mean that threats of violence were not permanent means for forcing populations to work for their victors. The Incas, in fact, repressed revolts in merciless fashion, deported whole populations, transferred loyal peoples to military colonies where a close eye was kept on disobedient tribes. But, so that the mode of production would reproduce itself in all ways and of its own accord it was found necessary to institute a well-conducted forced labour campaign, a bureaucracy, an auditing scheme, some means for keeping goods in stock and for transporting products, etc., in short new relations of production within which violence and armed control played a very important role, but did not get to the root of all problems.

In fact, as we have seen, for the system to function regularly, it was necessary that the surplus labour provided by the peasants did not seem like forced labour but like a 'duty', an 'obligation' accepted and carried out, a prestation calling for reciprocal action. Here the role of ideology was like a *constraint exercised without physical violence* on the mind and will of the Inca subjects. War, certainly, was a process which created *some of the conditions* for forming this new mode of production by detaching some of the elements, the production factors, from their general arrangements in the former structure and by liberating these elements in some way (land and labour became available production resources, partially detached from their former social relations). However, a new mode of production will only come about when the elements are combined in a new way. We should compare this process with that of the genesis of the capitalist mode of production, that which classical economists call the process of primitive accumulation of capital whereby peasants and artisans become dispossessed of the production and subsistence resources and, simultaneously, detached from their subjection to feudal relations of production, hence free yet compelled to sell their labour. Now, what war and the Inca conquest could not do, was to deprive communities directly of the means for ensuring their own subsistence; they could not completely separate individuals and groups from the *possession* of necessary subsistence resources. John Murra[1] emphasises that they could not seriously affect the Ayllu autonomy. The State was careful to exact only forced labour from the peasants and not to interfere with their autonomy. Briefly, therefore, the very possibility for the appearance of a mode of production of the Inca type, was the result of a certain level of productive forces, i.e., it was based on the technical possibility of direct producers being able to produce a regular surplus, and John Murra concludes that the existence and survival of a socio-political structure, such as the Inca State, technologically depends on an agriculture capable of regularly producing a surplus over and above the needs of the peasants' subsistence. Therefore, it was the development of productive forces in agriculture, which in the final instance, created the possibility for the appearance of a class society and a pluri-tribal, pluri-ethnic State. However, we should remember that the Andean agriculture was based on the production of potatoes and other tubers, maize, etc., in other words, it was extremely diversified. This allows us to answer a second question which also has immense significance in the theoretical knowledge of history. What was the role of vast labour projects in the birth and development of the State and the new mode of production? We have the answer already.

Great labour projects follow the appearance of the State: they are not the condition for its appearance. This again refutes the mechanist theory of Karl Wittfogel who considers that the necessity for organising vast labour projects (preferably hydraulic ones) actually created the condition for the appearance of the State (the oriental despotic type). In fact, it was the existence of an Andean agriculture capable of producing regularly a surplus which was the preliminary condition for forming a class and State society. What the conquest offered by expropriating local communities and instituting forced labour was the possibility of *concentrating* a vast quantity of production and subsistence resources and therefore having the material resources to organise, provided that they knew how to combine them, into gigantic forms of simple cooperation, and to tackle tasks outside the scope of any tribe and, *a fortiori*, any local community. But we should also stress that the very reproduction, the development, of the Inca mode of production, not only permitted but demanded the development of huge labour projects (which does not mean that the State both appeared and developed in order to carry them out), because if the mode of production was 'to develop' it needed roads, an army, a bureaucracy, clergy, etc. All these required the continual enlargement of agricultural and artisan surplus. The State thus favoured maize production; it was a plant easily stored and transported and a source of food and drink of high energy and ceremonial value, all qualities which tubers, the former traditional peasant staple food, did not possess. The State did its best to generalise maize culture and introduced it to numerous regions where it had not previously existed. At the same time they enforced the construction of sloped terracing, generally left fallow by the Andean communities because their traditional tubers grew better on the Andean plateau than on the slopes. Thanks to these terraces, now land was cultivated and the economic use of space enlarged. It was not therefore the need to carry out great works of collective interest which gave birth to class society and the Inca State, but it was the necessity to *enlarge* the conditions of reproduction in this class society which subsequently compelled great labour schemes. This naturally led to a greater complexity of the social stratification; it separated the distance between peasant and ruling class even further. And it is this increasing distance, which is glorified in the palaces, the temples, the gardens and tombs which exalt the superior essence of the ruling class, its ancestors and gods. In conclusion, a most important point in the analysis of the Inca economic and social formation and its internal hierarchy, the addition of a new and dominant mode of production to a former and dominated one, is that while the new relations of production *seem in embryo* to be contained in the old village and tribal relations (a simple development of them or the product of a continued evolution), in fact, the new mode of production when it appeared merely *suppressed* part of the former function of the old relations of production, by annihilating the dominant role which kinship relations had played. These did not altogether disappear, they continued but changed in content without changing in form. We see the danger in perceiving the passage of one mode of production to another in terms of embryonic evolution – like the development of a seed. This concept hides the non-lineal nature of evolution: *finding new starting points* plays a decisive role in this evolution. At the same time, we can immediately see the error in interpreting the Inca mode of production as a feudal-type society simply because a monarch, supported by an aristocracy, ruled and because the peasant masses were subjected to forced labour. The State structure in the Inca mode of production, in fact, expressed the *concentration of land ownership* on the level of the whole society in the form of a unique, collective, direct or pre-eminent ownership by a superior community, the dominant ethni-class. The structure of a feudal state, on the contrary, expresses the *hierarchistic association of multiple landlords.* In both cases, the nature of the State is different as are the terms and conditions of power in the State as well as the domination of the ruling class; they are based on different ways of extracting direct producers' surplus labour. Going further, we should analyse (by contrasting the example of the Inca mode of production) the modes of production which served as the basis for African States and pre-colonial class societies, such as the Mossi kingdoms of the Upper Volta, the Bamoun kingdom of the Cameroun, etc., and of course, the state-type societies of Asia.

9

The visible and the invisible among the Baruya of New Guinea†

I want to examine briefly some aspects of magic as practised by the Baruya, inhabitants of New Guinea. I shall offer a summary analysis of a complex domain, suggesting its contours and content, adding a few points for reflection such as the question of the relationship between a mythical and scientific consciousness of the world.[1]

FACTORS INVOLVED IN THE PRACTICE OF MAGIC

It needed more than a year's stay before the Baruya allowed me to visit their gardens while they performed magic rites for ensuring a plentiful harvest. They later disclosed the ritual formulae they had intoned in the fields, but on this occasion, too, they took extreme precautions, placing look-outs near the spots where these confidences were made. These men were responsible for warning us of passers-by who might overhear these secrets.

Comparing the information I managed to get, it appears that these magic practices follow the same plan and combine several similar elements.

These elements include, firstly, a ritual language; secondly, the use of ritual objects: plants, stones and magical pigments; thirdly, a series of gestures accompanying the planting of magical flowers, and the placing of stones covered with pigment. Spatial movements have a particular orientation. In order that a stream, flowing toward one end of the valley, does not carry away ritual words to other tribes or places inhabited by evil spirits and dead souls, the man shifts his position while pronouncing the magical formulae; he turns his back to the river and climbs up the slope of the garden usually situated on the mountainside. Fourthly, there is a series of rules of conduct relating to other people and himself.

Here I shall analyse two elements in these magical practices: the ritual language and the rules of conduct.

RITUAL LANGUAGE AND RULES OF CONDUCT

The ritual language consists of magical formulae composed from expressions of command or wish[2] with the invocation of the secret name of the being invoked. We shall give two examples.

The first formula is aimed at chasing away rats which lay waste the sweet-potato gardens. It might translate as follows:

'*Pranimayé* [the secret name for a species of rat], go far away, go and eat the *akila* and *wareuka* leaves [two trees in the forest which grow in the low, warm parts of the valley].'

The magician pronounces the formula while planting, inside the garden and near the enclosure, a stick cut from a tree called *bidanié*, which will bar the rats' way should they attempt to return and devastate the garden.

A second formula is used to protect sweet-potato gardens against the invasion of a species of spider commonly called *koulalinna*. According to the Baruya, sweet potatoes do not grow if these spiders spin their webs between the leaves and along the tuber stalks. They think that in most cases these spiders have cast an evil spell. Translated, it goes:

'*Ourourandavaiwé*' (the secret name of this species of spider, the profane name being *koulalinna*). This is followed by a series of names of trees from the primary forest, then:

'On the tree tops your food is placed, once upon a time the sun gave us sweet potatoes, to you he gave food in the bush on the tops of the *pangouté*, *pippéla*, *gananié* trees, etc. Why do you come to eat what is reserved for us? Go!'.

The essential element in these formulae is obviously the invocation of the secret name of the being addressed. In this way they can be sure of being heard, of having a hold over him, and the knowledge of these secret names constitutes the most important element in magical practices and ritual knowledge, which are passed on from generation to generation. Hence, the use of these secret names and the incantations imply that the being addressed is a twofold reality – both a visible, material reality (sweet-potato, taro, spider... – and an invisible reality, able to understand the appeals addressed to him and compelled in some way to reply, because the being has been addressed in terms that it 'understands', its real essence is referred to. Thus, to know the secret names of things is to have access to their invisible essence and to have a hold over them.

However, to be heard and to have the right to pronounce these words and formulae, the individual must have obeyed certain rules of conduct, which relate to himself and others. These rules consist of a series of prohibitions. Women, including the wife or wives of the man performing magic, are forbidden to be present during the ritual. No other men, except close kin, are allowed to be there. As far as the man performing the magic is concerned, he must be in a state of sexual purity and must therefore abstain from all sexual relations with his wives or other women during the previous days.

What would happen if these prohibitions were neglected? The harvest would be jeopardised, the family would suffer want, even starvation. Socially, the man would no longer be able to fulfil his responsibilities as head of the family or be a generous host to others. He would lose face and become a mere dependant of other people.

What are the implications of this system of prohibitions? It implies that human beings are conceived by the Baruya as being tied to nature by invisible links, making each individual *support* or *endanger* the order of things by his conduct. This confers a cosmic dimension to the individual's responsibility. By his actions he is responsible both to society and to Nature, understood by the Baruya to be a twofold reality, both visible and invisible, partly made up of evil spirits, such as the souls of the dead and other realities, which *we* call supernatural. In violating these prohibitions an individual will be guilty of creating disorder in Nature; a bad harvest, for example, will make him suffer the social consequences: hunger, shame, public accusation of bad conduct, censure, etc. A responsibility involving such cosmic dimensions explains the psychological force of the prohibition and the intensity of blame which the individual places on himself and which the group exercises over individuals.

This system of prohibitions appears to be dominated by sexual prohibitions. This implies that a human being's secret connection with the invisible depth of the universe is essentially connected with their sexual life. Baruya society is built on sexual repression, sex is a permanent threat to the order of nature and society. These representations allow us to catch a glimpse of the male–female relationship in Baruya society, men dominate the women and consider them a constant threat to the social order and to themselves, the guarantors of this order. We can see why the Baruya consider it their duty to separate young boys from their mothers and the female world about the age of nine in order to teach them gradually the rules of social life and the order of the universe; they are made to go through a cycle of initiations which last more than ten years at the end of which the child becomes an adult and is ready to return to the female world prepared for marriage and the dangers of sexual relations.

Who are the people among the Baruya who possess magical knowledge? This accomplishment is unequally distributed among individuals and social groups. First there is general disparity between men and women regarding the possession of knowledge and power, whether ritualistic, political or economic. Women have their own fertility magic which they pass from mother to daughter. Moreover women – even those who become shamans and therefore maintain unusual contact with the invisible – may never reach the higher ranks of the shaman hierarchy. Proof of this is shown when they take part in rites for curing diseases or chasing away evil spirits; they must remain seated and cannot stand in ceremonial enclosures or join in the dance of the male shamans who are fighting the evil spirits. Along with the inequality of the sexes, there is the inequality between men belonging to kinship groups possessing specific magical knowledge and powers and those who have little or none. Everyone knows for example that the Andavakia and Ndélamayé clans have special powers to make sweet potatoes grow. Everyone also knows that these clans may practise black magic to spoil the sweet potatoes in other people's gardens and so condemn them to shortage, even starvation. For example, Pandawé, an Andavakian, disclosed to me, that a few years ago, after his wife's suicide, he practised black magic to stop the growth of sweet potatoes in order to be free of the worries caused by this suicide. On another occasion, driven to despair by a friend's death, he again performed magic gestures during the funeral and near the house of the deceased; all the women assembled round the house to weep unwittingly carried away his curse with them, and spread it to their gardens when they returned to work after the ceremony. Very soon, sweet potatoes stopped growing or disappeared from the gardens. After a certain period rumour had it that Pandawé was responsible and he was reproached for having cast a spell. Later, he lifted his curse and the sweet potatoes multiplied, Pandawé allowing the women to use the sweet potatoes in his own gardens where they had never ceased to grow in abundance.

These examples confirm the hidden ties linking each person to the invisible world. We see that these links differ between persons, not only as individuals, but as members of the different social groups which make up the Baruya tribe. This inequality of magical powers between groups can only increase an individual's responsibility, specially those belonging to groups possessing the most powerful magic.

Where does magical knowledge come from and how do you explain its unequal distribution? Each person acquires this knowledge in the course of his life, or inherits it from the past. It is acquired mainly through a revelation in a dream or through a vision. In dreams or visions, invisible powers materialise and communicate to the individual some piece of knowledge. The next day, he goes to look for that special leaf in the forest, that particular bit of clay in the soil, pronouncing the formula revealed to him in the dream. However, by belonging to such and such a kinship group, some knowledge is passed on to him during his youth; here again the powers have come from some mythical period; they were conferred on Baruya ancestors by invisible powers as far back as the birth of the present world, and they were called Wandjinia or dream men. When accounting for the powers of each kinship group, we find that there is a certain hierarchy between them; on the other hand, everyone cooperates to make tubers grow in the gardens, to organise the ceremonial game hunts into fruitful expeditions, etc. – quite simply they cooperate to make society function.

Magic practices, in short, testify to the fact that a period dating from the beginning of the world has not completely disappeared and is present in the very fibre of the present order of things. How then, did the Baruya world come about?

THE INVISIBLE AND THE BEGINNING OF THE WORLD

We shall summarize only the essential points in Baruya myths about the beginning of the world.

In the beginning the Sun and Moon were merged with the earth. Everything was grey and all animal and plant species communicated in the same language. Men and spirits, animals and plants all lived together. These men were not like the men of today, their penises were not pierced and a woman's vagina was not open. The sexual organs of dogs were also closed. Then the Sun and the Moon decided to rise, pushing the sky up above them. From above the Sun said to the Moon that something would have to be done for men, and ordered the Moon to go back and look after them. The Moon stopped half way: and since then night has alternated with day and the seasons vary with rain and heat; animals became separated from men and went into the forest, while the spirits went off on their own into the depths where they remained hidden and threatening. Later the Sun invented an ingenious strategem for piercing men's penises and women's vaginas. Since then, man and woman have copulated and mankind has increased. But with this separation of all the species of the universe, their original common language disappeared. Men are now obliged to go into the forest and hunt the animals who have taken refuge there; they must plant sweet potatoes in order to survive and they are forced to protect themselves from spirits which became evil. While 'forced' to hunt, to farm and to perform rites, they are also helped by the Sun and Moon who guarantee to support the new order. If the Sun gets too close to the earth, he burns it and lays waste the gardens; if the Moon gets too close to the earth, she swamps everything in rain and darkness and makes the harvests rot. Thus, ever since mythical times when the Sun and Moon rose into the sky, the framework of the world has depended on a balance between the play of two opposing principal beings, the Sun and the Moon, from whence come heat, cold, dryness and humidity, fire and decay etc.

What light do these myths throw on the magical practices we have described above? The general connection between all beings who had existed in the beginning changed, after the Sun's ascent, but did not disappear. The original transparency and togetherness of beings and things disappeared and we have a world on two levels, the visible and the invisible, linked by hidden connections. Perhaps this explains the use of secret words in the magical formulae. These names are the esoteric doubles of everyday words used in describing things. In a way they are like the remnants or the reflection of an original language which permitted communication between everything. Uttering these secret words, a communication is re-established that had been broken; now there is certainty of being understood and therefore of having some hold over reality.

We can see now why these names are sacred to the Baruya. They are evidence of earlier times, dating back to the beginning of man, of the tribe, and also of the present invisible order of the world. They are a sacred trust, a heritage of powers permitting men, under their new conditions, to survive: a heritage whereby the dream men – the first ancestors, along with the Sun and Moon, father and mother of all things – are given recognition.

We found evidence of the sacred nature of these names when those who agreed to reveal the secret words, could not refrain from expressing the emotion they felt by this disclosure. All, without exception, a few hours after imparting their secrets, burst into a violent fit of weeping making me promise never at any price to reveal their name,[3] nor ever to make allusion to them or joke about them, for fear that famine would hit the villages and the fury of their ancestors would strike everybody. We may, therefore, state quite categorically, if our analysis is correct, that among the Baruya, magic and religion are not two separate domains, watertight compartments as we are generally led to believe from reading the works of many anthropologists since Frazer's *The Golden Bough*.

In ending this enquiry, several theoretical questions arise. We shall mention some briefly.

CONCLUSION. CAN WE MAKE COMPARISONS?

Among the Baruya, there is no significant economic inequality between individuals or between social groups. There are no chiefs nor any dominant social groups. But there is inequality in so far as there are individuals who are warriors or shamans, the two most highly prized statuses in Baruya society. There is also inequality between lineages: some lineages received from their ancestors the gift of providing society with the best warriors or the best shamans. We have seen that this inequality does not contradict – on the contrary, it strengthens – the social and cosmic responsibility of individuals as well as groups.

If we compare this with Malinowski's analysis of the chief Omarakana's privileges,[4] and Firth's on the powers of the chief in Tikopia,[5] we find that in the Melanesian and Polynesian societies – and it is greater in Tikopia than in Trobriand – there is an economic and political inequality which favours a tribal aristocracy. However, whereas economic differences between commoners and the aristocracy are a matter of degree rather than kind, there are, on the contrary, differences of kind to be found in the political and religious spheres. In both cases, political powers are justified by the monopoly which the most efficient chiefs hold over magic. The chief of Omarakana is the most powerful master of magic, commanding the rain and the sun; in Tikopia the chiefs are the sole intermediaries between human beings and supernatural forces. In both cases, chiefs and aristocrats are responsible for the wellbeing of the whole society, and they put their exceptional magical powers at the service of society as a whole. Like the Baruya, but more so, individuals and groups, at Kiriwina and in Tikopia have a social and cosmic responsibility. But, whereas among the Baruya, knowledge and responsibility are divided between individuals and groups, at Kiriwina and in Tikopia they are concentrated in the hands of a minority whose power is accepted. The question arises as to how such concentration and monopoly appeared and under what conditions; then, perhaps we shall have a partial explanation as to how primitive societies, which lack deep-seated inequalities and with no centralised power, become hierarchical with unequally privileged categories, where sometimes the power of a class or a caste is concentrated in a State apparatus.

Secondly, if we abstract the concrete details from the mythical universe of the Baruya and keep only the abstract principles which shape their universe, two are easily isolated. There is the hypothesis that reality is composed of several levels and that its essential basis is to be found beyond visible reality. This hypothesis could, in the abstract language of modern philosophy, be expressed in the formula that the essence of things is found outside their appearances. There is also the hypothesis that this multilevel reality is balanced in its own equilibrium and internal order by the play of two contradictory and complementary forces, the Sun and the Moon. Order reigns[6] when these two are at a fair distance from the earth, making it neither too hot nor too cold, neither too dry nor too wet, Order, therefore consists in the correct placement and the right distance of human beings in relation to the universe. In the language of western philosophy, this hypothesis could be expressed in the formula that the order of things lies in the balance of contradictory and complementary elements, a formula which constitutes one of the principles of dialectic thinking, the unity of opposites.[7]

If this is so, the difference between Baruya mythical thinking and modern scientific thinking is not to be sought on the level of those formal principles whereby experience is organised by thinking. The difference is to be found elsewhere but not, perhaps, until man stops being content with interpreting the world and starts experimenting with it in new and diverse ways.

For the Baruya, taking into account their technology and economy, the only experimentation possible is in the determined and extremely vast field of their practical knowledge of nature and social relations.

Nevertheless, they have to act on nature as a whole, on the network of hidden connections between things. For this reason productive work for the Baruya is thought of and performed as an activity where both magic and technique are indissociably involved. This is why where experiment is no longer possible they people the invisible part of their world with idealities created out of their own thoughts,[8] applying to these representations the elements of all possible experience, namely that the essence of things is not to be confused with their appearance and that the world obeys an order which subsists within certain limits only. Is this so very different from our own way of thinking, we who invented experimental scientific thinking?

10

Myth and History: reflections on the foundations of the primitive mind†

> Why should we examine seriously the spurious wisdom of myths?
>
> Aristotle, *Metaphysica*, Book IV

> The lesson to be drawn from the South American myths is then of specific value for the resolving of problems relating to the nature and development of thought.
>
> Claude Lévi-Strauss. *From Honey to Ashes*, Jonathan Cape, 1973, p. 474.

These thoughts are an attempt to clarify a problem which any anthropologist comes across in the exercise of his profession, the relations between mythical thinking, primitive society and history. It became practically inevitable for myself once I began analysing the myths and magico-religious practices of the Baruya of New Guinea. To give an idea of the kind of material, I shall present one version of the Baruya myth of the beginning of the world and mankind, a version put together from several variants:

In the beginning the Sun and the Moon were merged with the earth. Everything was grey and all animal and plant species communicated in the same language. Men and spirits, animals and plants all lived together. These men were not like the men of today; their penises were not pierced and a woman's vagina was not open. The sexual organs of dogs were also closed. Then the Sun and the Moon decided to rise, pushing the sky up above them. From above, the Sun said to the Moon that something would have to be done for men and ordered the Moon to go back and watch over them. The Moon stopped half-way: and since then night has alternated with day and the seasons vary with rain and heat; animals became separated from men and went into the forest, while the spirits went off on their own into the depths where they remained hidden and threatening. Later the Sun invented an ingenious stratagem for piercing the men's penises and womens' vaginas. Since then men and women have copulated and mankind has increased. But with this separation of all the species of the universe, their original common language disappeared. Men are now obliged to go into the forest and hunt the animals who have taken refuge there; they must plant sweet-potatoes in order to survive and they are forced to protect themselves from the spirits which became evil. While 'forced' to hunt, to farm and to perform rites, they are also helped by the Sun and the Moon who guarantee to support the new order. If the Sun gets too close to the earth, he burns it and lays waste the gardens; if the Moon gets too close to the earth, she swamps everything in rain and darkness and makes the harvests rot.

This text tells us about the origin of the world and the beginning of present-day man. They did not start from nothing, but from a primary state where distinct realities, the earth and the sky, the sun and the moon, man and spirits, plants and animals, etc., were not separated or disconnected from each other. This separation was carried out by the action of the sun and the moon and the world assumed its present configuration, its framework depending on the balanced play of these two opposing and principal characters, the sun and the moon, who brought warmth and cold, dryness and humidity, fire and decay, etc.

In a second stage, when the world took the shape men now recognise, the sun completed its work by making man and woman distinct, piercing the penis and the vagina. He thus reproduced them in the image of the world, both complementary and opposed in their differences. From that time mankind entered history, or at least history was possible for man who could now produce, multiply and be distinct as members of different tribes.

What is the nature of the idealities (characters and events) in this mythical discourse? It speaks of *primary causes* for the genesis of the world and the beginning of history, of *invisible* and ultimate forces which commanded and still command its form and growth. These causes are identified with the *actions* of the sun and moon, two beings endowed with knowledge and will, therefore *analogous* to man but different because of their *superior* power, because of their ability to act effectively over things which escape the control of man, or remain outside his grasp. The sun and moon, in Baruya language and ideology, are regarded as the father and mother of mankind and, in kinship terminology are designated by the terms of address applying to father and mother.[1]

Reduced to these *abstract* characters *alone*, which belong to the *form* of mythical discourse and to the formal properties of those idealities populating it (representation of primary causes in the shape of principal characters, analogous yet superior to man, etc.), the Baruya myth might be compared to the myths of many other peoples on condition that the abstract form *only* is retained.

What is the origin, therefore the foundation of the common presence of these abstract formal characters in the mythical discourse and idealities belonging to the ideology of societies differing profoundly in their ecology, economy, their social organization; in short, in all the positive determinations of their historical reality? How can different historical realities take account of these communal formal properties? Embarking on these reflections we are confronted with the general problem of the relations between mythical thinking, primitive society and History.

A direct relationship between myths and society can easily be proved once we undertake an exhaustive inventory of all the elements in myths transposed from aspects of the ecological environment: the social organisation, the historical traditions (migrations, wars, territorial alliances, etc.) of peoples where these myths have been studied or collected. We merely have to read *Les Mythologiques* of Lévi-Strauss to see with what minute precision he has located, isolated, refined and interpreted the multiple facts concerning fauna, flora, the environment, techniques, astronomy, etc., found in the myths of the American Indians; all these facts give sense to the numerous behavioural aspects and events ascribed to the ideal characters in these myths, the lynx, the owl, the great ant-eater, the capivara, the jaguar, the Pleiads, the moon, etc.

Alongside these aspects of man's relations with nature, carried over and transposed into myths, we also find a transposition of their social relations. One of the common features in North and South American myths is that the 'sociological armature' for these myths,[2] that is to say, the ideal social relations which link one imaginary protagonist to another in myth, takes the form of a kinship network, an ensemble of consanguineous and affinal relations. The conflicts, the agreements, between these characters are analogous with those facing the wife-givers and wife-takers, husbands and wives, parents and children, brothers and sisters, elder and younger sons, etc. This is why myths on the origin of cooking (the raw and the cooked) develop a veritable 'physiology of matrimonial alliance' and myths on other behaviour associated with cooking (table manners) are presented as a 'pathology' of this matrimonial alliance.[3] The form even, of myths varies with the nature of kinship relations and we find in numerous cases, that in the same myth (going from a version taken from a patrilineal society to another belonging to a matrilineal society) the signs are all inverted. If, instead of moving from one society to another within the same cultural group, we move from one cultural group to another, we discover that the same myth may undergo such distortions that it becomes difficult to recognise.

Through the identity of the sociological armature and the diversity in formal transformations of myths, we see a unique fact, a structural correspondence, an inner link between forms of mythical thinking and forms of primitive society which explain these phenomena. Kinship relations organise the scheme of mythical discourse and the representations of the world, because in real primitive societies, kinship relations are the dominant feature of the social structure. Here we have a structural correspondence which cannot be deduced from 'pure' categories of primitive thought or find an origin in Nature, its origin must be sought in the very structure of primitive societies. However, if the content of myths consists only of such objective elements, transposed from Nature or culture, it is difficult to understand how and why these myths become what they are: illusory representations of man and his world, inexact explanations of the order of things. How then do the objective materials of natural or social reality, transposed to mythical discourse, assume their phantasmic character? How do they become transmuted into illusory representations of the world?

The answer has been known for a long time and would seem to explain the principal characteristics of mythical idealities and the essential forms of mythical discourse: illusion is the child of analogy. Mythical thinking is human thought portraying reality by analogy.

Analogy is both a way of speaking and a way of thinking, a logic expressed in metaphor and metonym. Reasoning by analogy is to affirm a relationship of equivalence between objects (material or ideal), behaviour, the relationships of objects, the relationships of relations, etc. Reasoning by analogy is oriented. It is not the same to think of culture by analogy with nature (as for example in totemic institutions of the caste system), or to think of nature by analogy with culture. This possibility of following contrary and opposite ways manifests the theoretical, and generally unlimited, ability of thought to reason by analogy and to find equivalences between all aspects and levels of natural and social reality. We should remember this before tackling the problem of how analogy produces an illusory representation of the world.

We shall try to understand the category of representations of nature devised analogously with culture and analyse the effects of this type of analogous representation in and on behalf of the consciousness. What we must try to clarify is the mechanism of 'transmutation' – through this kind of analogy (Nature analogous with Culture) – of an objective element, *present* in human experience, into an illusory, therefore subjective, representation of the real. We shall start from a universally objective fact: human experience is divided spontaneously and inevitably into two spheres – what in nature and society, is directly controlled by man and what is not.

What is controlled, of course, and what is not, differs according to various societal forms and periods of historical development. Given the low level of development in their production techniques and in spite of significant differences in levels of development found in the various modes of production of primitive peoples (hunters, gatherers, fishermen, farmers), the control which they exercise over Nature remains very limited. In these circumstances, the sphere which man does not control can only appear, *present itself*, spontaneously to the consciousness, as a sphere of *powers superior* to man which he must represent to himself, explain and reconcile himself to and, therefore, control indirectly.

Once again we must stress the fact that the objective data, presented to the consciousness, is here a *negative* determination of the content of man's relations with man and Nature, a determination of the objective *limit* of this content. The basis for this determination is therefore, not found *in* but *outside* the consciousness. We should also note that the sphere of latent natural causes, of invisible forces not controlled by man, is presented spontaneously in the consciousness as a sphere of powers *superior* to man; it *does not produce* any further illusory representations of reality or causality in the world order. On the contrary, this representational content, this form of world presence corresponds to an objective fact of social and historical reality.[4]

How then are the objective facts of this representation transmuted into an illusory representation of the world? The transmutation takes place as soon as the mind represents the invisible forces and realities of Nature as beings analogous to men. Similarly, the invisible causes and forces which give rise to and regulate the non-human world (Nature) or the human world (culture) *assume the attributes* of man, i.e., present themselves spontaneously in the consciousness as beings endowed with *consciousness, will, authority and power*, therefore as beings analogous to men, but *different* in that they know what man does not know, they do what man cannot do, they control what he cannot control; they are different from man and are superior to him.

The immediate effect of a thought process which represents Nature as analogous with culture, human society, is to treat the superior and mysterious powers of Nature as *subjects*', hence '*personifying*' these powers as natural beings, animals, plants, stars, and they, as a result divide in two (like the whole of Nature) into both sentient and supersentient superhuman beings, becoming the superhuman characters in myth whose actions are responsible for the present world order.[5]

By representing Nature as analogous to man, the primitive mind treats the world of things as a world of persons, it regards the objective and unintentional relations between things as the intentional relations between persons. At the same time, in opposition yet complementary to it, the primitive mind regards the subjective world of its idealities as objective realities outside men and his thoughts, with which it is possible and necessary to communicate when wanting to influence the order of things and using them as intermediaries. Analogous thinking, by monopolising the objective data of experience, present in the consciousness, gives rise therefore to a double illusion, an illusion about the world and an illusion about itself; an illusion about itself because the mind attributes idealities with an existence outside man and independent of him: these idealities are engendered spontaneously and the mind therefore alienates itself by its own representations; illusion about the world because the mind peoples it with imaginary beings similar to man, capable of understanding his needs and replying to them in a favourable or hostile fashion.

Two consequences may be seen from this analysis. Mythical thinking (and this includes all religious thought) derives its impulse from the desire to *know* reality, but in the process it arrives at an illusory explanation for a series of causes and effects which establish the order of things. At the same time, because it perceives the world of the invisible in the form of imaginary realities endowed with consciousness, will and, particularly, abilities analogous yet superior to man's, mythical thinking *calls for* and *sets up* magical practices as a means of influence over the consciousness and will of these imaginary characters who regulate the course of things. Analogous thinking establishes therefore both a theory and a practice, religion and magic. Or, at least, religion exists spontaneously in a theoretical form (representation, explanation of the world) and in a corresponding practical form (magic and ritual influence over the real); thus, a means of explaining the world (in an illusory way) and changing the world (in an imaginary way.)[6]

We could extend this analysis further and show that all religious intervention in the world is simultaneously 'an influence over itself'. All magical practices and all ritual are accompanied by some kind of restriction or prohibition on the actions of the officiant and/or the public. All religious influence over the secret forces which rule the world, implies and demands man's influence over himself if he is to *communicate* with these forces, reach them, be heard by and obey them.[7] Magical power is paid for by some restriction on man concerning food, sex or something else. The reverse of authority is obligation. From this standpoint the restrictions, the constraints, the prohibitions, the taboos are not a restriction of authority, but an accumulation of power (imaginary). Analogous thinking produces therefore two complementary, yet opposite, effects: the mind humanises Nature and its laws by endowing it with man's attributes, but from this very fact, it spontaneously and *inevitably* endows man with supernatural powers, i.e., with power and efficacity comparable (and thus illusory) with those of natural phenomena.[8] It thus creates 'This reciprocity of perspectives in which man and the world mirror each other and which seems to us the only possible explanation of the properties and capacities of the savage mind.'[9]

In this mythical reciprocity of perspectives between man and the world we can confirm that there is a twofold illusion about the world and about man: the illusion of a false explanation and the illusion of man's imaginary influence over the world and over himself. This illusion becomes greater as the reciprocity of perspectives between man and the world becomes more complex and complete. Now, to reach this completion, mythical thinking must explore and exploit all internal possibilities; it must systematically traverse all possible routes of analogical interconnection. These routes, as we have already pointed out, may take, theoretically, four different directions: from culture to Nature (1), from Nature to culture (2), from culture to culture (3), from Nature to Nature (4).

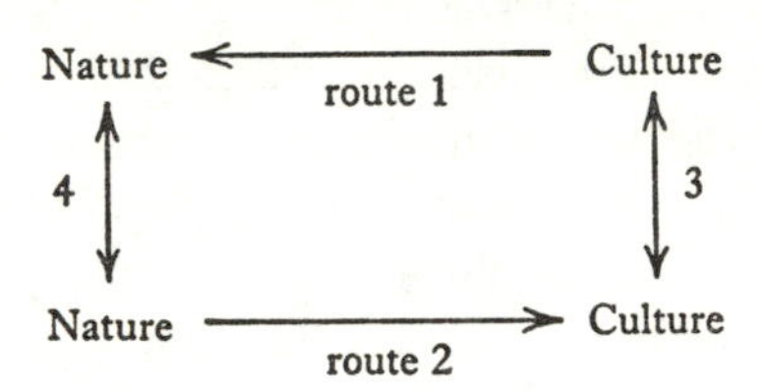

Using these four fundamental axes, a multitude of analogous comparisons may be deployed and combined in some sort of phantasmic vectorial algebra conferring on mythical thinking and discourse an inexhaustible symbolic wealth and polysemy.

We have already analysed a progression of type 1, which projects culture over Nature and whose general effect is thc anthropomorphisation of Nature, the humanisation of its laws, but at the same time, in complementary and contrary fashion, naturalises human influence in magic (effect of route type 2). To give an idea of the multitude of effects possible from route type 2, (Nature over culture) we should have to go into the whole of Lévi-Strauss's analysis concerning institutions such as the totemic and caste systems; this is where they are most clearly seen. Lévi-Strauss has shown that totemic institutions imply, on the level of thought, the *representations and assumption* of a homology between two series of relations, two systems of differences situated, the one in Nature, between natural species, and the other in culture, between social groups (clans, phratries, etc.).[10] Going further, he brings together and compares all totemic groups and caste systems, showing that here there are inverse effects of the same principle according to whether the postulated analogy between human groups and natural species is formal or substantial.[11]

Through totemic institutions, primitive thinking is seen to *borrow*, in order to think about *social life* (culture), an objective combination *given* in Nature, the natural distinction between biological species. Helped by this scheme of differences in natural species, the mind is open to exceptional theoretical possibilities because 'considered in isolation, a species is a collection of individuals; in relation to other species, however, it is a system of definitions.'[12] The notion of 'species' is at one and the same time precept and concept, the intuitive image of the discontinuity of the real with its combinatory aspects and abstract operator; it permits the unity of multiplicity to pass for the diversity of identity and offers primitive thinking a basic principle for classifying the facts of experience, of natural and social reality. In analogous thinking, the notion of species, under certain conditions, becomes a 'totemic operator' serving as the mediatory link between Nature and culture and bringing the reciprocal perspectives concerning man and the world closer.[13]

We could go further still and analyse the example of analogy in types 3 and 4. For example the analogy found in all studied societies between sexual and food relations (type 3), but here we shall only show something of the complexity analogous thinking may attain and the degree of illusion which mythical thinking contributes to man and the world.

How far have we come? So far we have been trying to find the reasons and conditions, therefore the mechanisms, for the transmutation into illusory representations of the world and man, the phantasmic explanation of the real, for the multiple objective facts of Nature, primitive societies and history which are present in the content of myths and which mythical thinking seizes hold of in order to construct its 'palace of ideas'.

Briefly, and this principle was already known by the 19th century, this transmutation occurs every time the objective materials of representation enter into *forms* of reasoning by analogy. The primitive mind spontaneously grasps these materials, conceals them, carries them away to help cover the distance which separates nature from culture and, more importantly, the distance separating all levels of human and natural reality. In this process of transport and employment, the objective materials are changed into simple props for a system of fantastic and illusory representations of the world, for which finally they seem to be only alibis or pretexts.

Can we now reply to our general question about the relations between myth, society and history which came up in analysing the Baruya myths and in Lévi-Strauss's work on American Indian mythology and the essentials of *The Savage Mind*? The answer may be presented in this way: myths originate *spontaneously at the intersection* of the networks of effects; effects *in* the consciousness of man's relations with man and Nature and effects *of* Thought on these representational facts which enter the complex machinery of reasoning by analogy.

EFFECTS IN THE CONSCIOUSNESS OF THE CONTENT OF MAN'S HISTORICAL RELATIONS WITH MAN AND NATURE

In myths, the content of man's historical relations with man and Nature is present both in its *positive* determinations and, within limits, in its *negative* determinations. We have already indicated the presence of mutilple elements of objective knowledge in myths – fauna, flora, the environment, astronomy, techniques – which express the positive content of primitive man's relationship with Nature. We have seen from the 'sociological armature' of American Indian myths, based essentially on imaginary kinship relations, that there is an effect in the consciousness (= transposition, representation), of the content of the Indians' social organisation; now, by investing imaginary societies where mythical ideal characters live, die and are eternally resuscitated, with an organisation based on relationships of blood and alliance, does not mean that the origin can be traced from 'pure principles' of thought, nor from models in Nature. For the basis of this conceptual usage of kinship relations, we must look elsewhere than in the empty and timeless[14] forms of thought or models offered us by Nature. This can only be in society and history.

In society, since, in the majority of primitive societies (as distinct from class, slave, feudal or other societies), kinship relations are objectively the dominant form of social relations; in history, because (for reasons and conditions that have to be determined) the dominance of kinship relations disappears from many primitive societies as new social relations develop, such as caste, class, State.

Understandably, the dominance of kinship relations in primitive societies means that the effect in consciousness is to invent ideal societies in which mythical characters are developed in accordance with the kinship model (hence analogous to the real). This effect in the consciousness, therefore, has its origin outside consciousness, in society and history, and it explains the structural correspondence, which often exists between forms of mythical thinking and forms of society; we have seen how, by passing from a patrilineal form of society to a matrilineal one, the same myth can change and invert its signs.

With regard to the effect in the consciousness of the *limits* of the content of man's historical relations with man and Nature – the negative determinants of this content – we have analysed, taking account of the low level in the development of techniques characteristic of primitive economies, the fact that the sphere of laws and invisible forces of nature and society not controlled by man, appears to him as a sphere of *powers superior* to man. This effect in the consciousness expresses an objective fact, however, and the representation too has its basis outside consciousness in objective social reality and its content changes with the development of productive forces in history.

Whether they are positive or negative determinants of the social and historical reality, these effects in the consciousness *do not in themselves create myths* – on the contrary – nor do they constitute illusory representations of Nature and history. An additional factor, the intervention of another mechanism is required, before mythical representations of the real come about; this mechanism has its origin outside man himself.

THE EFFECT OF ANALOGOUS THINKING ON THE CONTENT OF ITS REPRESENTATIONS

This other mechanism we have called '*the effect of analogous thinking on content*', on the objective data of its representations. Spontaneously, by systematically covering all the possible analogous parallels between Nature and Culture, thought constructs a gigantic mirror-effect, where the reciprocal image of man and the world is reflected *ad infinitum*, perpetually decomposing and recomposing in the prism of Nature–Culture relations. Using analogy to bring together all aspects and levels of Nature and culture, thought in its spontaneous or primitive state is immediately and simultaneously *analytic* and *synthetic*[15] and has the ability both to *totalise* all aspects of the real in mythical representation and to *pass* from one level of the real to another by the reciprocal *transformations* of its analogies.[16] By analogy the whole world makes sense, everything is significant, everything can be explained within a symbolic order, where all the positive known facts transposed into subject matter for myths, may take their place with all their rich abundance of detail.[17]

If these are the characteristics of mythical thinking, thinking which is both analytic and synthetic, totalisatory and worked by rules of transformation, a whole series of facts may be explained.

(*a*) All mythology tends to become a closed system with neither beginning nor end. 'The world of myths is round', says Lévi-Strauss and simultaneously 'it is hollow'.[18] Here are implied the basic principles of structural methods in the analysis of myths, methods which reproduce in an ideal form the very properties of the system of objects studied and which allow us to perceive, among other things, the canonical laws of the groups of transformations of myths.[19]

(*b*) Mythical thinking can only appear as temporal thought tracing the origins of things, unmasking original and still present origins – it is both analytic and synthetic, going back to a past but living history, back to the eliminated but eternally present genesis in order to explain the present world order.[20] Confining its discoveries to the closed systems of its representations, mythical thinking possesses all the characteristics of religious and philosophical systems of representation.

(*c*) Since it is able to classify its representations, to exchange one for another and to totalise them into a system, thinking by analogy establishes formal principles in the development of myths and rules of operation which imply an algebraic equivalent[21] – understanding by algebra a series of operative rules permitting us to constitute all the objects of a domain in such a way that they always belong to that domain and can be exchanged one with another. Thinking by analogy, therefore, establishes principles which constitute the formal conditions, *a priori*, of all demonstrative reasoning revealed in a linked and coherent discourse, whether the content of this discourse be mythical, religious, philosophical or scientific.

We must therefore be aware of the fact that primitive thinking, in spontaneous practice, uses two operative systems which should not be confused.

(*a*) One, directly founded on the principles and forms of reasoning by analogy;

(*b*) The other, spontaneously and automatically involved in the exercise of any form of thinking which constructs its idealities according to transformational rules and ideally aspires to the 'closure' of this domain of idealities. In so far as mythical thinking formally manifests itself as a closed world of idealities strictly bound together, it inevitably produces this second system which does not merge with analogy, nor is it established solely by means of analogy.

What then, is the origin of these operations which thought spontaneously applies to the ideal substance of its representations?

At first it would seem that thought has an innate capacity to reason by analogy about the content of human experience. Can we assume, however, that thought has invented this ability itself? We should remember that thinking by analogy means grasping a certain 'relationship of equivalence' between distinct social and material realities, or more abstractly, relationships of equivalence between relations, etc. Now, it is not only the exercise of abstract thinking that infers a grasp of relationships of equivalence. In order to have a perception of objects and forms, or at a more complex level, movement in space and motor-sensory behaviour, relationships of equivalence must be perceived and controlled in a certain way. The possibility that thought represents itself in a relationship of equivalence is external to thought itself, and is based on the properties of living matter found in complex forms of organisation, the nervous system and the brain.

We now have what Lévi-Strauss has called: 'An original logic, a direct expression of the structure of the mind and behind the mind, probably, of the brain.'[22]

The origin of spontaneous thought processes at the primitive level involves a history which is something apart from the history of man; this is the 'natural' history of the species, laws involving the evolution of matter and of nature. What is revealed by analysing myths is, beyond the thought of 'savages' themselves, thought 'in its primitive state'. In this sense, thought in its primitive state is not historic, rather, it is 'trans-historic'. It has existed since the beginning of history. It constitutes the condition for the existence of human history, for the practical development of relationships between men and the world; it is not, however, the result of this practical development: 'But in order for *praxis* to be living thought, it is necessary first (in a logical and not a historical sense) for thought to exist: that is to say, its initial conditions must be given in the form of an objective structure of the psyche and brain without which there would be neither praxis nor thought.'[23]

Our analysis of 'primitive' thinking and mythical thinking has arrived at a paradoxical conclusion; it has made us discover and consider thought 'in its primitive state', in a kind of pre-historic reality. But this is only half the paradox; by presenting itself as an *ensemble of formal conditions* whereby thought can ideally apprehend and organise relationships of equivalence and link judgments in demonstrative discourses, by presenting itself both as a logic of equivalence and as a formal logic, thought 'in its primitive state' is present today in history and is the *same* as it was on the threshold of history. The final paradox is therefore, that thought, as a condition of history, has no history (or at any rate its history does not belong to the history of man but to the history of matter).

On this point Lévi-Strauss and Marx would agree. For Lévi-Strauss: 'All social life, even elementary, presupposes an intellectual activity in man of which the formal properties, consequently, cannot be reflection of the concrete organization of the society.'[24] For Marx: 'Since the thought process itself grows out of the conditions, is itself a *natural process*, thinking that really comprehends must always be the same, and can only vary gradually according to maturity of development, including that of the organ by which the thinking is done. Everything else is drivel.'[25]

History has not disappeared from our analysis. On the contrary, its exact *place* has been marked and its proper *reality* demonstrated. The body, the brain, thought, consciousness and unconsciousness all constitute human nature, but this human nature does not constitute the whole of man's nature, because History must be added to human nature. At least History adds something at the outset, the transformation of man's relations with Nature and man's relations with man;[26] this is made possible by the evolution of Nature, which, throughout history, has been the laboratory where man exercises his practical activities and gives him, moreover, the possibility and conditions of thinking.

We should try to consider two facts together, although at first sight they may appear contradictory, if not mutually exclusive: the fact that thought, in its *formal structure*, has remained the same throughout history (and, in this sense, has no history) and the fact, and this is more obvious, that there is transformation of ideas throughout history and progress in different branches of learning.

In fact, there is neither contradiction nor paradox here, since it is history, it is the transformation of man's relations with Nature and man's relations with man, which gives thought a content (to think of) and it is history which changes the content. To illustrate this fact, we merely have to return to one of our previous analyses. We showed in the South-American myths, that the existence of a 'sociological armature', constructed primarily from imaginary kinship relations, brought us up against an element in myth which derives its origin neither from the formal structure of the mind, pure structure and to a certain degree ahistorical, nor from models drawn from Nature, since in Nature there is no equivalent for the exchange of women, i.e. alliance relationships which, together with consanguineous relations, go to make up the *human* fact of kinship. And, with this example we see History, the life of hunters, farmers – their way of life, their forms of social organisation, their marriage rites, rites of initiation, etc. – all crowded into 'Thought'. In short, everything which we call 'effects in the consciousness' of 'primitive' peoples' relationships between themselves and Nature. This is why, and here perhaps we part company with Lévi-Strauss,[27] mythical thinking is both thought in its *primitive state* and the thought *of* 'primitives'. Let us pause for a moment here.

It goes without saying that analogy, an operative scheme based on formal structures of thought, and therefore expressing capacities of thought in its primitive state, is at hand, at any epoch in History, for man to describe the domains of his experience. Modes of thought based on analogy do not *exclusively* characterise *primitive* forms and stages of historical development. Moreover, Lévi-Strauss mentions among contemporary forms of analogous thinking: 'Art...and so many as yet 'uncleared' sectors of social life, where through indifference or inability, and most often without our knowing why, primitive thought continues to flourish.'[28] We could, of course, mention religious representations, even political ideologies, etc.

In fact, speaking simply and universally, since it occurs in every individual and at all epochs, there exists a field of *perception*, an observation of the perceived world in which, continuously and spontaneously, analogies with forms, objects and actions present themselves to our consciousness. Today, and this is a crucial point, within the framework of our industrial society, and taking into account the development of natural and 'human' sciences, analogies drawn from the domain of *perception* no longer constitute the *essential stuff* for man's *dominant* representation of Nature and history.[29] Conversely – and this is the direct result of practical relations with the world characterised by the low level of development in productive forces and non-empirical knowledge – in primitive societies, as Lévi-Strauss has shown, it is those analogies drawn from the field of perception, from sentient knowledge, which constitute the basic material with which the mind of 'primitives' (spontaneously subject to formal principles of thought in the primitive state), construct their 'palace of ideas', where the reciprocal image of man and the world is reflected to infinity and where the illusions which primitive man holds about himself and the world originate and are maintained. Nourished by a wealth of knowledge derived from a thousand-year familiarity and commerce with Nature, the mind of 'primitives', in order to represent *the invisible but necessary relationships* between things, relationships *not observable on the level* of perception, could only avail themselves of the resources of analogy, an analogy which derived a great deal of its images and processes from the very content of sentient knowledge.[30] But within these limitations, the positive results obtained by mythical thinking were immense.

Myths and rites are far from being, as has often been held, the product of man's 'myth-making faculty', turning its back on reality. Their principal value is indeed to preserve until the present time the remains of observation and reflection which were (and no doubt still are) precisely *adapted* to discoveries of a *certain* type: those which nature authorises from the starting point of a *speculative* organization and exploitation of the *sensible world in sensible terms*. This science of the concrete was necessarily restricted by its essence to results other than those destined to be achieved by the exact natural sciences but it was no less scientific and its results no less genuine. They were secured ten thousand years earlier and still remain at the basis of our own civilisation.[31]

Thought in its 'primitive' state and scientific thought are not therefore, 'two unequal stages in the development of the human mind', since thought in its primitive state (the mind in its formal structure) does not develop and operates the same at all periods and on all material which history provides. There is no progress of the Mind, only progress in knowledge and learning. This means it would be an error to identify the thought of 'primitives' with primitive thinking. The thought of primitives differs in its representation of the cosmos from Ionian physicists in ancient Greece or 18th-century post-Newtonian philosophers. But how do these differences arise? Take for example the Greeks: today we know a few more reasons why the Milesian philosophers repudiated the old cosmogonies, or rather mythical theogonies of the oriental model.[32] One fundamental reason was the development of geometry and, with it, a mathematical representation of the universe which 'consacre l'avènement d'une forme de pensée et d'un systeme d'explication sans analogie dans le mythe'.[33] A second reason, whose results converge with the first, was that man's relationship with man had also changed with the appearance of a new form of society, the *polis*, and that a régime of *isonomy* took the place of *monarchy* in the cities as well as in representations of Nature.[34]

It was as a result of this twofold process, (which led to a partial decline in mythical thinking in the Ionian 'physics' and 'politics', of Greek 'citizens'), that philosophy was born and a new mode of reflective thought, with vast repercussions, was established at the beginning of the 6th century in Ionia. This brings us to a fundamental problem in our understanding of the history of mankind: the exact nature of philosophical thought, its specific difference from mythical thinking and the historic conditions for its appearance. We can therefore understand why 'The lesson to be drawn from the South American myths is then of specific value for the resolving of problems relating to the nature and development of thought'[35] and why Aristotle, who was aware of the novelty brought by the first Ionian physicists, should have said: 'why should we examine seriously the spurious wisdom of myths?'[36]

There is no question of entering into the problem of the relationship between mythical and philosophical thought. It would need more than one book. However, we may draw on the Greeks for an observation which suggests a general line of analysis. In discovering that Nature, beyond *its visible forms*, was organised according to essential relationships of a mathematical order, Greek thought partially and locally burst through the network of intentional causalities; analogical representations drawn from perception were abandoned in favour of other relationships of equivalence expressing this new field of human experience.[37]

Generally speaking, progress, as far as knowledge of Nature and history is concerned, has consisted in erasing from the surface of things, the network of intentions which man had initially ascribed to them in his own image; in destroying fragment by fragment, level by level, the imaginary representations of 'intentional' causes and replacing these with the representation of unintentional and inevitable relationships. From a certain point of view, there was progress in the ability to represent the unintentional system of objective relationships existing in Nature and history, when semi-abstract, semi-concrete speculative concepts of mythical thought were substituted for purely abstract speculative concepts in philosophy: concepts of cause, purpose, reason, origin, principles, analyses and the classification of different types of causes, primary, secondary, motivating, final, material, formal, etc. Naturally, there is no point in denying the speculative nature of concepts and movements in philosophical thought which endeavour, like mythical, analytic and synthetic thought, to arrive at the first and ultimate origins of the order of things.[38]

In short, in order to think about the specificity of mythical thinking and its conditions for reproduction or decline in History, and thus to think about the relations between myth, society and History, we must discover scientifically the *raisons d'être* and the inevitability of History's multiple momentum which provides new subject matter for human thought, bearing in mind that this last remains essentially the same. On this point – the analysis of unintentional inevitabilities which are manifest in History and profoundly actuate it – we again part company with Lévi-Strauss who has spoken about history[39] in a way we cannot ultimately accept and which seems to us not to be entirely founded on principles of the structural method.

For Lévi-Strauss, 'it is tedious as well as useless to amass arguments to prove that all societies are in history and change: that this is so is patent'.[40] This kind of history is not just 'cold' history, in which the same structures are reproduced without notable variations. History is also made from those 'non-recurrent chains of events whose effects accumulate to produce economic and social upheavals.'[41] Here, Lévi-Strauss raises the question of the relationship between thought and History, and we have seen that he adopts a position close to Marx for whom thought in its *formal* structure had no history; thought does not 'develop' in history, but assumes different modalities according to the tenor of history. 'Reason develops and transforms itself in the practical field: man's mode of thought reflects his relations to the world and to men. But in order for *praxis* to be living thought, it is necessary first . . . for thought to exist.'[42] Going further still, Lévi-Strauss accepts as a law of 'order', 'the undoubted primacy of infrastructures',[43] and he writes:

> I do not at all mean to suggest that ideological transformations give rise to social ones. Only the reverse is in fact true. Men's conception of the relations between nature and culture is a function of modifications of their own social relations . . . we are merely studying the shadows on the wall of the Cave.[44]

We have shown at some length what Lévi-Strauss has contributed to a theory of 'ideological superstructures'. And he refers to himself as a materialist and determinist: 'whereas in the public mind there is frequently confusion between structuralism, idealism, and formalism, structuralism has only to be confronted with true manifestations of idealism and formalism for its own deterministic and realistic inspiration to become clearly manifest.'[45] Even in *Structures élémentaires de la parenté*, Lévi-Strauss quotes Taylor's phrase: 'If law is anywhere, it is everywhere.'

From this point of view, with which we heartily concur, it becomes difficult to follow Lévi-Strauss in his conclusion to *Du miel aux cendres*. In the upheaval, at the end of which: 'along the frontiers of Greek thought (when) mythology gave way to philosophy and the latter emerged as the necessary precondition of scientific thought,' he sees this as 'one historical occurrence which can have no meaning beyond all actual happening at that place, and in that time,'[46] 'and if history retains its paramount place it is one which rightfully belongs to irreducible contingency.'[47]

Yet, in a sense, this conclusion was necessary. In identifying mythical thought and thought in its primitive state, by leaving aside the specific differences between modes of philosophical and scientific representations, so that they do not appear to be 'interlocked with each other' in mythical thinking, we are only stripping history of all creativity and necessity. History is no more than an external catalyser which haphazardly releases possibilities which 'lie dormant in the seeds' of mythical thought. Perhaps this representation of history can be seen as the ultimate triumph of mythical thinking over the science which analyses it, since it has made the scholar look at History as primitive societies see it; who 'want to deny it and try, with a dexterity we underestimate, to make the states of their development which they consider 'prior' as permanent as possible.'[48]

Notes

INTRODUCTION

1 Article published in *Annali*, review of the Instituto Giangiacomo Feltrinelli, Milan, 1971. Special number entitled 'Ricerca dei presuppositi e dei fondamenti del discorso scientifico in Marx', pp. 7–21.

2 We have explained this itinerary at the beginning of *Rationalité et irrationalité en économie*, Maspero, Paris, 1966.

3 From the article 'Objet et méthode de l'anthropologie économique', which appeared in *L'Homme*, No. 2, 1965, and later in *Rationalité*. . . ., op. cit., pp. 232–93.

4 See Ch. 1, p. 15 *et seq.* We refer to our brief analysis of the economy and society of the Mbuti Pygmy hunters, in which we try to discover this system of simultaneous effects of inner constraints in the mode of production on kinship relations, political relations and their symbolic and ritualistic relationships with the outer world.

5 Cf. Engels' remarks, still of topical interest, when writing to Joseph Bloch, 22 September 1890: 'According to the materialist conception of history, the ultimately determining element in history is the production and reproduction of real life. More than this neither Marx nor I have ever asserted. Hence if somebody twists this into saying that the economic element is the *only* determining one, he transforms that proposition into a meaningless abstract, senseless phrase. . . Unfortunately it happens only too often that people think they have fully understood a new theory and can apply it without more ado from the moment they have assimilated its main principles, and even those not always correctly. And I cannot exempt many of the more recent "Marxists" from this reproach, for the most amazing rubbish has been produced in this quarter, too.' (*On Religion*, Lawrence and Wishart, 1957.)

6 Cf. Symmes C. Oliver, *Ecology and Cultural Continuity as Contributing Factors in the Social Organization of the Plains Indians*, University of California Press, 1962, pp. 1–5, 66–8.

7 Cf. Preston Holder, *The Hoe and the Horse on the Plains. A study of Cultural Development among North American Indians*, University of Nebraska, pp. 23–88.

8 In order to examine further these studies we have devoted two papers to John Murra's works relating to the Inca economy and society. We have attempted to locate and explain the elements in former modes of production and social organisation which the new mode of production, the state, retained, yet changed, in order to adapt to its own process of reproduction. Cf. chs. 2, 9.

9 The distinction – a basic one for us – between these two types of contradiction, intra- and interstructural, has been outlined in our article 'Système, structure et contradiction dans *Le Capital* de Marx', published in *Temps Modernes*, 1966, special no. devoted to 'Problèmes du structuralisme'. This gave rise to a lively attack from Lucien Sève and a subsequent response from us.

10 Soeren Kierkegaard, *The Concept of Dread*, Oxford University Press, 1944.

11 A complete translation, in two volumes, appeared in *Anthropos* in 1967 and 1968, under the title, *Fondements de la critique de l'économie politique*.

12 Cf. the second part of this book 'Dead sections and living ideas in Marx's thinking on primitive society.'

13 Here we have adopted Jean T. Desanti's well-formulated phrase from his article, 'Sur la "production" des concepts en mathématiques', in the journal *Les Etudes philosophiques,* October–December, 1969, pp. 475–97. Of course, to understand in context Marx's ideas on primitive society presupposes that it is not enough to quote from Engels on the subject in his *Origins of the family, private property and the state.* On the contrary what is interesting about Marx and Engels' attitude concerning this subject is their constant ability to absorb avidly and consider seriously the new ideas contained in the works of Maurer, Kovalevski, Morgan, Taylor, etc.

14 Marx, *Pre-Capitalist Economic Formations,* Lawrence and Wishart, 1964, p. 71.

15 See ch. 6, a paper J.-B. Pontalis asked us to write for a special number of *Nouvelle revue de psychanalyse,* No. 2, 1970, on 'Objets du fétichisme'.

16 We chose the example of the Mbuti for two reasons: Firstly, because their economic system (based on hunting and gathering within a fairly widespread ecosystem, the Congolese primary forest) is relatively simple and, secondly, and more particularly, because – as distinct from innumerable ethnographic works which provide vague information on the societies treated – the works of Turnbull are of outstanding quality and rich in detail, happily complemented by the notable discoveries of Richard Lee, Lorna Marshall, Julian Steward working on other hunter–gatherers, the Boshimans, Shoshones, etc. We should like to thank Colin Turnbull, who answered, with great kindness and clarity, the numerous questions we put to him, correcting the interpretations we made of his material and work.

17 From H. Frankfort's and T. Jacobsen's *Before Philosophy* (Pelican, 1949), a book quite old, but still important. It would be interesting to make a list of the various imaginary or real functions which the state and state representative carried out in ancient Egypt and Mesopotamia. It is remarkable that in the myths summarised by these two authors, the Cosmos itself is represented after the *manner* of a state, and that the forms of state constitute the sociological scheme which organises the representation of the Universe. On the other hand, in the Amerindian myths of stateless societies, it is kinship relations which play the role of the sociological scheme. It should also be noted that any *extra* work – in the form of special hunting forays, where game is consumed after the hunt as with the Mbuti – becomes, forced surplus labour, in Egypt and among the Incas, to feast the gods and support their earthly representatives, kings and priests.

1 ANTHROPOLOGY AND ECONOMICS

† Paper read at the Conference: *L'Unité de l'homme. Invariants biologiques et universaux culturels.* An international seminar held by the CIEBAF, (Centre international d'études bio-anthropologiques et d'anthropologie fondamentale), Abbaye de Royaumont (6–9 September 1972).

1 Malinowski, before going to the field, had already published an article on 'The Economic Aspect of the Intichiuma Ceremonies', *Festskrift tillägnad, Eduard Westermarck,* Helsingfors, 1902, and on his return, he published 'Primitive Economics in the Trobriand Islands', *Economic Journal* XXXI, London, pp. 1–16.

2 Maurer, *Einleitung zur Geschichte der Mark-Hof-Dorf und Stadtverfassung und der öffentlichen Gewalt,* München, 1854.

3 Maine, *Ancient Law,* John Murray, Albemarle Street, London, 1861, ch. 8: 'The Early History of Property', pp. 244–303.

4 M. M. Kovalevski, *Tableau des origines et de l'évolution de la famille et de la propriété,*

Lorensak Stiftelse, No. 2, 1890, Stockholm. Morgan, of course, should also be mentioned, *Ancient Society*, 1877, Part IV: 'Growth of the Idea of Property', and Engels' commentary on it in *Origins of the Family, Private property and the State*, 1884. See our preface to *Sur les sociétés précapitalistes*, Editions sociales, 1970.

5 R. Firth, Preface to the second edition (1964) of *Primitive Polynesian Economy*, p. xi, Routledge and Kegan Paul (Godelier's italics).

6 André Leroi-Gourhan, *Le Geste et la Parole*, Albin Michel, 1964, Vol. 1, p. 210. (Godelier's italics).

7 Karl Marx, *A Contribution to a criticism of Political Economy*, Lawrence and Wishart, 1971, pp. 20–21.

8 In this connection see M. Sahlins, 'Economic Anthropology and Anthropological Economics', *Social Science Information*, 8 (5), 1969, p. 13.

9 Lionel Robbins, *The Subject Matter of Economics*, Macmillan, 1952, Ch. 1. The formalist theses are to be found in E. Leclair and H. Schneider, *Economic Anthropology*, Holt Rinehart, New York, 1967.

10 As found in the Introduction to Samuelson's famous work, *Economics*, A. Colin (2 vols.), 1943.

11 K. Polanyi, *The Great Transformation. The Political and Economic Origins of our Time*, Beacon, 1957; C. Dalton, *Economic Anthropology and Development. Essays on Tribal and Peasant Economics*, Basic Books, 1971.

12 Piero Sraffa, *De la production des biens de production*, Dunod, 1970.

13 M. Godelier, *Rationalité et irrationalité en économie*, Maspero, Paris, 1966; M. Sahlins, *Stone Age Economics*, Aldine, 1972; E. Terray, *Le Marxisme devant les sociétés primitives*, Maspero, 1968.

14 M. Godelier, 'Qu'est-ce que définir une "formation économique et sociale": l'exemple des Incas', *La Pensée*, No. 159, October 1971, pp. 99–106; the text is reproduced here, pp. 63–9.

15 See our critique of Lange and the praxeology of Kotarbinski in *Rationalité et irrationalité en économie*, op. cit., Ch. 1.

16 H. K. Schneider, *The Wahi Wanyaturu: Economics in an African Society*, Aldine Publishing Co., Chicago, 1970.

17 Ibid., p. 4.

18 K. Polanyi, 'The Economy as Instituted Process', in *Trade and Market in Early Empires*, The Free Press, Glencoe, Illinois, 1957.

19 This is the case with E. Terray, when he 'reconstructs' Meillassoux, *Anthropologie économique des Gouro de Côte-d'Ivoire*, Mouton, 1964, in the second part of his book *Le Marxisme devant les sociétés primitives*, op. cit., pp. 95–173.

20 This point is specifically illustrated in a recent anthropological manual published in the United States, *An Introduction to Cultural and Social Anthropology*, The Macmillan Company, New York, 1971, 456 pages, in which the author, Peter B. Hammond, having defined anthropology in vague and general terms as 'the study of man', and having divided, as is usual in American methods, physical, archaeological anthropology from social and cultural anthropology, dedicates his well-written book to the customary study of hunting, agricultural, pastoral, etc., societies, without any analysis of Western societies.

21 Cf. John Howland Rowes's very useful article 'Ethnography and Ethnology in the Sixteenth Century', *The Kroeber Anthropological Papers*, No. 30, 1964, pp. 1–19, and his address, in April 1963, to the same society, 'The Renaissance Foundations of Anthropology'. Only in 1590 did José de Acosta invent the term 'moral history' to designate what was to be called 'ethnography', i.e., 'the description of customs, rites, ceremonies, laws, government and wars' of Indian peoples. Before him, in

1520, Johann Boem had published a general work comparing the customs of Europe, Asia and Africa, *Omnium gentium mores, leges et ritus ex multis clarissimis rerum scriptoribus... super collectos.* See also a posthumous and incomplete work of J. S. Slotkin, *Readings in Early Anthropology*, Methuen, 1965, and James H. Gunnerson's address 'A Survey of Ethnohistoric sources' to the Kroeber Anthropological Society in 1958.

22 A Van Gennep's work illustrates these efforts.

23 As did the two founders of anthropology, in their own way: E. B. Tylor in 1865 with his *Researches into the Early History of Mankind and the Development of Civilization*, London; and L. Morgan, in 1877, with *Ancient Society*, op. cit.

24 Cf. Chapter I of Georges Lefebvre's course of lectures at the Sorbonne in 1945–6, re-edited in 1971 by Flammarion under the title *La Naissance de l'historiographie moderne.*

25 Cf. De Vore and Lee, *Man the Hunter*, Aldine, Prentice-Hall, 1968.

26 For this new orientation, see the works of J. Le Goff, E. Le Roy-Ladurie, J.-P. Vernant, P. Vidal-Naquet, M. Détienne, N. Wachtel, C. Parain, etc.

27 M. Godelier, *Rationalité et irrationalité en économie*, op. cit., pp. 230–1.

28 Sol Tax, 'Primitive Peoples', and Lois Mednick, 'Memorandum on the use of Primitive', *Current Anthropology*, September–November 1960, pp. 441–5; Francis L. Hsu, 'Rethinking the Concept "Primitive"', *Current Anthropology*, Vol. 5, No. 3, June 1964, pp. 169–78.

29 E. Wolf, *Peasants*, Prentice-Hall, 1966, pp. 3, 4.

30 Ibid., pp. 57, 58.

31 George Dalton, 'Peasantries in Anthropology and History', *Current Anthropology*, 1971, and *Traditional Tribal and Peasant Economies: an Introductory Survey of Economic Anthropology*, A. McCaleb Module in Anthropology, Addison-Wesley Publishing House, 1971.

32 Daniel Thorner, 'L'Economie paysanne, concept pour l'histoire économique', *Annales*, May–June, 1964, pp. 417–32.

33 K. Marx, *Introduction to a criticism of Political Economy*, in *Contribution to a criticism of political economy*, op. cit., p. 153.

34 F. Engels, *Anti-Dühring*, op. cit. p. 117.

35 M. Sahlins, 'Poor Man, Rich Man, Big-Man, Chief: Political Types in Melanesia and Polynesia', *Comparative Studies in Society and History*, vol. v, No. 3, April, 1963, pp. 285–303.

36 R. Firth, *Primitive Polynesian Economy*, op. cit., p. 14.

37 Robert McC. Netting, 'The Ecological Approach in Cultural Study', *Current Topics in Anthropology*, Vol. I, Addison-Wesley Modular Publications, 1971, Module 6, pp. 3, 4.

38 The formula is R. Firth's in *Primitive Economics of the Maori*, Owen, Wellington, 1929, p. 32.

39 M. J. Herskovits, *The Economic Life of Primitive Peoples*, A. A. Knopf, New York, 1940.

40 Murdock, G.P., *Social Structure*, Macmillan, 1949, p. 200.

41 Harold E. Driver and Karl F. Schuessler, 'Correlational Analysis of Murdock's 1957 Ethnographic Sample', *American Anthropologist*, 1967, Vol. 69, No. 3. 'For the world as a whole, it is apparent that descent has shifted from matrilineal to patrilineal (sometimes with a bilateral stage in between) more often than it has changed in the opposite direction. The 19th century evolutionists were partly right about the major sequence of change, but their reasons for the change were wrong. It is the evolution of technology and government that favours patrilineal over

matrilineal descent, not the recognition of biological fatherhood and the abandonment of promiscuity or 'group marriage'. However, after societies have attained an advanced level of technology and political organisation, unilineal descent groups of all kinds tend to disappear, as they have done in most of Europe and its derivation cultures.' Op. cit., p. 345. Driver and Schuessler continue with the findings of David Aberle regarding 'Matrilineal Descent in Cross-Cultural Perspective', *Matrilineal Kinship*, Schneider and Gough, University of California Press, 1961, pp. 655–727.

42 Evans-Pritchard, *Social Anthropology*.

43 A bibliography of all these works can be found in Robert McC.Netting's article, previously quoted, 'The Ecological Approach...'.

44 Ruth Benedict, 1946, p. 169.

45 With the notable exception of Roy Rappaport.

46 Harris, M., *Current Anthropology*, vol. 7, 1966, p. 51.

47 Lévi-Strauss, *Anthropologie structurale* (Plon, 1958), p. 17.

48 M. Sahlins, 'Economic Anthropology and Anthropological Economics', *Social Science Information* 8 (5), 1969, p. 30.

49 Marvin Harris: 'Dependent as we are on the unfolding of the natural continuum of events, our generalizations must be courbed in probabilities derived from the observation of the frequencies with which predicted or retrodicted events occur' (*The Rise of Anthropological Theory*, T. Y. Cromwell, New York, 1968, p. 614.).

50 Cf. M. Sahlins, 'Economic Anthropology and Anthropological Economics', op. cit., p. 80. 'The new materialism seems *analytically* innocent of *any concern for contradiction* – although it sometimes figures itself a client of Marxism (minus the dialectical materialism). So it is unmindful of the barriers opposed to the productive forces by established cultural organizations each congealed by its adaptive advantages in some state of fractional effectiveness.'

We compare this comment from Marshall Sahlins with an extract from a remarkable letter which Engels addressed to Lavrov on 12th November, 1875. Lavrov had asked him for his views on an article entitled 'Socialism and the struggle for life', which had appeared in the journal *Bnepëd* on 15th September 1875. Engels did not attack Darwin himself, since he considered him, like Marx, one of the masters of modern scientific thought, but he did take up with the 'bourgeois Darwinists' on specific points.

'Of the Darwinian doctrine I accept the *theory of evolution*, but Darwin's method of proof (struggle for life, natural selection) I consider only a first, provisional, imperfect expression of a newly discovered fact. Until Darwin's time the very people who now see everywhere only *struggle* for existence (Vogt, Büchner, Moleschott, etc.) emphasized precisely *cooperation* in organic nature, the fact that the vegetable kingdom supplies oxygen and nutriment to the animal kingdom and conversely the animal kingdom supplies plants with carbonic acid and manure, which was particularly stressed by Liebig. Both conceptions are justified within certain limits, but the one is as one-sided and narrow-minded as the other. The interaction of bodies in nature – inanimate as well as animate – includes both harmony and collision, struggle and cooperation. When therefore a self-styled natural scientist takes the liberty of reducing the whole of historical development with all its wealth and variety to the one-sided and meagre phrase 'struggle for existence', a phrase which even in the sphere of nature can be accepted only *cum grano salis* such a procedure really contains its own condemnation...'

'The essential difference between human and animal society consists in the fact that animals at most *collect* while men *produce*. This sole but cardinal difference alone makes it impossible to transfer laws of animal societies to human societies.

Marx–Engels Correspondence, Lawrence and Wishart, 1956, pp. 367–8.

51 Radcliffe-Brown, in D. Forde and A. R. Radcliffe-Brown (ed.), *African Systems of Kinship and Marriage*, 1950, p. 82. 'The components of the social structure are human beings', the social structure itself being 'an arrangement of persons in relationships institutionally defined and regulated.' F. Nadel, *The Theory of Social Structure*, Cohen and West, London, 1957, Preliminaries.

52 E. Leach: *Political Systems of Highland Burma*, Bell and Sons, 1964, pp. 4–5, Introduction: 'I hold that social structure in practical situations (as contrasted with the sociologist's abstract model) consists of a set of ideas about the distribution of power between persons and groups of persons.' Then turning away from the model of informants to that of the anthropologist, Leach, somewhat like Radcliffe-Brown, states: 'We may discuss social structure simply in terms of the principles of organisation that unite the component parts of the system.' And in conclusion, as distinct from Radcliffe-Brown: 'The structures which the anthropologist describes are models which exist only as logical constructions in his own mind'.

53 K. Marx, *Contribution to a criticism of Political Economy*, op. cit., p. 20: 'The relations of production (correspond) to a given stage in the development of the material forces of production. The totality of these relations of production constitutes the economic structure of society, the real foundation, in which arises a legal and political superstructure and to which correspond definite forms of social consciousness.' And in *Capital*, op. cit., vol. I. p. 82: 'Don Quixote long ago paid the penalty for wrongly imagining that knight errantry was compatible with all economical forms of society.'

54 C. Lévi-Strauss, *The Savage Mind*, Weidenfeld and Nicholson, 1966, p. 234.

55 C. Lévi-Strauss, *Conversations with G. Charbonnier*, Jonathan Cape, 1969, p. 33.

56 C. Lévi-Strauss, *The Savage Mind*, op. cit., p. 235.

57 Ibid, p. 130.

58 Ibid. p. 117.

59 C. Lévi-Strauss, *La Pensée sauvage*, p. 178.

60 C. Lévi-Strauss, *From Honey to Ashes*, Jonathan Cape, 1973, p. 473.

61 Ibid., p. 474.

62 C. Lévi-Strauss, 'Les Limites de la notion de structure en ethnologie', *Sens et usage du terme structure*, ed. Roger Bastide, Mouton, 1962, p. 45. The passage from Leach quoted by Lévi-Strauss comes from *Political Systems of Highland Bura*, Bell and Sons, 1964, p. 283.

63 The same as Leach who states clearly: 'The generation of British anthropologists of which I am one has proudly proclaimed its belief in the irrelevance of history for the understanding of social organisation... We functionalist anthropologists are not really 'antihistorical' by principle; it is simply that we do not know how to fit historical materials into our framework of concepts.' E. Leach, *Political Systems of Highland Burma*, op. cit., p. 282.

64 C. Lévi-Strauss, 'Les Limites de la notion de structure en ethnologie', op. cit. p. 44.

65 C. Lévi-Strauss, *Les Structures élémentaires de la parenté*, PUF, 1949, p. ix.

66 *Elementary Structures of Kinship*, Eyre and Spottiswoode, 1968, p. 116. Lévi-Strauss refers to G. P. Murdock's text, 'Correlation of Matrilineal and Patrilineal Institutions', *Studies in the Science of Society*, presented to A. G. Keller, New Haven, 1937.

67 K. Marx, Letter to the Editor of *Otechestvenniye Zapisky*, late 1877, addressed to Chukovsky in reply to Mikhailovsky, one of the Narodnik socialist party leaders: 'But that is too little for my critic. He feels he absolutely must metamorphose my

historical sketch of the genesis of capitalism in Western Europe into an historic-philosophic theory of the general path every people is fated to tread, whatever the historical circumstances in which it finds itself, in order that it may ultimately arrive at the form of economy which ensures, together with the greatest expansion of the productive powers of social labour, the most complete development of man. But I beg his pardon. (He is both honouring and shaming me too much).

Marx–Engels Correspondence, Lawrence and Wishart, 1956.

68 C. Lévi-Strauss, p. 390. (Godelier's italics). *Elementary Structures of Kinship*, op. cit., p. 390.

69 Maurice Godelier, 'Mythe et histoire, réflexions sur les fondements de la pensée sauvage', *Les Annales*, special issue, 'Histoire et structure', August 1971, pp. 541–68.

70 C. Lévi-Strauss, *Totemism* Pelican, 1969, p. 163.

71 K. Marx, *Le Capital*, Vol. 1, Sect. 4, chap. 15. Ed. sociales, Vol. 2, p. 50. (trans. from French).

72 One cannot but admire the offhand way in which Edmund Leach, having shown that the analysis of property relations is 'of the utmost importance' for his general argument, writes in 'Political Systems...' (op. cit., p. 141): 'In the *last* analysis the power relations in *any* society must be *based* upon the control of real goods and the primary sources of production, but this Marxist generalisation does not carry us very far.' (!) (Godelier's italics)

73 We refer here to general works, books and articles by Colin Turnbull, and particularly to *Wayward Servants*, Eyre and Spottiswoode, London, 1966.

74 That is to say, having a large number of animal and vegetable species, allowing only a limited number of individuals. Cf. David S. R. Harris 'Ucko and Dimbleby', *Domestication and Exploitation of Plants and Animals*, Duckworth, 1969.

75 In correspondence with C. Turnbull over a period of some ten or twelve months, we were able to clarify some points which the author did not raise or develop in his published works, particularly with regard to kinship relations, mobility between bands, the bow-and-arrow hunters, etc. We thank C. Turnbull warmly for his patience and cooperation.

76 C. Turnbull, op. cit., p. 149.

77 Ibid., p. 174.

78 C. Bettelheim, *Calcul économique et formes de propriété*, Maspero, 1969.

79 C. Turnbull, op. cit., p. 110.

80 Ibid., p. 141.

81 Ibid., p. 132.

82 Ibid., pp. 251–3.

83 Ibid., p. 262.

84 With the notable exception of Roy Rappaport in his book *Pigs for the Ancestors*, Yale University Press, New Haven and London, 1967.

85 Claude Meillassoux, for example, in his article on Colin Turnbull's works.

86 Except for some valuable works, e.g.; Pierre Bonnafé, 'Un aspect religieux de l'idéologie lignagère: le nkira des Kukuya du Congo-Brazzaville', *Cahiers des religions africaines*, 1969, pp. 209–96, or those, in France of Marc Augé and P. Althabe.

87 C. Meillassoux, *Anthropologie économique des Gouro de Côte-d'Ivoire*, op. cit., is an example of this: it leaves to one side any thorough analysis of kinship relations, representations and religious activities.

88 A task which can only be carried out gradually, by posing new questions. For example, from our analysis of kinship and political relations among the Mbuti, the problem arises to discover under what circumstances kinship groups become *closed* and exchange is made in a regular and direct way, as is the case in moiety systems,

sections or subsections of Australian aborigines, who are also hunter–gatherers like the Mbuti. Under what conditions do truly segmentary societies appear in which instead of a discontinuity between generations or a fluidity of social relations, (characteristic of the Mbuti or the Bushmen) closed groups appear based on a continuity between generations and permanent social relations.

One could say that instead of an irregular exchange of women between, at least, four 'open' bands, we have a regular exchange between four closed groups. Then a system of kinship in sections like the Australian one seems to have been generated. For a general reappraisal of problems in anthropology the best method is one which constructs transformational matrixes.

89 *Anti-Dühring*, op. cit. p. 169.

2 THE CONCEPT OF 'SOCIAL AND ECONOMIC FORMATION': THE INCA EXAMPLE

† This text appeared in the journal *La Pensée*, No. 159, October 1971, entitled 'Qu'est-ce que définir une "formation économique et sociale": l'exemple des Incas'.

1 K. Marx, *Capital*, op. cit., vol. 1, p. 77.

2 Cf. *Capital*, op. cit., vol. 1, p. 78: 'Let us now picture to ourselves a community of free individuals carrying on their work with the means of production in common, in which the labour-power of all the different individuals is consciously applied as the combined labour-power of the community.'

3 Even Las Casas, a fierce opponent of *encomienda* and a pathetic defender of the enslaved Indians, ceaselessly reaffirmed to his opponents, (who were all for enslaving and even massacring the Indians) that evangelisation should precede subjugation; this was the only justification for the king of Spain's sovereignty over the Indians: 'These, my Lord, are the most convenient ways and means of penetrating this country: the people must first recognise our God for their own by accepting the faith and then the king as sovereign. Because the ultimate cause, the whole basis for His Majesty's intervention in this country, as king of Castille, and the claims he has over them, must be the spreading of the faith'. (Letter to a person of the court, 15th Oct., 1535, BAE T.110; p. 67 a.)

4 References to the Incas, derive mainly from Professor John Murra's brilliant work: *The Economic Organization of the Inca State*, an unpublished thesis submitted in 1956 to the University of Chicago, a microfilm of which the author kindly entrusted to us. We should like to express here our warm gratitude to him.

3 THE CONCEPT OF THE 'TRIBE'

† Part of this text appeared in the *Encyclopaedia universalis*, 1973, for the entry 'Tribu'.

1 Elliott Skinner, 'Group Dynamics in the Politics of Changing Societies: The Problem of "Tribal" Politics in Africa,' Essays on the Problem of Tribe, Proceedings of the *American Ethnological Society*, 1968, pp. 170–85.

2 *Le Vocabulaire des institutions indo-européénes*, Editions de Minuit, Paris, 1969, vol. 1, p. 258.

3 John J. Honigmann, *Dictionary of the Social Sciences*, 1964, p. 729.

4 M. Sahlins, 'The Segmentary Lineage: an Organization of Predatory Expansion', *American Anthropologist*, 1961, p. 324; E. R. Service, *Primitive Social Organization*, Random House, New York, 1962, p. 111.

5 M. Sahlins, 'The Segmentary Lineage...' op. cit., p. 326.

6 Ibid. p. 143.

7 Ibid., p. 324.
8 Ibid., p. 354.
9 M. Sahlins, *Tribesmen*, Prentice Hall, 1968, p. 20.
10 Ibid.
11 Ibid., p. 48.
12 Ibid., pp. 74–5.
13 *The Nuer*, Clarendon Press, Oxford, 1940, p. 144.
14 *Tribesmen*, op. cit., p. 24.
15 A. Strathern, *The Rope of the Moka*, Cambridge University Press, 1971.
16 M. Sahlins, 'Poor Man, Rich Man, Big-Man, Chief: Political Types in Melanesia and Polynesia', op. cit.
17 *Tribesmen*, op. cit., p. 26.
18 Steward in Y. Cohen, *Man in Adaptation*, Aldine Publishing Company, 1968, I, p. 81.
19 On the Incas, cf. Murra, op. cit.; on the Aztecs, cf. J. Soustelle, *La Vie quotidienne des Aztèques à la veille de la conquête espagnole*, Hachette, 1955.
20 K. Marx, *Contribution to a criticism of political economy*, op. cit., pp. 150–3.
21 P. Clastres, 'Ethnographie des Indiens Guayaki', *Journal de la Société des américanistes*, Plon, 1968.
22 D. W. Lathrap, 'The "Hunting" Economies of the Tropical Forest Zone of South America: An Attempt at Historical Perspective', in De Vore and Lee, *Man the Hunter*, op. cit., pp. 23–9.
23 Introduction to a *Contribution to a Criticism of Political Economy* (*The German Ideology*), Lawrence and Wishart, 1970, p. 149.

4 AN ATTEMPT AT A CRITICAL EVALUATION

† This is an extract from the long preface (pp. 14–142) which we wrote to introduce and comment on texts chosen from Marx and Engels, published under the title: *Sur les sociétés précapitalistes*, Editions sociales, 1970.
1 Letter to Kautsky, 26 April 1884, *Marx–Engels Correspondence*, Lawrence and Wishart, 1956, p. 446.
2 F. Zeuner, *A History of Domesticated Animals*, Hutchinson, 1963, pp. 59, 63.
3 Mourant, Zeuner, *Man and Cattle*, Proceedings of a Symposium on domestication at the Royal Anthropological Institute, 24–6 May 1960, R.A.I., 1963, p. 15.
4 Fuhrer-Haimendorf, 'Culture, History and Cultural Development', *Yearbook of Anthropology*, 1955, pp. 149–68; L. Krader, 'Ecology of Central Asian Pastoralism'; *South-west Journ. Anthro.*, 1955, pp. 301–26.
5 R.-J. Braidwood, *Reflections on the Origin of the Village-Farming Community* and *The Aegean and the Near West*, Locust Valley, New York, 1956, pp. 22–31; Braidwood & Reed, *The Achievement and Early Consequences of Food Production: A consideration of the Archaeological and Natural-Historical Evidence*, Long Island Biological Association, 1957, pp. 25–7.
6 L. Dumont, *Homo Hierarchicus*, 1956, pp. 36–50.
7 Morgan, on the prohibition of marriage between brothers and sisters which, according to him, characterised the Punaluenne family discovered in Hawaii, says: 'This is an excellent illustration of the way in which the principle of natural selection works'. (Cf. also *Origins of the Family*, p. 36).
8 Cf. Robin Fox, *Kinship and Marriage*, Pelican, 1967, p. 29. Engels cites the contradictions in Letourneau, Saussure, Espinas when they refer to animal society, concluding: 'But the only conclusion I can draw from all these facts, so far as man

and his primitive conditions of life are concerned, is that they prove nothing whatever...For the present, therefore, we must reject any conclusion drawn from such completely unreliable reports' (*Origins of the Family* op. cit. pp. 30, 32). See also a recent discussion on the behaviour of primates, *Current Anthropology*, June 1967, pp. 253–7.

Lévi-Strauss, in his preface to the 2nd edition of *Structures élémentaires de la parenté*, emphasises that recent works on chimpanzees, baboons, gorillas at the savage state require us to draw a finer and more tortuous line of demarcation and contrast between nature and culture. 'Vingt ans après', *Les Temps modernes*, September 1967, p. 368.

9 Cf. Lévi-Strauss, *Les Structures élémentaires de la parenté*, op. cit., pp. 52–3.

10 R. Fox, *Kinship and Marriage*, op. cit., pp. 120–1.

11 Cf. a criticism of Morgan by Rivers, one of his disciples, in *Social Organization*, New York, 1924, pp. 85–90.

12 This explains why the statistical correlations established by Murdock between groups of variables taken in pairs (kinship and residence, kinship and economics, etc.) does not prove a necessary correlation between these variables; similarly such a theoretical step cannot, in principle, prove the *inexistence* of such correlations. Cf. G.-P. Murdock, *Social Structure*, op. cit., 1947, p. 192.

13 Leslie White, *The Evolution of Culture*, McGraw-Hill, 1959, p. 133–40.

14 One of the best known examples of the bilateral system is that of the Yako of Nigeria, where land is inherited through patriclans (kepun), while all goods, silver, cattle belong to matriclans (yeponama). The Yako lived for the most part in one town only, Umor, and were studied by D. Forde, *Yako Studies*, Oxford University Press, 1964.

One of the best known examples of cognatic systems is that of the inhabitants of the Caroline Is., studied by W. Goodenough in *Property, Kin and Community on Truk*, Yale University, New Haven, 1951.

15 R. Fox, *Kinship and Marriage*, op. cit., p. 132.

16 Cf. J. Barnes, *African Models in the New Guinea Highlands*, in *Man*, 1962, pp. 5–9.

17 Bertha Surtees Phillpots, *Kindred and Clan in the Middle Ages and After*, Cambridge University Press, 1913, and R. Fox, 'Prolegomena to the Study of British Kinship', in *Penguin Survey of the Social Sciences*, 1956.

18 Cf. M. Sahlins, *Social Stratification in Polynesia*, 1958, Seattle, pp. 13–22.

19 Cf. Lévi-Strauss, 'Régimes harmoniques et régimes disharmoniques', ch. 12, *Structures élémentaires de la parenté*, op. cit., p. 274; W. Shapiro, 'Preliminary Report on Fieldwork in Northeastern Arnhem Land', *American Anthropologist*, 1967, pp. 353–5.

20 H. E. Driver & K. F. Schuessler, 'Correlational Analysis of Murdock's 1957 Ethnographic Sample', op. cit., p. 345–51.

21 The Nayar of Malabar, famous for being both matrilineal and matrilocal, were a warrior caste in south-west India. The Menangkabau of Sumatra also belonged to a relatively complex society.

22 J. Steward, *Theory of Culture Change*, Urbana, 1955.

23 Malinowski, *Moeurs et coutumes des Mélanésiens*, 1923 p. 20. Malinowski was criticising Rivers, Morgan's discipline, who in *Psychology and Politics* spoke of 'socialist behaviour, indeed communist, in societies such as those found in Melanesia'.

24 Salisbury, *From Stone to Steel*, Melbourne, 1962.

25 M. Godelier, 'Economie politique et anthropologie économique, *L'Homme*, 1964, pp. 118–32.

26 Cf. Gluckmann, *Essay on Lozi Land and Royal Property*, Rhodes Livingstone

Institute, 1943, No. I, pp. 11–27, No. II, pp. 70–81; J. Murra, 'Social Structures and Economic Themes in Andean Ethnohistory', *Anthropological Quarterly*, April 1956, pp. 47–59.

27 Cora Dubois, 'The Wealth concept as an Integrative Factor in Tolowa-Tututni Culture', from *Essays in Anthropology*, presented to A. L. Kroeber, Berkeley, 1936, pp. 49–66.

28 See Firth's criticism of the concept of subsistence economy, in *Primitive Polynesian Economy*, op. cit., p. 17, and our criticism of Cl. Meillasoux, 'Anthropologie économique des Gouro de Côte d'Ivoire', op. cit., in *L'Homme*, 1967, pp. 78–91.

29 The non-existence of universal currency in primitive societies is explained therefore, both by the absence of developed market production and, simultaneously, by the necessity to control access to women and power. This would lead to *choosing* 'rare' goods corresponding to the limited number of women and roles of authority, and to *separating* their circulation from that of other goods, placing them under the control of individuals who represent the community's interests. This control is both an attribute of their function and a symbol of their status.

30 Cf. K. Bücher, *Die Entstehung der Volkwirtschaft*, 1893, ch. 1.

31 McCarthy & McArthur, *The Food Quest and the Time Factor in Aboriginal Economic Life*, 1960.

32 Leslie White, *The Evolution of Culture*, op. cit., 1949, p. 372. In a provocative and charming way M. Sahlins sees henceforth in societies of hunter–gatherers the true representatives of the 'Affluent Society'. See 'La première Société d'abondance', *Les Temps Modernes*, No. 268, Oct. 1968, pp. 641–80.

33 This example shows, as Engels pointed out, that primitive societies exercise a conscious control over their social life, more so than any society where private ownership and market production have been developed. However, the image is a dangerous one, because it suggests that society is a subject whose development merely obeys its will. In fact, the norms of collective or individual behaviour recognised by society, explain the nature of the social relations which characterise that society and the *dominant* role played by some (kinship, religion, etc.).

34 M. Sahlins, 'Poor Man, Rich Man, Big-Man, Chief: Political types in Melanesia and Polynesia', op. cit.

35 The concept of 'tribe' has undergone severe criticism recently in so far as it is often difficult to see in it any 'substantial' reality, unified by custom, language, etc. Cf. Leach 'Political Systems', op. cit., pp. 321–2.

36 Engels, *Anti-Dühring*, op. cit., p. 201.

37 M. Fried, *The Evolution of Political Society*, op. cit., pp. 182–91.

38 Max Gluckman declares that 'the paramount Chief' of Malinowsky is close to becoming the 'Piltdown Man' of anthropology. Preface to Uberhof's book, p. vi. The 'Piltdown Man' is a fossil whose identification was the object of fierce debate between palaeontologists in the 19th century.

39 J. P. Singh Uberoï, *Politics of the Kula Ring, An Analysis of the Findings of Bronislaw Malinowski*, Manchester University Press, 1962, p. 46.

40 *We, the Tikopia*, Allen and Unwin, 1936.

41 Preface to the 2nd edition, 1965, p. xi. Religious practices and institutions were analysed in 1940. Cf. the *The Work of the Gods in Tikopia*, The Athlone Press, 1967.

42 *Primitive Polynesian Economy*, op. cit., p. 17.

43 Cf. M. Sahlins' synthesis, *Social Stratification in Polynesia* op. cit., pp. 13–22.

44 R. Karsten, *A Totalitarian State of the Past; the Civilization of the Inca Empire*, 1949, Helsingfors Societas, ch. 7, p. 99.

45 Lucy Mair, *An Introduction to Social Anthropology*, Oxford, 1965, p. 113.
46 Lucy Mair, *Primitive Government*, 1962, p. 247.
47 Radcliffe-Brown, preface to *African Political Systems*, by Mayer Fortes and Evans-Pritchard, Oxford University Press, 1970, p. xxi; see also G. Balandier, 'Réflexions sur le fait politique: le cas des sociétés africaines', *Cahiers internationaux de sociologie*, XXXVII, 1964.
48 Eric Wolf, *Peasants*, op. cit., p. 10, goes so far as to say: 'It is this production of a fund of rent which critically distinguishes the peasant from the primitive cultivator.' Compare Engels' letter to Bernstein, 9 August 1882: 'It's the same old story of peasant peoples. From Ireland to Russia, and from Asia Minor to Egypt in peasant nations, the peasant exists only to be exploited. It has been thus since the Persian and Assyrian State.'

The existence of this fundamental relation of the village community exploited by the State, refutes the validity of certain studies in rural ethnology or sociology where rural communities are treated as microcosms more or less disconnected from the outside world.
49 Note that traditional patterns of obligation and custom are often used by the State as a means for extracting this surplus Cf. John Murra apropos the Inca State, 'On Inca Political Structure', *Human Societies*, special No., 'Systems of Political Control and Bureaucracy', 1958, pp. 30–41.
50 Lucy Mair, *Primitive Government*, op. cit., p. 187.
51 Cf. K. Polanyi, *Trade and Market in Early Empires*, Aldine, 1957, ch. XI, pp. 218–37.
52 E.g., the Arusha of Tanzania. Cf. P.-H. Gulliver, *Social Control in African Society*, 1963.
53 To cite only Pedro Carrasco, Morton Fried, Hackenberg, G. P. Murdock, J. Steward and, in opposition, E. Leach, 'Hydraulic Society in Ceylon', *Past and Present*, 1959, No. 15, pp. 2–26.
54 Engels, *Anti-Dühring*.
55 It has become more and more evident, with recent archaeological finds, that in Mesopotamia and the Indus valley, agriculture in the first epochs based its development on the use of spontaneous flooding. Canals came much later; in Egypt, irrigation by flooding remained the basic form, though reinforced by canals.
56 See a fine analysis of traditional Tibet, in Carrasco, *Land and Policy in Tibet*, Seattle, 1959, pp. 79, 85, 207–24. 'There is no separation between economic power and political power. The same people who control the land also control the State; in fact they *are* the State; and the State, that is, its personnel as a group, owns the land. The collective rule of the upper class also finds its political expression in the Dalai Lama, his personal ownership of all the land and the subordination of all the people as his subjects.'
57 Cf. apropos the Burmese Shan States, E. Leach, *Political Systems...*, op. cit., pp. 247–62; Leach sees these as a 'feudal' structure.
58 R. Karsten, *A Totalitarian State of the Past: the Civilization of the Inca Empire*, Helsingfors Societas, 1949, p. 266; L. Baudin, *L'Empire socialiste des Incas*, 1928, p. 226.
59 G. Childe, *Social Evolution*, 1950; Clark, *World Prehistory* (cf. our summing up in *La Pensée*, 1963, No. 107.).
60 See J. Needham's masterly writings on Chinese learning and society, demonstrating the superior development of Chinese learning up to the time of the Renaissance in Europe, and in particular the birth of 'experimental' sciences.
61 Cf. M. Godelier, *La Notion de mode de production asiatique et les schémas marxistes d'évolution des sociétés*, CERM, 1946, p. 34.

62 Cf. M. Godelier, *Rationalité et irrationalité en économie*, op. cit., pp. 90–98 and 229–231.
63 *Capital*, op. cit., vol. 1, p. 82.
64 C. Lévi-Strauss, *Du miel aux cendres*, op. cit., p. 37, 97, 113, 124, 241.
65 Whence the error of anthropologists who like to treat the symbolic function of kinship purely in linguistic terms, and those who, on the contrary, seek to define its content by *subtracting* its economic, political and religious functions. Cf. M. Godelier, 'Système, structure et contradiction dans *Le Capital* de Marx', *Les Temps modernes*, Nov 1966, pp. 828–64.
66 C. Lévi-Strauss, *Les Structures élémentaires de la parenté*, op. cit., p. 48.
67 Referring to the rank and importance of social structures in a particular society, Marx wrote in his *Introduction to a Criticism of Political Economy* (1859): 'It is as though light of a particular hue were cast upon everything tingeing all other colours and modifying their specific features; or as if a special ether determined the specific gravity of everything found in it' (p. 146).
68 Smelser, 'Mécanismes du changement et de l'adaptation au changement', *Industrialisation et société*, Mouton, 1963, pp. 29–53.

5 'SALT MONEY' AND THE CIRCULATION OF COMMODITIES AMONG THE BARUYA OF NEW GUINEA

† *Cahiers Vilfredo Pareto*, No. 21, Droz, Geneva, 1970. The material for this study was put together during a mission to New Guinea (1967–9) subsidised by the *Centre national de la recherche scientifique*. The author would also like to thank the Wenner Gren Foundation for the personal help extended to him. A more descriptive version of this study was published in *L'Homme*, Vol. IX, No. 2, 1969, pp. 5–37.
1 Boas, 'The Social Organization and the Secret Societies of the Kwakiutl Indians', *Report of the U.S. National Museum for 1895*, Washington, 1897, pp. 341–59.
2 Malinowski, 'The Primitive Economics of the Trobriand Islanders', *Economic Journal*, 1921, pp. 1–15; 'Kula', *Man*, art. 51, 1920–1.
3 Mauss, 'Essai sur le don, forme archaïque de l'échange', *Année sociologique*, 1923–4.
4 Firth, 'Currency, Primitive' and 'Trade, Primitive', *Encyclopaedia Britannica*, pp. 345, 346, 881.
5 Einzig, *Primitive Money*, Eyre & Spottiswoode, 1948.
6 Polyani, 'The Semantics of Money Uses', *Primitive, Archaic and Modern Economies*, 1968.
7 Dalton, 'Primitive Money', *American Anthropologist*, vol. 67, 1965, pp. 44–65.
8 Sahlins, 'On the Sociology of Primitive Exchange', *The Relevance of Models for Social Anthropology*, ASA Monographs, New York, Praeger, 1965.
9 Herskovits, *Economic Anthropology*, New York, A. Knopf, 1952, pp. 487–8.
10 Goldmann, 'The Kwakiutl of Vancouver Island', *Cooperation and Competition among Primitive Peoples*, Margaret Mead (ed.), McGraw-Hill, 1937, pp. 180–209.
11 Moore, 'Labor Attitudes Toward Industrialization in Under-Developed Countries', *American Economic Review*, No. 45, 1955, pp. 156–65.
12 Forde, 'Primitive Economies', *Man, Culture and Society*, NY Oxford Press, p. 342. See particularly: L. Lancaster, 'Crédit, épargne et investissement dans une économie non monétaire', *Archives européennes de sociologie*, III, 1962, pp. 156–65.
13 Dalton, *Primitive Money*, op. cit., p. 59.
14 Davenport, 'Red Feather Money', *Scientific American*, vol. 206, March 1962, pp. 94–105.

15 A. Senft, 'Ethnographische Beitrage über Karolinen-Insel Yap', *Dr A. Petermann's Mitteilungen*, 1903, pp. 50–151, and W. H. Furness, *The Island of Stone Money*, Philadelphia, 1910, p. 96.
16 K. Polanyi, Arensberg, Pearson, *Trade and Market in the Early Empires*, Glencoe, 1957.
17 M. Godelier, 'Objet et méthodes de l'anthropologie économique', *L'Homme*, vol. v, No. 2, 1965, and *Rationalité et irrationalité en économie*, op. cit., pp. 262–79.
18 Einzig, *Primitive Money*, op. cit., pp. 24–5.
19 Sahlins, 'Exchange value and the Diplomacy of Primitive Trade', *American Ethnological Society*, 1965 annual meeting, pp. 95–129.
20 See the use of the concept of capital by Salisbury, *From Stone to Steel*, op. cit.; and our critique in 'Economie politique et anthropologie économique', *L'Homme*, vol. IV. no. 4, 1964, pp. 118–32; and Bessaignet, 'An Alleged Case of Primitive Money', *Southwestern Journal of Anthropology*, 1965, pp. 333–45.
21 Take the case of the Tolaï in New Britain: cf. T. S. Epstein, 'European Contact and Tolaï Economic Development, A Schema of Economic Growths', *Economic Development and Cultural Change*, April 1963, pp. 283–307; and R. Salisbury, 'Politics and Shell-Money Finance in New Britain', *Political Anthropology*, Aldine, 1966, pp. 113–28.
22 Davenport, 'When a Primitive and a Civilized Money Meet', *Proceedings of the American Ethnographical Society*, Spring Meeting Symposium, Seattle, 1961, pp. 64–8.
23 On the gift and trade in Homeric times, see M. Finley, *The World of Odysseus*, Viking Press, NY, 1954, ch. 3; E. Will, 'De l'aspect éthique des origines grecques de la monnaie', *Revue Historique*, 1954, pp. 212–31; and Benvéniste, *Le Vocabulaire des institutions indo-européenes*, Editions de Minuit, Paris, 1969, vol. 1, ch. 2: 'Donner et prendre', and ch. 11: 'Un métier sans nom: le commerce'.
24 Salt usage in different societies and at different times should be compared. See Mahieu, *Numismatique du Congo*, 1924, p. 57; and for the salt bars in Abyssinia, Salviac, 'Les Gallas', *Geographical Journal*, 1901, p. 159.
25 The Baruya were discovered by J. Sinclair in 1951. He called them Batia in his book, *Behind the Ranges* (ch. 3: 'The Saltmakers'). Cf. J. Sinclair, *Behind the Ranges*, Melbourne Univ. Press, 1966.
26 S. A. Wurm, 'Australian New Guinea Highlands Languages and the Distribution of their Typological Features', *Amer. Anthrop.*, New Guinea, August 1964, pp. 77–97.
27 J. P. Murray, *Papua or British New Guinea*, T. Fischer-Unwin, 1912, pp. 170–1.
28 Cf. Demaitre, *New Guinea Gold: Cannibals and Goldseekers in New Guinea*, London, Geoffrey Bles, 1936. The only scientific publications concerning the Kukakuka are those of B. Blackwood, 'Use of Plants among the Kukakuka of Southeast Central New Guinea', *Proceedings of the Sixth Pacific Science Congress*, IV, Berkeley, 1939, pp. 111–26 and *The Technology of a Modern Stone Age People in New Guinea*, Oxford, Pitt-Rivers Museum 1950 (60 p.). Note also H. Fischer, 'Ethnographien von de Kukukuku' *Baessler Archiv.* 7 (neue Folge), pp. 99–122; description of a collection in the Hamburg museum by a missionary, J. Maurer.
29 Cf. J. M. Meggitt, 'Salt Manufacture and Trading in the Western Highlands of New Guinea', *The Australian Museum Magazine*, XII, 10, 1958, pp. 309–13.
30 Spectroscopic examination shows that this salt has a high percentage of potassium and, in high doses, is a violent poison.
31 A. Freund, E. Henty, M. Lynch, 'Salt Making in Inland New Guinea', *Transactions*, Papua and New Guinea Scientific Society, 1965, pp. 16–19.

32 In their language the Baruya distinguish: *moumbié*, bartering in the sense of both buying and selling; and *yanya*, giving; the generous man is the one who goes halves.

33 From A. L. Rand and E. T. Gilliard, *Handbook of New Guinea Birds*, Weidenfeld and Nicholson, London, 1967 (612 p.).

34 A. Deluz & M. Godelier, 'A propos de deux textes d'anthropologie économique', *L'Homme*, vol. VII, 3, 1967, pp. 78–91.

35 When the Baruya were paid for the first time in cash, they did not understand the utility of the coins. Some threw them in the bush, others pierced them and wore them round their necks like shells. However as soon as a 'counter' was opened at Wonenara, where for these pieces, they were offered shorts, shirts, canned foods, chewing-gum, they had no doubts about the usefulness of this metallic money. Perhaps the above anecdote explains why the Baruya, in their language, designate for the White Man's money, the very same term they give to their cowries: *nounguyé*; no one has been able to tell us the reasons for this assimilation. It is useful to note that when the Baruya want to make the value and functions of salt understood, they like to compare it with the White man's 'big money', i.e., pound sterling notes or dollar bills.

36 This merits separate treatment which is beyond the scope of this article.

37 Marx clearly indicated the *restrictive* conditions under which, in a developed market economy, a commodity may be exchanged for its value: 'For prices at which commodities are exchanged to approximately correspond to their values, nothing more is necessary than (1) for the exchange of the various commodities to cease being purely accidental or only occasional; (2) so far as direct exchange of commodities is concerned, for these commodities to be produced by both sides in approximately sufficient quantities to meet mutual requirements; (3) so far as selling is concerned, for no natural or artificial monopoly to enable either of the contracting sides to sell commodities above their value or to compel them to undersell.' *Capital*, op. cit., Vol. 1, p. 175. See also M. Godelier, 'Théorie marginaliste et théorie marxiste de la valeur et des prix: quelques hypothèses', article cited.

38 M. Sahlins, 'Poor Man, Rich Man, Big-Man, Chief: Political Types in Melanesia and Polynesia', *Comparative Studies in Society and History*, 5, op. cit., pp. 285–303. See also by the same author 'On the Sociology of Primitive Exchange'; M. Banton, ed., *The Relevance of Models for Social Anthropology*, New York, Praeger, 1965.

39 In the Baruya language, work is not an abstract notion, unaffected by the concrete matter of laborious activity. The verb *waounié*, to work, to make, is always used in a practical context: make a house, salt, palisade, etc. Let us remember what Marx said, having stressed the immense progress made by A. Smith, when the latter broke away from the ideas of the physiocrats in order to define work simply and independently of its concrete forms: agricultural (to the physiocrats the only productive kind of work), manufacturing, commercial work: 'It might seem that in this way merely an abstract expression was found for the simplest and most ancient relation in which human beings act as producers, irrespective of the type of society they live in. This may appear true, but is, in fact false. 'Labour' from the simplest economic point of view is a category just as modern as the social relations which give rise to this pure and simple abstraction.' Cf. Introduction to a Criticism of Political Economy, from *The German Ideology*, Lawrence and Wishart, 1970 and *Capital*, Book III, 1, pp. 173–94.

6 MARKET ECONOMY AND FETISHISM, MAGIC AND SCIENCE ACCORDING TO MARX'S *CAPITAL*

† *La Nouvelle Revue de psychanalyse* No. 2, Autumn 1970, Special No.; 'Objets du fétichisme', pp. 197–213.

1 References to Marx, *Capital*, that have been traced in the English edition are given as here throughout this chapter (i.e. *Capital*, Vol. 1, p. 35). References not traced are listed in the notes, and are to the French edition.

2 K. Marx, *Le Capital*, Bk. 1, Vol. 3, p. 246 (Marx's italics).

3 *Le Capital*, 1, 3, p. 249 (Marx's italics).

4 Marx quotes a remarkable piece of anonymous writing from 1739 or 1740, where it was already stated that: 'The value of them (the necessaries of life) when they are exchanged the one for another, is regulated by the quantity of labour necessarily required, and commonly taken in producing them' (*Some Thoughts on the Interest of Money in general, and particularly in the Publick Funds*..., London, p. 36.).

5 *Le Capital*, 1, 1, p. 74.

6 *Le Capital*, 1, 3, p. 247.

7 The price is the exchange value of a commodity expressed in terms of money. It may or may not correspond to the 'value' of the commodity. Cf. 1, 1, p. 83.

8 Karl Marx, *Le Capital*, 1, 1, p. 64.

9 *Le Capital*, 1, 1, p. 63.

10 Sometimes even earlier as in Italy. Cf. *Le Capital*, 1, 1, p. 156. n. 1.

11 *Ibid.*, 1. 1, 3, pp. 155–6.

12 We do not refer to the origin and nature of antedeluvian forms of capital: commercial, finance, etc., which Marx examines in *Le Capital* book III, Vol. 2. Here we wish only to deal with productive capital (industrial and agricultural).

13 Cf. also *Capital* Vol. III: 'The way in which surplus-value is transformed into the form of profit by way of the rate of profit is, however, a further development of the inversion of subject and object that takes place already in the process of production... On the one hand the value of the past labour, which dominates living labour is incarnated in the capitalist. On the other hand, the labourer *appears* as bare material labour-power, as a commodity. Even in the simple relations of production this *inverted relationship necessarily produces* certain *correspondingly inverted conceptions*, a *transposed consciousness* which is further developed by the metamorphoses and modifications of the actual circulation process.' (C, III, 45) (Godelier's italics).

14 And this link is indicated by Marx himself in a letter to Engels 24 August 1867. 'The best points in my book are: (1) the *double character of labour*, according to whether it is expressed in use value or exchange value (*all* understanding of the facts depends upon this, it is emphasised immediately in the *first* chapter); (2) the treatment of *surplus value independently of its particular* forms as profit, interest, ground rent, etc.' (Marx's italics) (*Marx–Engels Correspondence*, op. cit. p. 232.)

15 Perhaps from this point of view we can now explain Marx's meaning in a letter to Kugelmann, 11 July 1868, after Book 1 of *Capital* had been published: 'Since the thought process itself grows out of the conditions, is itself a *natural process*, thinking that really comprehends must always be the same, and can only vary gradually according to maturity of development, including that of the organ by which the thinking is done. Everything else is drivel.' (Marx's italics) (*Marx–Engels Correspondence*, op. cit.)

16 Marx to Engels, 24 August 1867: 'I sweated plenty ascertaining *the things themselves*, i.e., their *interconnection*.' (Marx's italics). (Ibid., p. 232).

17 Aristotle, *Ethics*, Book v, Penguin, 1964, p. 154.
18 *Introduction to a criticism of political economy*, op. cit., p. 145.

7 FETISHISM, RELIGION AND MARX'S GENERAL THEORIES CONCERNING IDEOLOGY

1 K. Marx, 'Notes on Wagner', 1881–2. *Le Capital*, Book I, vol. 3, p. 247.
2 References to Marx, *Capital*, that have been traced in the English edition are given as here throughout this chapter (i.e. *Capital*, Vol. III, p. 809). References not traced are listed in the notes and are to the French edition.
3 Marx, *Pre-Capitalist Formation*, op. cit., p. 71.
4 Engels, letter to Schmidt 27 October 1890, *On Religion*, op. cit., p. 281.
5 Friedrich Engels, *Anti-Dühring*, Lawrence and Wishart, 1943, p. 346.
6 Engels, *Anti-Dühring*, op. cit., p. 346–7. Marx, in *Capital*, explicitly links the forms taken by Christianity at its inception with the immense development of market exchange in Mediterranean Antiquity. The appearance and domination of capitalist modes of production, the most developed form of market production, unsettled Christianity again with the appearance of its 'bourgeois' forms: 'Suppose a society made up of the producers of commodities, where the general relations of social production are such that (since products are commodities, i.e. values) the individual labours of the various producers are related one to another in the concrete commodity form as embodiments of undifferentiated human labour. For a society of this type, Christianity, with its cult of the abstract, human being, is the most suitable religion – above all, Christianity in its bourgeois phases of development, such as Protestantism, Deism, and the like.' (*Capital*, op. cit., Vol. I, p. 71.) And Engels completed this analysis in *Anti-Dühring* when he declared: 'At a still farther stage of evolution, all the natural and social attributes of the innumerable gods are transferred to one almighty god, who himself once more is only the reflex of the abstract man. Such was the origin of monotheism, which was historically the last product of the vulgarised philosophy of the later Greeks and found its incarnation in the exclusively national god of the Jews, Jehovah. In this convenient, handy and readily adaptable form, religion can continue to exist as the immediate, that is, the sentimental form of men's relation to the extraneous natural and social forces which dominate them, so long as men remain under the control of these forces. We have already seen, more than once, that in existing bourgeois society men are dominated by the economic conditions created by themselves, by the means of production which they themselves have produced, as if by an extraneous force. The actual basis of religious reflex action therefore continues to exist, and with it the religious reflex itself.' (*Anti-Dühring*, op. cit., p. 347.) Nevertheless, concerning the exact conditions for the appearance of Christianity, it should not be forgotten that Engels wrote: 'It arose in a manner utterly unknown to us' (*On Religion*, op. cit., p. 206). Since, thanks to archaeological discoveries in Palestine and the Dead Sea scrolls, some progress has been made.
7 In fact, we should compare Engels' remarks on the role of Christian philosophy and the Church in the development of the feudal mode of production with the medieval ideal of Islam as a lay theocracy with no true clergy, total application of the Sharî-a religious law within the social and political organisation. Several times in history an attempt was made to govern a society or State with Moslem Sharî-a alone; not to mention Saudi-Arabia – a country with archaic structures – we merely cite Pakistan, a new country which wanted to build itself on the foundations of Islam.
8 Marx, *On Precapitalist Societies*, op. cit., p. 68

9 Ibid., p. 73.

10 'Engels: 'In all earlier periods the investigation of these driving causes of history was almost impossible – on account of the complicated and concealed interconnections between them and their effects' (*On Religion*, op. cit., p. 255).

11 Cf. Engels: 'It is clear that all the generally voiced attacks against feudalism were above all attacks against the Church, and all social and political, revolutionary doctrines were necessarily at the same time and mainly theological heresies' (*On Religion*, op. cit., p. 98). We should analyse, from this point of view, the conditions for the birth of Confucianism, the official religion of China, or the Hinduism and Buddhism which divided the Hindu and Indo-China sub-continents during the development of caste and, later, class societies after the Aryan invasions of India.

12 Marx, *On Religion*, op. cit., p. 93.

13 For example, see Condorcet, *Esquisse d'un tableau historique des progrès de l'esprit humain*, 1795, English translation, Weidenfeld and Nicholson, 1955, p. 18: 'This distinction, whose relics we are still now offered by priests, at the end of the eighteenth century, is found amongst the least civilized savages who already have their charlatans and their sorcerers. It is a distinction so general, one meets with it so constantly in all stages of civilization that it must have a foundation in nature itself; and thus we shall discover in our examination of the faculties of man in the early days of society the cause of the credulity of the original dupes and the cause of the crude cunning of the original imposters.' Diderot and other Encyclopaedists maintained the same point of view.

8 THE NON-CORRESPONDENCE BETWEEN FORM AND CONTENT IN SOCIAL RELATIONS

† The material in this text has been used elsewhere in the chapter 'Anthropologie économique', from *Manuel d'anthropologie*, published by A. Colin in 1973, collection U, edited by Robert Cresswell.

1 John Murra, *The Economic Organization of the Inca State*, op. cit. pp. 73, 166 and 34.

9 THE VISIBLE AND THE INVISIBLE AMONG THE BARUYA OF NEW GUINEA

† Published in the 2nd volume of tributes to André G. Haudricourt, Editions Klincksieck, 1972, entitled *Langues et Techniques. Nature et Société.*

1 Some material has been removed from this text and can be found in the article, 'Salt Money and the circulation of goods among the Baruya of New Guinea', above pp. 127–51.

2 In expressing these wishes, analogies and metaphorical comparisons are used..., for example one of the formulae heard from a member of the Ndélamayé group, asks for sweet potatoes to grow in as great a number as the youkouri eggs: the youkouri is a jungle bird who builds a nest with earth and lays a large number of eggs.

3 That is to say, not to disclose the names to any Baruya belonging to the same kinship group or to members of any neighbouring tribes. Some intended this interdiction to apply to all the tribes in New Guinea, permitting me only to tell their secrets to Whites.

4 B. Malinowski, *Argonauts of the Western Pacific*, Routledge, London, 1922, *passim*. And particularly, *Coral Gardens and their magic*, George Allen and Unwin, London, 1935.

5 R. Firth, *Primitive Polynesian Economy*, op. cit., ch. v: 'Ritual in Productive Activities', pp. 168–86.
6 Among the Baruya, it would appear that there is no notion of the beginning of a world, starting from nothing. Before the Sun and Moon went up into the sky, another order existed. The concept of *creatio ex nihilo*, creation from nothing, which since Saint Augustine, has been foremost in Christian philosophy, would mean nothing to a Baruya. The Greek notion of chaos preceding the present world order has nothing in common with Baruya notions either, though both believe that there is no absolute beginning starting from nothingness.
7 As distinct from the principle of the *identity* of opposites, first principle of Hegel's dialectical logic and the final basis of his absolute idealism; cf. Hegel, *Science de la logique*, Aubier, Vol. 1, p. 43.
8 It is worth remembering that Hegel, like Aristotle two thousand years before, rejected with the same contempt mythical forms of thinking; he also rejected the principle on which Kant built his criticisms of all metaphysics, which today is standard modern scientific thought, in other words that knowledge begins with experience and can only develop within fixed limits by and through experience. 'Kantian philosophy – that the understanding ought not to go beyond experience, else the cognitive faculty will become a theoretical reason which by itself generates nothing but fantasies of the brain – this was a justification from a philosophical quarter for the renunciation of speculative thought'. (Preface to 1st edition of the *Science of Logic*, Allen and Unwin, 1969, p. 25). Since it is true that from Plato through to Hegel and Heidegger, western philosophy – born out of its distrust for the old 'mythical' philosophies – had devoted much effort to building and destroying 'metaphysical' systems, we must therefore attempt to define the specific differences between myth, religion and philosophy and discover the reason for their different developments in History.

10 MYTH AND HISTORY: REFLECTIONS ON THE FOUNDATIONS OF THE PRIMITIVE MIND

† Published in *Annales*, special No. entitled 'Structure et Histoire', Armand Colin, Paris, May–August, 1971.
1 In another, more secret variant, pertaining particularly to the shamans, the sun and moon are designated in the kinship terms used for eldest and youngest brothers.
2 Apropos notions of 'armature', 'code', 'message' in myths, see Claude Lévi-Strauss, *Le Cru et le Cuit*, p. 205.
3 Claude Lévi-Strauss, *Du miel aux cendres*, op. cit., p. 240–2, 404–5.
4 Since this article was published and following discussions with Lévi-Strauss, we feel we should warn the reader that we are not satisfied with the last three paragraphs, becuse they involve two different problems. The problem here is the general effect on the mind of recognising the *existence* of limits on the control which members of a particular society exercise over Nature and for Society; whether this control is illusory or actual is less important to us than the fact that there is a socially recognised limit to it.

The analysis of the *real*, objective *content*, i.e., defined according to modern scientific data, of this limit in a given society, is outside the scope of our problem and extends to another field of investigation.
5 This provides an answer to the question we asked after citing the Baruya myth on the origin of the world: the question concerning the origin and basis of *formal*, *abstract*, characteristics (and these only) in mythical discourse and idealities which

are common to the myths of peoples profoundly different in the fields of ecology, economy and social organization, thus in all the positive determinations of their historical reality.

6 As Lévi-Strauss has demonstrated in *Totemism*, the essential link in the religious experience of the world is found in representation, in the principles and content of the representation of the world and not in man's effective relationship with Nature. It is not because primitive man originally identified himself affectively with Nature (by some kind of emotion and diffuse participation) that he represents this Nature by analogy with himself. Contrary to Lévy-Bruhl's thesis 'primitive mentality' is the child of the intellect, according to Lévy-Bruhl: 'When confronted by something that interests, disturbs, or frightens it, the primitive's mind does not follow the same course as ours would do. It at once embarks upon a different channel...The natural world he lives in presents itself in quite another aspect to him. All its objects and all its entities are involved in a system of mystic participations and exclusions; it is these which constitute its cohesion and its order.' (*Primitive Mentality*, Allen and Unwin, p. 35.) Levi-Strauss contradicts this: 'Actually, impulses and emotions explain nothing: they are always *results*, either of the power of the body or of the impotence of the mind. In both cases they are consequences, never causes. The latter can be sought only in the organism, which is the exclusive concern of biology, or in the intellect which is the sole way offered to psychology and to anthropology as well.' (*Totemism*, Merlin Press, London, 1964, p. 71).

7 We may also analyse from this aspect the practice of sacrifice. In *The Savage Mind*, op. cit., Lévi-Strauss has outlined a general analysis as follows: 'In sacrifice, the series of natural species (continuous and no longer discontinuous, oriented and no longer reversible) plays the part of an intermediary between two polar terms, the sacrifices and the deity, between which there is initially no homology, nor even any sort of relation. For the object of the sacrifice precisely is to establish a relation not of resembling but of contiguity, by means of a series of successive identifications. These can be made in either direction depending on whether the sacrifice is expiatory or represents a rite of communion...Its object is to bring to pass the fulfilment of human prayers by a distant deity. It claims to achieve this by first bringing together the two domains through a sacralised victim (an ambiguous object, in effect attaching to both), and then eliminating this connecting term. The sacrifice thus creates a lack of contiguity and by the purposive nature of the prayer, it induces (or is supposed to induce) a compensating continuity to arise on the plane where the initial deficiency experienced by the sacrificer traces the path which leads to the deity, in advance and as it were, by a dotted line.' (*The Savage Mind*, Wiedenfeld & Nicholson, 1966, pp. 224–6.)

8 Cf. Lévi-Strauss, his critical reply to A. Comte's thesis on religion as the anthropomorphism of Nature: 'The mistake made by Comte and the majority of his successors was to believe that man could at all plausibly have peopled nature with wills comparable to his own without ascribing some of the attributes of this nature, in which he detected himself, to his desires.' (*The Savage Mind*, op. cit., p. 220).

9 *The Savage Mind*, op. cit., p. 222.

10 *La Pensée Sauvage*, p. 152.

11 Ibid., p. 169.

12 *The Savage Mind*, op. cit., p. 136.

13 See, for example, Lévi-Strauss's analysis of a myth from the Murngin living in Arnhemland: 'The mythical system and the modes of representation it employs serve to establish homologies between natural and social conditions or, more accurately, it makes it possible to equate significant contrasts found on different planes: the

geographical, meteorological, zoological, botanical, technical, economic, social, ritual, religious and philosophical.' (*The Savage Mind*, op. cit., p. 93.)

14 In the sense of 'transhistoric'.

15 See *La Pensée Sauvage*, p. 290.

16 Ibid., p. 228.

17 Lévi-Strauss, *The Savage Mind*, p. 223. 'Attentive, meticulous observation turned entirely on the concrete finds both its principle and its results in symbolism'.

18 *Du miel aux cendres*, p. 7, 201, 216.

19 See, for example, the canonical law of transformation of myths for the Bororo mythology as Lévi-Strauss reconstructed them in *Du miel aux cendres*, p. 15, 17, 20. We should, of course, mention methods of myth analysis by syntagmatic and paradigmatic chains, the distinction between formal and semantic, analysis, etc., but this goes beyond our aim which is to give a simple outline of relations between myth, society and history. However, we should stress, as Lévi-Strauss does, that the structural method, far from neglecting or belittling the content of myths, constitutes: 'a new way of apprehending content which translates it into structural terms.' (*From Honey to Ashes*, op. cit., p. 466). Thus, comparative mythology was founded, not as the 19th-century mythographers would have wished, but as Van Gennep wanted it; this time '[It is not] comparison that supports generalisation but the other way round.' (Lévi-Strauss, *Structural Anthropology*, Penguin Books, 1972, p. 21.).

20 *La Pensée Sauvage*, pp. 313, 348.

21 At any rate an Algebra of cyclical transformations.

22 Lévi-Strauss, *Totemisé*, op. cit., p. 90. See also *The Savage Mind*, op. cit., p. 242. 'As the mind too is a thing, the functioning of this thing teaches us something about the nature of things: even pure reflection is in the last analysis an internalization of the cosmos.' We might compare this theory with Marx's thesis in *Capital* on the nature of religious idealities: 'In the mist-enveloped regions of the religious world . . . the productions of the human brain appear as *independent* beings endowed with life and *entering into relation* both with one another and the human race.' (*Capital*, op. cit. Vol. 1, p. 72) (Godelier's italics). Here we find the whole problem of analogy (route 1) as we have shown it.

23 *The Savage Mind*, op. cit., pp. 263–4.

24 *Totemism*, op. cit., p. 96.

25 'Letter to Kugelmann, 11 July 1868' (Marx's italics).

26 Which is also the transformation of man and the transformation of Nature; this is remarkably illustrated in the process of domesticating plants and animals with all its consequences regarding man's relations with man and Nature (genetical transformations of domesticated species, etc.).

27 'This "savage mind" is not that of primitive or archaic humanity, but rather mind in its untamed state as distinct from mind cultivated or domesticated' (*The Savage Mind*, op. cit., p. 219).

28 *The Savage Mind*, op. cit., p. 219.

29 We should compare these observations with what Michel Foucault has to say in *The Order of Things*, Tavistock, 1970, when he analyses the constructive role of 'resemblance' in knowledge and learning of western culture up to the end of the 16th century: 'It was resemblance that organized the play of symbols, made possible knowledge of things visible and invisible, and controlled the art of representing them . . . And representation – whether in the service of pleasure or of knowledge – was posited as a form of repetition: the theatre of life or the mirror of nature, that was the claim made by all language, its manner of declaring its

existence and of formulating its right of speech' (p. 17). Of course, certain resemblances and analogies drawn from the domain of perception disappeared before the 16th century in some sectors of learning and it is possibly because of this that mathematics among the Greeks, even philosophy, was born.

30 For this very reason numerous analogies, appearing in the myths, seem to bring out the associative principles of English empirical philosophy. Lévi-Strauss notes in *Le Totémisme aujourd'hui*, pp. 129–30, that Radcliffe-Brown in considering the Australian myths and the use of oppositions relying on pairs of opposites (high and low, dry and wet, etc.), regarded them as a special case of 'association by contradiction', and he partially rehabilitated the associationist doctrines. David Hume in *Enquiries concerning the Human Understanding*, 1748, section III, 'The Association of Ideas', declared: 'To me, there appear to be only three principles of connexion among ideas, namely, *Resemblance*, *Contiguity* in time or place and *Cause* or *Effect.*' (Clarendon Press, 1966, p. 24.).

31 *The Savage Mind*, op. cit., p. 16 (Godelier's italics).

32 Cf. glimpses into the mythologies of Mesopotamia and ancient Egypt in *Before Philosophy* by Henry Frankfort and T. Jacobsen, ch. 1, 'Myth and Reality', Penguin, 1949, pp. 11–36.

33 J.-P. Vernant stresses the significance of Anaximander thus: 'Anaximandre situe le cosmos dans un espace mathématique constitué par des relations purement géométriques. Par la se trouve effacée l'image mythique d'un monde à étages où le haut et le bas, dans leur opposition absolue, marquent des niveaux cosmiques differenciant des puissances divines et où les directions de l'espace ont des significations religieuses opposées.' *Les Origines de la pensée grecque* PUF, 1962, (p. 117).

34 J.-P. Vernant: 'Le nouvel espace social est centré. Le *kratos*, *l'arché*, la *dunasteia* ne sont plus situés au sommet de l'échelle sociale, ils sont déposés *es mason*, au centre, au milieu du groupe humain... Par rapport à ce centre les individus et les groupes occupent tous des positions symétriques... et entrent les uns les autres dans des rapports de parfaite réciprocité. (*Les Origines de la pensée grecque*, p. 122.)

35 Lévi-Strauss, *From Honey to Ashes*, op. cit., p. 474.

36 Aristotle, *Metaphysics*, B.4. Aristotle is referring to 'The contemporaries of Hesiod and all theologians' and advises, 'We should learn rather from those who can reason by demonstration'.

37 C. Lévi-Strauss referred us to G.E.R. Lloyd, *Polarity and Analogy. Two Types of Argumentation in Early Greek Thought*, Cambridge University Press, 1966; in this he enumerates examples of the use of pairs of contradictory terms and analogy as a mode of inference and a method of discovery in all fields of Greek philosophy and science up to the time of Aristotle.

38 Recalling Burnet's contrasting ideas, partisan of the 'Greek miracle' theory whereby, suddenly, 'on Ionian land the logos would break free from the myth as scales fall from the eyes of the blind', and of Cornford, for whom the first philosophy was nearer to mythical construction than scientific theory – J.-P. Vernant, while accepting Cornford's analyses, concludes: 'Cependant, en dépit de ces analogies et de ces réminiscences, il n'y a pas entre le mythe et la philosophie réellement continuité. Le philosophe ne se contente pas de répéter en termes de *phusis* ce que le théologian avait exprimé en termes de puissance divine. Au changement de registre, à l'utilisation d'un vocabulaire profane, correspond une nouvelle attitude d'esprit... Ainsi *s'affirme une fonction de connaissance dégagée de toute préoccupation d'orare rituel.* Les "physicians" *délibérement* ignorant le monde de la religion. Leur recherche n'a rien à voir avec ces procédures du culte auquel le mythe, malgré sa relative autonomie, restait toujours plus ou moins lié.' (*Les*

Origines de la pensée grecque, p. 102.) Desacralization of knowledge and a laicisation of social life appear to be the conditions, therefore, of the birth of philosophy.

39 'History' as reality (*Geschichte*) and not as a scientific discipline (*Historie*).

40 *The Savage Mind*, op. cit., 234.

41 Ibid., p. 235.

42 Ibid., p. 263.

43 Ibid., p. 173.

44 Ibid., p. 155. As a parallel we quote Marx's famous text: 'In direct contrast to German philosophy which descends from heaven to earth, here we ascend from earth to heaven . . . We set out from real, active men, and on the basis of their real life-process we demonstrate the development of the ideological reflexes and echoes of this life-process . . . Morality, religion, metaphysics, all the rest of ideology and their corresponding forms of consciousness, thus no longer retain the resemblance of independence. They have no history, no development; but men developing their material production and their material intercourse, alter, along with this their real existence, their thinking and the products of their thinking. Life is not determined by consciousness, but consciousness by life.' *The German Ideology*, op. cit., pp. 37–8.

45 Lévi-Strauss, *The Raw and the Cooked*, Jonathan Cape, 1970, p. 27; 'Structural thought now defends the cause of materialism.'

46 *From Honey to Ashes*, op. cit., p. 473.

47 Ibid., p. 474.

48 *The Savage Mind*, op. cit., p. 234.